THE UNITED STATES MARINES
1775–1975

This book is printed on 100 percent recycled paper

The United

States

MARINES

1775-1975

by Brigadier General
EDWIN H. SIMMONS
U.S. Marine Corps (Retired)

Foreword by
General R. E. Cushman, Jr.
25th Commandant
of the Marine Corps

Maps by
Major Charles Waterhouse
USMCR
from sketches by the author

THE VIKING PRESS
New York

To Captain John C. Shelnutt, USMC
Killed in Action, Hagaru-ri, Korea,
29 November 1950

359.960973

Si4m

101967

aug 1977

LIBRARY OF CONGRESS CATALOGING IN PUBLICATION DATA
Simmons, Edwin H   1921–
    The United States Marines, 1775–1975.

    Bibliography: p.
    Includes index.
    1. United States. Marine Corps—History. I. Title.
VE21.S55   359.9′6′0973   75-35719
ISBN 0-670-74101-9

Printed in U.S.A.

CONTENTS

FOREWORD

The Marine Corps owes a lot to Brigadier General Ed Simmons.

He gave the Corps thirty years of distinguished active service, personally fighting in three wars. In retirement, he is making a lasting contribution as the Marine Corps' Director of History and Museums by putting together a comprehensive museum program . . . our first.

Now he has added luster to those achievements with the publication of this highly-readable bicentennial history of the United States Marines.

His concise and cogent descriptions of the giants of our Corps, and of the fights that made them giants, make good reading for any military buff. For Marines who actually walked across any of his history's pages, however, his work has special value. It is punctuated with enough pithy detail to cut through the fog of elapsed time—bringing back into focus such vivid images as, "the weird scene of Marines fighting in bandages and underwear" to stop the Japanese counterattack which had reached their division hospital during the recapture of Guam. He upholds some Marine legends, such as the one about Archibald Henderson's portrait crashing to the floor when General Holcomb announced the formation of the Women's Reserve in 1943. He explodes others, such as the one about a Marine throwing a grenade from the rigging of the *Bonhomme Richard* to explode a magazine on the main gun deck of the *Serapis*, leading to her defeat at the hands of John Paul Jones. "It was a seaman, not a Marine . . ." General Simmons says, flatly.

Pride has never been a short suit with Marines. This book's combination of painstaking research and historian's hindsight—and insight—gives us something more to hang our hats on. It is a fine effort by a fine Marine.

R. E. Cushman, Jr.
General, U. S. Marine Corps
Twenty-Fifth Commandant
of the Marine Corps

1

1775–1785

"... to serve to advantage by sea ..."

Congress Passes a Resolution

In the fall of 1775, the Second Continental Congress, then sitting in Philadelphia, blew hot and cold on the debated proposition to create a Continental Navy. On 30 October the Congress named a Naval Committee (also called, in those confused and imprecise times, the Marine Committee) with John Adams of Massachusetts as one of its seven members. Tradition has it that the committee met in Peg Mullan's Beef-Steak House. The tavern, at the corner of King Street and Tun Alley, once the best in the city, was now of declining reputation but it was conveniently close to the State House.

If there were to be a Continental Navy, then there would have to be Continental Marines. Marines were as much a part of a man-of-war's furniture as its spars or sails or guns. They preserved internal order and discipline and gave national character to a ship. In sea battles they took their muskets and grenades into the fighting tops and also saw to it that the sometimes polyglot ship's crew stayed at its guns. Marines were also useful in amphibious expeditions, being half-soldier, half-sailor. Britain's colonial wars had given ample evidence of their usefulness, not only English Marines (who were now annoyingly present at Boston) but also the several regiments of American Marines which in earlier wars had been raised to help fight England's New World battles.

So must have gone the committee's discussion in Peg Mullan's second-floor rooms. General George Washington, the Virginian who commanded the Continental Army then besieging Boston (and whose half brother Lawrence had served in Gooch's Regiment of Marines at Cartagena in 1740, and who had later named his plantation after the English admiral, "Old Grog" Vernon), had already raised a small Navy of his own, complete with Marines. Besides Washington's Navy— armed fishing schooners manned for the most part by Marblehead fishermen—eleven of the Colonies had organized navies and most of these had Marines; so did many of the privateers and letters of marque. Accordingly, the committee put together a resolution and on 10 November 1775 it was passed by the Congress:

Resolved, *that two Battalions of Marines be raised consisting of one Colonel, two lieutenant Colonels, two Majors & Officers as usual in other regiments, that they consist of an equal number of privates with other battalions; that particular care be taken that no person be appointed to office or inlisted into said Battalions, but such as are good seamen, or so acquainted with maritime affairs as to be able to serve to advantage by sea, when required. That they be inlisted and commissioned for and during the present war between Great Britain and the colonies, unless dismissed by order of Congress. That they be distinguished by the names of the first & second battalions of American Marines, and that they be considered a part of the number, which the continental Army before Boston is ordered to consist of.*

John Hancock, president of the Congress, on 28 November 1775 signed a captain's commission (with the same bold signature that on 4 July 1776 would appear on a better-known document—the Declaration of Independence) for thirty-one-year-old Samuel Nicholas whose family owned the tavern Conestogoe Waggon on Market Street. Fifers and drummers were sent out to drum up recruits for the new corps. The drums, as noticed by Benjamin Franklin, were painted with a coiled rattlesnake and the motto "Don't Tread on Me."

While Nicholas was assembling his Marines, the Continental Navy was putting together its first squadron. During November a number of merchant ships had been purchased for conversion. At a Philadelphia wharf, under the critical eye of a demanding young Scot named John Paul Jones, the 450-ton *Black Prince* had her sides pierced for twenty guns and became the flagship *Alfred*. Profane old Commodore Esek Hopkins, forty years a sailor and a privateer in the French and Indian Wars, came hell-roaring down from Rhode Island and on 3 December took command of the squadron on the deck of the *Alfred* while Marine fifers and drummers whistled and banged away. Three weeks later Dudley Saltonstall of Connecticut arrived to be captain of the *Alfred*. John Paul Jones, reverting to first lieutenant, disliked the new flag captain on sight, calling him the "sleepy gentleman."

The New Providence Raid

Commodore Hopkins took his makeshift squadron down the Delaware into the Bay on 7 January 1776. Here he waited for a month, hampered by ice and a fractious crew, until he had collected eight ships, all conversions, ranging from the 20-gun *Alfred* to the 6-gun *Fly*. The squadron put to sea on 17 February. Altogether there were about fifteen hundred men in the eight ships and of these about three hundred were Continental Marines. Captain Nicholas was in the *Alfred* as senior Marine officer. Pennsylvania's resourceful Committee on Public Safety had provided them with muskets and necessary accouterments.

The sailing orders given Hopkins were hopelessly ambitious. He was to clear the British Navy from the Chesapeake, make himself master of the North and South Carolina coasts, and then "attack, take, and destroy all the Enemy's Naval force you may find" in Rhode Island. However, in the event of bad winds, stormy weather, or any other unforeseen accident of disaster, he was permitted "to follow such Courses as your best Judgement shall suggest."

"The Wind after we came out came on to blow hard," reported Hopkins later to the Congress and this gave him the excuse to pursue his own more modest plan, a raid into the Bahamas to get gunpowder for Washington's army. Nassau Town, a sunburnt little colonial port set down on the flat and scrubby island of New Providence, was protected by two stone forts, Nassau and Montagu, fairly formidable, but the garrison of British regulars had been taken off and the sloop-of-war, HMS *Savage*, usually on station, was also gone. The defense of the island rested in the hands of some half-pay officers and two hundred of what Hopkins called the "Inhabitants."

Hopkins' first plan was to put two hundred Marines under Captain Nicholas along with fifty seamen into two captured sloops and try for a surprise attack against the town. But they were seen, there was no surprise, and Fort Nassau warned them off with a couple of cannon shot. The two sloops now proceeded to the eastern end of the island, and on 3 March 1776, covered by the 12-gun *Providence*, the landing party went ashore, was unopposed, and marched against Fort Montagu.

The British Governor, Montford Browne, sent out an emissary who cautiously inquired of their intentions.

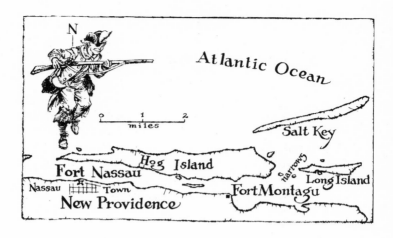

Nicholas replied that he was to take "possession of all warlike stores belonging to the crown, but had no desire of touching the property of any of the inhabitants." The defenders of the fort let fly with three rounds of 12-pound shot. That was the only resistance; then, honor served, they spiked their cannon and withdrew. Nicholas ran up the Grand Union flag (not yet the Stars and Stripes) and spent an undisturbed night in the fort. Then, as he reports it:

The next morning by daylight we marched forward to take possession of the Governor's house . . . and demanded the keys to the fort, which were given to me immediately and then took possession of Fort Nassau. In it were 40 cannon mounted and well loaded for our reception with round, langridge, and canister shot. All this was accomplished without firing a single shot from our side. We found in this fort a great quantity of shot and shells, with 15 brass mortars, but the grand article, powder, the Governor sent off the night before, viz. 150 casks.

Governor Browne had indeed used the night well. The powder had gone out in a merchant vessel through the unguarded eastern channel. Hopkins' squadron now came into the harbor and the next two weeks were spent in loading the spoils. The squadron headed for home on 17 March; Rhode Island was the destination. On 4 and 5 April, south of Block Island, they took four small prizes. At one in the morning on the sixth, with a full moon and a north wind, *Glasgow*, a 20-gun English corvette, crossed the squadron's bows. Not recognizing the squadron as hostile, *Glasgow* came alongside *Cabot*, 14, to hail, in answer got a hand grenade on her deck from a Marine in the maintop. *Cabot* touched off a broadside and got back two in return which put her out of action. A cannon ball carried away the *Alfred*'s wheel block and tiller lines. *Andrew Doria*, 16, closed on *Glasgow*'s port quarters, but her guns were too light and too few. *Columbus*, 28, came up next. *Glasgow*, expecting to be boarded, broke off and ran for Newport, much cut up. At dawn, Hopkins collected his scattered squadron and his prizes, and on 8 April took them into New London, Connecticut. Marine Lieutenant John Fitzpatrick was dead. So were six other Marines with four more wounded.

At first there were congratulations. Then there were second thoughts. The showing against the *Glasgow* had been poor and, if Hopkins were to be excused for taking liberties with his orders, where was the powder? There were investigations in Philadelphia. Hopkins, who deserved better, was censured and eventually dismissed from the service. Nicholas emerged not only with his reputation intact but on 25 June was promoted to major, with pay increased to $32.00 a month and orders to raise four companies of Marines. Tun Tavern (another name for the Beef-Steak House) was named the recruiting rendezvous, and Peg's son, Robert Mullan, got one of the new captain's commissions.

On 5 September the Naval Committee came out with

uniform regulations for the Continental Marines: green coats with white facings, a round hat with the left brim pushed up and pinned to the crown with a cockade. Also prescribed was a leather stock, borrowed from the British, regarded by some as vestigial bit of body armor to protect a man's throat from a cutlass slash and by others as simply a device to keep a man's head erect. Whatever its use, the stock, praised by the officers and damned by the men, would persist until after the Civil War, its memory still preserved by the best known of Marine nicknames: "Leatherneck."

Princeton

In December 1776, "the Enemy having overrun the Jerseys, & our Army being greatly reduced," Nicholas was ordered to join Colonel John Cadwalader's Philadelphia brigade with three of his companies. (Total strength was only eighty men, so they hardly could be called a battalion.) On Christmas night when Washington crossed the Delaware and captured the Hessian garrison at Trenton, Cadwalader's brigade was blocked by the ice farther south on the river. But it was already on the Jersey side at the year's end when Washington crossed at Trenton a second time. Cadwalader, promoted to brigadier general and his command grown by attachments to division size, marched to join Washington and this brought up the American strength to about six thousand men.

Cornwallis, after the capture of the Hessians, had hurried across New Jersey with eight thousand men. By the night of 2 January 1777 the two armies were on opposite banks of the Assunpink Creek, outside Trenton. Cornwallis's staff urged a night attack, but the English lord said that he would "bag the old fox" in the morning. Leaving his campfires burning, Washington made a night march around Cornwallis's flank and engaged his rear at Princeton. Lieutenant Colonel Charles Mawhood was there with three regiments of foot

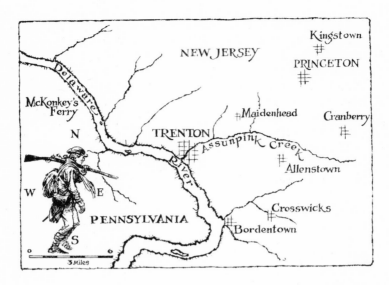

—the 17th, 55th, and 40th. Mawhood's brigade was giving Cadwalader's division a rough handling when Washington came riding up and rallied them with a display of the famous Washington temper. The three English regiments were then rolled up and routed before Cornwallis could join with his main body.

Washington now marched unimpeded to Morristown, where he made his winter camp. The Marine "battalion" stayed with him until the end of February. Some of the Marines joined Washington's artillery; the rest went back to Philadelphia with Nicholas. That summer and fall the few who were left found employment in the defense of the Delaware and the fighting preceding the British capture of Philadelphia.

With John Paul Jones

John Paul Jones had gone to Portsmouth, New Hampshire, in July 1777 to take command of the new sloop-of-war *Ranger. Ranger* was rated at 20 guns (although Jones prudently reduced his ordnance to eighteen 9-pounders). This meant, by rule-of-thumb— one Marine for every gun or a little more—a Marine guard of twenty-two or twenty-four. Jones chose a friend, Captain Matthew Parke, to be his senior Marine. Samuel Wallingford of Portsmouth was named lieutenant. Captain Parke was told to take "a Drum, Fife, and Colours" and go recruit his Marines.

The *Ranger*'s first mission was to carry to Dr. Benjamin Franklin in Paris the first dispatches reporting the surrender of Burgoyne at Saratoga. *Ranger* put to sea on 1 November and reached France in thirty-one days. The crew and officers were mostly Portsmouth men. They did not like Captain Parke, so Jones removed him from command of the Marines and put Wallingford in his place. After some tentative cruising off the French coast in February and March, Jones sailed on 10 April 1778 from Brest for the Irish Sea. In the next ten days the *Ranger* took two merchant ships, brushed against a revenue cutter, and sank a Scots schooner loaded with oats and barley. On 20 April they spoke with a fishing boat who told them that HMS *Drake*, 20 guns, was in Belfast Lough.

Jones then mounted a raid on Whitehaven in Solway Firth. He had sailed from there as a boy of thirteen. His Portsmouth crew wanted no part of the venture; there was almost a mutiny, stopped by Jones putting a pistol to a recalcitrant's head. A landing party of two boats' crews was made up, about twenty men in each, Jones commanding one, Wallingford the other. At midnight on 22 April the boats pulled away from the *Ranger*, three hours of hard rowing to the harbor. Jones went up the wall of the south battery, found the gunners asleep, took them prisoner, and spiked the guns. He repeated the performance at the north battery. Then an Irishman broke away from his crew and raced down the street, banging on doors and shouting that Yankee pirates had come to burn their homes and ships. It was now five in the morning and broad daylight. With the town thoroughly roused, the two boat crews reassembled and pulled safely back to the *Ranger*.

Jones now crossed Solway Firth to St. Mary's Isle with the idea of carrying off the Earl of Selkirk as a hostage who could be traded for American prisoners. Mid-morning on the twenty-third he put a cutter in the water, taking with him the sailing master, David Cullam, Wallingford, and a dozen hands. Posing as a press gang, they learned from the head gardener that the Earl was away, benefiting from the waters at Buxton. Jones gave Cullam and Wallingford permission to carry off the family silver so as not to go back to the *Ranger* empty-handed. The Countess of Selkirk afterward wrote that the sailing master "had a vile blackguard look," but the other officer "was a civil young man in a green uniform, an anchor on his buttons which were white."

With the *Ranger* safely back in Brest on 8 May, Jones wrote to the Countess telling her of his intentions of buying the plate when it was sold and restoring it to her. He also told her of his encounter with the *Drake* the day following the visit to St. Mary's. The English ship had struck her colors after an engagement lasting sixty-five minutes, her captain killed by a Marine musket ball through the head. Among the American dead, as Jones could have told the Countess, was the civil young man in the green uniform.

Penobscot Bay

Leave Jones there, cross the Atlantic once again, and move forward a year: It is now June 1779. Brigadier General Francis McLean has come down from Halifax to Penobscot Bay in Maine with seven hundred troops —including four hundred fifty Argyle Highlanders and two hundred members of the 82d Foot—three sloops-of-war, and orders to build a fort and naval base. Maine is a province of Massachusetts and the move causes

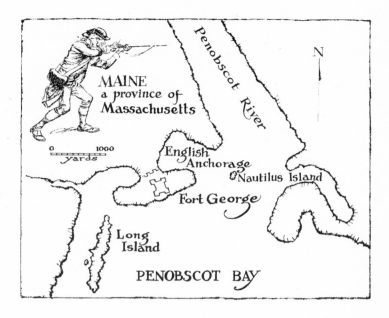

consternation in Boston. The State Board of War plans an expedition to be prosecuted with or without the help of the Continental Congress in distant Philadelphia.

There are three ships of the Continental Navy in Boston harbor. Captain Saltonstall, late of the *Alfred*, has the fine new frigate, *Warren*, 32, and is named commodore. The Massachusetts State Navy provides three 14-gun brigs. New Hampshire adds an 18-gun brig. There are also twelve privateers and nineteen transports and store ships. The landing force is under Brigadier General Solomon Lovell of the Massachusetts militia. He wants fifteen hundred militiamen but has to be content with nine hundred. His chief of artillery is the Boston silversmith, Lieutenant Colonel Paul Revere.

This formidable force gets under way on 19 July 1779, and by the twenty-fourth is in the mouth of Penobscot Bay. That night a Marine reconnaissance party goes ashore and learns that the British are well along in the construction of Fort George on a fishhook-shaped promontory sticking out into the bay. Next day Commodore Saltonstall takes his ships past the fort and the English sloops pop away at them for an indecisive two hours. The militia make a hesitant effort to land, lose an Indian scout, and come back to their transports. To stiffen the militia, both the Continental and State Marines are combined into a "landing division" under Captain John Welsh of the *Warren*. They land on Nautilus Island, nine hundred yards offshore from Fort George, on the twenty-sixth, chase off twenty British Marines, who abandon their four small field guns, and secure the island as a site for Revere's artillery.

Assault of the fort is to come on 28 July, the landing to be west of the fort in three columns, the Marine column on the right. The Marines get ashore, the militia lagging somewhere to the left rear. The beach is badly chosen. The Marines have in front of them a 45° wooded slope and at the top the 82d Foot is waiting for them. As the Marine bugler from the *Providence* remembered it, "Our brave general did not lead the van in the ascent, neither did he bring up the rear. Probably he and the commodore were walking the *Warren's* quarterdeck with their spy-glasses to see the fun."

The Marines get to the crest losing fourteen killed—including Captain Welsh—and have twenty more wounded out of a total of three hundred. The English retire to their fort and the militia comes ashore. The fort, as Paul Revere saw it, was ". . . as high as a man's chin and built of square logs." A militiaman disdainfully remarked he could "jump over the walls with a musket in each hand."

The attack got under way next day; the Marine line in the advance. Five hundred yards from the fort they were halted by order of General Lovell. In the fort, General McLean waited wonderingly: "I was in no situation to defend myself; I meant only to give them one or two guns, so as not to be called a coward, and then to have struck my colours. . . ."

But Lovell would not assault until Saltonstall brought his ships in close enough to join the barrage and Saltonstall refused to close because of the three British sloops-of-war. ("I am not going to risk my shipping in that damned hole.") The impasse persisted for sixteen days. Then on the afternoon of 13 August, the privateer *Active* came flying in through the fog with the news that a British squadron was entering the bay. It was the 64-gun *Raisonable*, four frigates, and three sloops-of-war. Saltonstall spent an apprehensive night. Next morning at first light he flew the signal, "All ships fend for yourself." Setting the example, he took the *Warren* upstream, drove her into the bank, and set her afire. The Americans lost nineteen ships, two of them surrendered to the British, the rest abandoned and burned. Marines, militiamen, and seamen floundered through the Maine wilderness. Most found their way back to Boston. There was, of course, a board of inquiry. Findings were such that the "narrow-minded" Saltonstall was brought before a court-martial and cashiered.

Bonhomme Richard v. Serapis

In France, John Paul Jones had gotten a new ship, *Bonhomme Richard*, formerly an East Indiaman, built in 1766, and now somewhat tired. In her conversion to a man-of-war she received a mixed battery of 44 guns.

John Adams dined with Jones in Lorient on 13 May 1779. That night he entered in his diary, "After Dinner walked out, with Captains Jones & Landais to see Jones's Marines—dressed in the English Uniforms, red & white. . . ." Marines in red coats instead of green? Adams disapproved but Adams was in error; the Marines were French, not American, and they were in proper uniform of the Walsh Regiment of the Irish

Brigade of the French Army. There were 137 of them under command of two French lieutenant colonels—an unusually large complement, but Jones had originally envisioned the *Bonhomme Richard* as a kind of amphibious command ship and had put in extra berthing when she was being converted.

On 14 August 1779 the *Bonhomme Richard*, in company with the new American-built frigate *Alliance*, 36, and the *Pallas*, 26, sailed from Lorient, embarked on the great clockwise cruise around the British Isles. The final, climactic battle took place off Yorkshire's Flamborough Head on 23 September. At three in the afternoon, Jones sighted the *Serapis*, new, copper-bottomed, rated a 44 but carrying 50 guns, and the *Countess of Scarborough*, 20. Two hours later Jones's French-Irish Marine drummers beat the roll to General Quarters. At about seven in the evening the battle began with an exchange of broadsides between *Bonhomme Richard* and *Serapis*. Outgunned and against a better ship, Jones's one chance was to hold tight to the Englishman and depend, as much as anything, upon the marksmanship of his French Marines. It was a seaman, not a Marine as sometimes reported, who dropped a hand grenade from the yard of the *Richard* into an open hatch of the *Serapis* and exploded a magazine. Captain Richard Pearson, his ship on fire, his mainmast giving way, at ten-thirty tore down the Red Ensign from where it had been nailed to its staff.

Last Days

In September 1781, while Cornwallis pondered surrender at Yorktown, Robert Morris, the Finance Minister and Rothschild of the American Revolution, had a secret mission in Philadelphia, one last adventure for his friend Major Samuel Nicholas and his few remaining Marines. There were a million silver crowns (a loan from Louis XVI) waiting at Boston. Nicholas brought it down by ox cart, three hundred fifty miles, much of the way through Tory country, arriving safely on 6 November. Two months later, 7 January 1782, Morris opened the Bank of North America, its assets secured by the French silver.

In 1783 Great Britain recognized the United States as a sovereign and independent power and the war was over. On 3 June 1785, Congress authorized the selling of the decommissioned *Alliance*, the last vessel of the Continental Navy. The Continental Marines had already disappeared.

The original resolution of Congress had the sound idea of a corps of Marines from which battalions could be formed for expeditionary service and from which detachments could be spun off for service afloat. Somehow, the idea got lost: insufficient resources, distances that were too great, communications that were too slow. After Penobscot, there was no major effort at an amphibious operation. Records show that 131 officers held Continental Marine commissions. Major Samuel Nicholas is held by the U. S. Marines to be their first Commandant. He never actually was so designated, but he was the only field-grade officer and the duties as "Muster Master" give some legitimacy to the tradition. The number of Continental Marines enlisted is not exactly known, but probably did not exceed 2000. In all, counting States' navies and privateers, perhaps 12,000 had some claim to the title "United States Marine."

2

1798–1811
"... to be called the Marine Corps..."

Quasi-War with France (1798–1801)

Troubles with Algerian corsairs began before the ink was dry on the Peace of Paris. But there was no Navy and not much of an Army, nothing more than a few quartermasters and a sergeant's guard or two. As for the Marines, only the slenderest thread of continuity can be claimed by virtue of "Marines" serving in the Revenue Cutter Service. Nothing was done until the Naval Act of 27 March 1794 authorized the building of six frigates, and before they could be completed an ignominious treaty with Algiers was reached in September 1795 at a cost of a million dollars in ransoms and bribes.

The next vexation was Revolutionary France, piqued because the United States would not join her against Great Britain. From July 1796 until the end of 1797, French raiders took 316 merchant ships flying the American flag. American attitudes stiffened. There was a new slogan: "Millions for defense, but not one cent for tribute." Work on three of the frigates, *United States*, *Constitution*, and *Constellation*, was resumed and other ships were authorized for building or conversion. There were to be Marine quotas for the new ships, "quotas" not "detachments" because there was no corps from which they could be detached. Samuel Sewall, chairman of the House Naval committee, arguing that all Marines should be in one corps for better discipline, order, and economy, offered the following resolution:

> Resolved, *That, in addition to the present Military Establishment, there shall be raised a battalion, to be called the Marine Corps, to consist of a Major, and suitable commissioned and non-commissioned officers, five hundred privates, and the necessary musicians, including the marines now in service; and the marines which shall be employed in the armed vessels and galleys of the United States shall be detachments from this corps.*

Sewall's bill quickly passed the House, moved to the Senate (where there were amendments), and on 11 July 1798, the true birthday of the Corps, President John Adams approved "An act for establishing and organizing a Marine Corps" and it became law. (Unfortunately, the Senate amendments had taken out the provision for battalion organization and had perpetuated the Revolutionary War practice, copied from the English custom, that Marines were to be governed by the Articles of War when ashore and Naval Regulations while afloat.) Next day the President appointed William Ward Burrows of Philadelphia the Major of the new Corps. On 23 August 1798, Burrows opened his headquarters in Philadelphia, at that time still the nation's capital. An economical administration gave the new Marine Corps a stock of uniforms left over from "Mad Anthony" Wayne's Legion, blue with red facings, and this was the beginning of the U. S. Marines' familiar "dress blues." A round hat, edged in yellow, and with the brim turned up over the left ear, went with the uniform. It gave trouble at sea, was difficult to store and easily blown over the side.

In May 1799 another Philadelphian, Daniel Carmick, was ordered to the frigate *Constitution*. After viewing his fifty-man Marine detachment he wrote to the Major Commandant, "I think it is not possible to produce such another shabby set of animals in this world."

Most of the French raiders, mixed up with Spanish privateers and some regular French Navy ships, were in the Caribbean. *Constitution*, 44, commanded by Captain Silas Talbot, took station there with orders to cooperate with Toussaint L'Ouverture, the black Haitian general who had expelled the French and Spaniards from almost all of Santo Domingo. Talbot learned that the 14-gun French privateer *Sandwich* (that un-French name because she was a captured English packet) was loading coffee and sugar at Puerto Plata, a north coast Dominican port still in Spanish hands. Talbot commandeered the American merchant sloop *Sally*, put his first lieutenant, Isaac Hull, and Carmick into it with ninety Marines and sailors, and at high noon, 12 May 1800, they sailed into the harbor and lay alongside the *Sandwich*. They caught the crew below decks at mess, one or two rounds went off by accident, but there was no resistance. Carmick now loaded his Marines into the *Sandwich*'s boat and pulled for Fortaleza San Felipe on the eastern arm of the harbor. Here again there was no opposition, although the French and Spaniards were supposed to have five hundred men in and around Puerto Plata. Guns of the fort spiked, the Americans hurriedly rerigged the *Sandwich* and sailed her out of the harbor. Thus went the first of many U. S. Marine landings to be made on the beautiful, unhappy island of Hispaniola.

In June 1800 the national capital was moved from Philadelphia to the new Federal city of Washington. Major Burrows brought his Marines down from Philadelphia and set them up in a temporary camp (not far from today's Lincoln Memorial). In France, Bonaparte was now First Consul. No great friend of the Americans but a realist who did not want a continuing enemy in the New World, he caused the war which was never declared to end. The Peace Establishment Act drastically cut away at the Navy. The Marines were reduced from a strength of about 1100 to 700.

Burrows was giving permanent shape to the Corps. The law included provision for a "drum major, a fife major and thirty-two drums and fifes." Burrows was determined to have a proper Marine Band. He assessed his officers $10.00 each to buy additional instruments. The Band gave its first open-air concert on 21 August 1800, and made its debut at the President's House on New Year's Day, 1801. Thomas Jefferson had defeated John Adams in the election of 1800, and the Band played at his inauguration in March 1801 (as it has played for every inauguration since, becoming the "President's Own").

On 31 March Burrows rode out with the new President to look "for a proper place to fix the Marine Barracks on." They chose a square in Southeast Washington, bounded by 8th and 9th Streets, and G and I Streets, because "it lay near the Navy Yard and was within easy marching distance of the Capitol." The quadrangle was to be laid out in typical nineteenth-century barracks style. On the north side, on G Street, would be the Commandant's House.

Burrows, whose title had become Lieutenant Colonel Commandant, could also sternly instruct a junior officer, struck by a Navy lieutenant, to "wipe away this Insult," citing approvingly that "On board the *Ganges*, about 12 mos. ago, Lt. Gale, was struck by an Officer of the Navy, the Capt. took no notice of the Business and Gale got no satisfaction on the Cruise; the moment he arrived he call'd the Lieut. out and shot him; afterwards Politeness was restor'd. . . ."

Barbary Wars (1801–1815)

With the war with France behind them, there was work
for the Navy in the Mediterranean against the Barbary
pirates. Yusef Karamanli had made himself Bey of
Tripoli by murdering one older brother and chasing a
second brother out of the country. Looking at the
favors given Algiers and Tunis and greedy for his share
of the same, in May 1801 he cut down the flagstaff in
front of the American Consulate and declared war on
the United States.

President Jefferson dispatched a squadron to the
Mediterranean, the forerunner in almost unbroken line
to the Sixth Fleet of today, but not much was done with
it until, in September 1804, Commodore Samuel Barron
came out with fresh ships and took command of the
squadron. He brought with him Mr. William Eaton,
Arabic scholar, eccentric, and one-time captain in the
U. S. Army. Eaton had just been appointed Naval
Agent for the Barbary States and he had a secret plan
approved by Jefferson. He proceeded in the brig *Argus*
(commanded by Isaac Hull, Carmick's companion in
the cutting-out at Puerto Plata) to Egypt, found Hamet
Karamanli, Yusef's deposed brother, living several
hundred miles up the Nile with the Mamelukes and
persuaded him to join in an expedition against the Bey.
A polyglot "army" was put together in Alexandria,
most of it made up of Arabs, but also some European
soldiers-of-fortune, thirty-eight Greek mercenaries,
and Marine Lieutenant Presley N. O'Bannon with a
sergeant and six privates from the *Argus.*

Counting camel drivers and camp followers, the
column numbered perhaps four or five hundred. There
was a lurid march of six hundred miles across the
Libyan desert, punctuated with demands for more
money, murders, mutinies, and fights between the two
factions: Christian and Muslim. On 27 April 1805
Argus, 18, *Hornet*, 10, and *Nautilus*, 12, bombarded the
walled city of Derna while Eaton launched his attack

from the desert. Hamet and his Arabs came in from the southwest, while O'Bannon and his "Christians" attacked from the southeast. O'Bannon charged through the town, seized the harbor fort, and turned the guns on the governor's palace. In two hours the palace was taken and Hamet's Arabs were pursuing the defeated defenders across the desert. The Christians had lost thirteen men, including two Marines killed, and one wounded. On 3 June a peace treaty was concluded at Tripoli with Yusef. Hamet, who had expected to become the Bey, was mollified by the promise of a U. S. pension. O'Bannon came away with a Mameluke sword, reputedly a present from Hamet. (The regulation Marine officer's sword was patterned after O'Bannon's Mameluke scimitar in 1826 and the design has persisted except for one brief interlude. In 1859 the Mameluke pattern was abandoned for the heavier, more businesslike U. S. Army infantry officer's saber. In 1875 the Mameluke sword was restored, the saber being continued for noncommissioned officers. In World War II, Marine officers were officially encouraged to turn in their swords for scrap metal. There is no record of any officer being so foolish as to do so, and after the war the sword was quickly restored as a required item for regular officers.)

In Washington, ill-health forced the resignation of Lieutenant Colonel Commandant Burrows on 7 February 1804 (he would be dead within the year). His successor was Franklin Wharton, another Philadelphian. At the Marine Barracks, Wharton pushed the construction of the Commandant's House. The design was Georgian-Federal: two stories and an attic with dormer windows, and a hipped roof. The soft salmon-color bricks were baked on the site from clay dug in a pit halfway between the Barracks and the Navy Yard.

In March 1804 new uniform regulations came out. The colors were still blue for the coat, white for the pantaloons, and scarlet for the facings, but the cut was along latest European lines, with a high collar, black calf-length gaiters, and, most impressive of all, a tall shako with a red plush plume, and a large octagonal brass plate on the front embossed with an eagle and bearing the word "Marines" and the motto *Fortitudine* (with Fortitude).

Early in 1804 Captain Daniel Carmick was sent with 122 Marines to garrison New Orleans which had just become American by way of the Louisiana Purchase. In the next several years he put down bits and pieces of revolt and insurrection, and was promoted to major in 1809. Larger employment for him and his Marines was in the offing.

3

1812–1815
"Shall I board her, sir?"

War of 1812

Impressment was the device by which Britain's Royal Navy was kept manned. Distinctions between American and Briton were slight. The language was the same and appearance not much different. (Although officers in charge of press gangs were advised that "the typical American has a degenerate, hangdog air quite different from that of our noble British tars. . . .")

The new President, James Madison, was a scholarly, mild-mannered man who did not want war, but by 1812 the number of impressed American seamen had grown to 6000 and it was claimed there were more Americans in the Royal Navy than in the U. S. Navy. Madison, forced to choose between war and further degradation, asked Congress for a declaration of war and he got it on 18 June 1812.

The Marine Corps was at about half strength; the muster rolls for 30 June 1812 show only 10 officers and 483 enlisted men. Of these, more than half were on board ship or serving in the near-useless gunboats built by the inventive Jefferson for coast defense. In East Florida, among the swamps and alligators, a small

expeditionary force was campaigning variously against
Spaniards, Indians, and pirates. The few other Marines
were strung out in small detachments from Boston to
New Orleans.

The war started with the great frigate duels. On 19
August the *Constitution*, cruising off Newfoundland
met the *Guerrière*, 38. After an hour of maneuver and
bombardment the two frigates came together. Marine
Lieutenant William S. Bush went up on the rail, called
to Captain Isaac Hull, "Shall I board, sir?" and was
shot dead by a Royal Marine. The *Guerrière*'s own
decks were swept clear by musket fire from the
Constitution's decks and tops. Hullshot, sinking, and
allowed no chance to board, the *Guerrière* surrendered.
Too damaged to bring into port, she was burned.

Next honors went to the *Wasp*, an 18-gun sloop
under command of Master-Commandant Jacob Jones.
She intercepted *Frolic*, 20-gun brig-of-war, convoying
fourteen merchantmen, southwest of Bermuda on 18
October 1812. In a rough-weather battle of less than an
hour, in which Lieutenant John Brooks and his sixteen
Marines did their share, the *Frolic* was taken. But
before battle damage could be repaired and the *Wasp*
could get away with her prize, the 74-gun *Poictiers*
came bearing down and captured them both.

A week later the *United States*, captained by Stephen Decatur, met the *Macedonian*, 38, a strong new
frigate in the mid-Atlantic. The *Macedonian* was forced
to strike and was brought safely into port.

Meanwhile, the *Constitution* was at sea again. The
more senior William Bainbridge had replaced Isaac
Hull in command. On 29 December 1812, off the coast
of Brazil, the *Constitution* encountered the frigate
Java, 38. In a particularly bloody two-and-a-half-hour
fight, the Englishman was battered into surrender.

Three British frigates lost in four months? Nothing
like that had happened in fourteen years of naval war
with France. The London *Times*, which at the war's
beginning had sneered at the American Navy as a

"Handful of fir-built frigates with bits of striped bunting at their mast-heads, manned by bastards and outlaws," now cried, "Good God! Can such things be?"

At the end of October 1812, with 318 souls on board, the 32-gun frigate *Essex*, under Captain David Porter, cleared Delaware Bay with orders to rendezvous in the South Atlantic with the *Constitution*. Porter's Marine officer was Lieutenant John Marshall Gamble. On 12 December 1812, the *Essex* took His Majesty's packet *Nocton*, 10, and found $55,000 in gold in her strongbox. Porter then zigzagged across the South Atlantic but could not find the *Constitution* (which was on her way home for repairs), so he decided to take the *Essex* into the Pacific to go after the British whaling trade.

After a hard passage around the Horn, the *Essex* reached the whaling grounds in and around the Galapagos Islands. Prizes, in the shape of British whalers and privateers, came thick and fast. Porter kept six ships and eighty guns and made himself commodore of a squadron. Running out of Navy officers to command the prizes, he gave the privateer *Greenwich* to Gamble, who with it captured the biggest prize of all, the 22-gun *Seringapatam*.

His Majesty's frigate *Phoebe*, 36, and two 24-gun sloops, *Raccoon* and *Cherub*, were now in the Pacific with orders to find the *Essex*. Porter decided he had done a good year's work and retired discreetly to the Marquesas. He went in at Nukuhiva Island, impressed the natives with a parade of his Marines, and possessed it in the name of the United States. One tribe remained rebellious. Porter launched an amphibious landing. Slung stones and spears proved tougher opposition than he anticipated and for a time the expedition was down to Porter, Gamble, and the ship's doctor firing from behind one small tree. The next day Porter went back with two hundred Americans, burned ten villages in as many skirmishes, and peace settled on the island. Six weeks later, after refitting, Porter sailed off with the *Essex* and most of his force, leaving Gamble behind with three ships and twenty-two men. The *Essex* was scarcely over the horizon before there was a native rebellion. Gamble put it down but his own men were becoming mutinous.

Gamble hung on grimly in the Marquesas, but on 7 May 1814 the mutineers gained the upper hand, set sail in the *Seringapatam* (flying the Union Jack), and held Gamble, a musket ball in his heel, a prisoner. The mutineers put Gamble in an open boat with a few loyal hands. He managed to get back to Nukuhiva and after more hostilities sailed in the *Sir Andrew Hammond* with seven men for the Hawaiian Islands, where they were taken prisoner by the *Cherub*. They learned that on 28 March 1814, the *Essex* had been caught in Valparaiso harbor by the *Phoebe* and *Cherub*. The English ships stood off, using their long guns. The *Essex* caught fire; there was an explosion below decks and she was finished. Eventually, Gamble and his survivors were put ashore under parole at Rio de Janeiro and at the war's end made their way back to New York.

On the Great Lakes

While these events were taking place at sea, the U. S. Army's ambitious land campaign against the Canadian border had failed disastrously. One of the causes was continued British control of the Great Lakes. The first step taken to challenge this control was to establish a U. S. naval base at Sacketts Harbor on the eastern end of Lake Ontario, and by April 1813 there was a flotilla of fourteen more-or-less effective lake ships and a Marine force mustering three officers and 121 men. Because of the Niagara Falls, it was not possible to transit ships to the equally vital Lake Erie; hence, a separate squadron had to be established there. A fortunate choice as commander was Commodore Oliver Hazard Perry. He set up his base at Erie and began construction of his fleet.

Perry's friend, James Lawrence, commanding the *Hornet*, the 18-gun sister to the *Wasp*, had on 24 February 1813 sunk the brig *Peacock*, also 18 guns, in a fourteen-minute battle. Lawrence was promoted, given command of the *Chesapeake*—that unlucky 36-gun frigate which had been humiliated by HMS *Leopard* in 1807—and ordered to put to sea at once from Boston. He did so reluctantly. The *Chesapeake* was not ready. On 1 June 1813, she was met off Boston by the frigate *Shannon*, 38, Captain Philip B. V. Broke. There was an exchange of broadsides. Lawrence was struck in the hip, then hit again. Mortally wounded, he was carried below. "Don't give up the ship," he pleaded. "Sink her. Blow her up." Ten minutes after the action began, *Shannon*'s nine-pounders had cleared the American Marines from the fighting tops and Captain Broke was leading a boarding party onto the *Chesapeake*. Fifteen Marines were killed, including Lieutenant James Broom, and twenty more were wounded.

On Lake Erie, Perry, with ten vessels and a total of 54 guns, on 12 August 1813 met the British squadron of six ships and 61 guns. Perry's flagship was the new 20-gun brig *Lawrence*, named for his friend, and from her masthead flew a blue battle flag crudely lettered "Don't give Up the Ship." The English commodore, Robert H. Barclay, was in the *Detroit*, a 20-gun corvette and a fair match to the *Lawrence*. Lieutenant John Brooks had the Marine detachment in the *Lawrence*. Exchanged since his capture by the *Poictiers*, he had been sent west in April with twelve Marines and orders to recruit more along the way. He had no success with his recruiting and the dozen Marines had to be augmented with Army volunteers, some of them Kentucky riflemen. In the fight between the squadrons, Brooks had his hip taken away by a round shot and bled to death. When it was all over, and the British squadron had surrendered, Perry in his report would coin another American naval slogan: "We have met the enemy and they are ours."

Britain's Strategy

After Napoleon was exiled to Elba in May 1814, England could give larger attention to the troubles in America. Her strategy had three parts: invasion of New York by way of Lake Champlain (reminiscent of Burgoyne's vain venture), a tightened blockade against the Atlantic seaboard with forays against the principal cities, and an expedition against New Orleans to detach the Mississippi Valley from the Union.

Sir George Prevost marched down from Canada with 11,000 troops and halted outside the American works at Plattsburg to await the arrival of the British lake fleet. Commodore George Downie had contrived a first-class 38-gun frigate, the *Confiance*, in addition to a brig, two sloops, and twelve row-galleys. On the American side, Lieutenant Thomas Macdonough had the 24-gun *Saratoga*, a brig, a schooner, and ten gunboats. He had asked for Marines and had gotten none, so soldiers had to serve as such. The squadrons came together on 11 September 1814 off Valcour Island. Commodore Downie was killed early in the action and at the end there was not a mast left in either squadron sound enough to bear sail, but the Americans had won. General Prevost was watching from shore, and next day began his march back to Canada.

On the Atlantic coast, early in 1813, Rear Admiral George Cockburn had raided the Chesapeake and burned Havre de Grace, Maryland. He then began operations around Norfolk, Virginia. The *Constellation* and twenty of Jefferson's gunboats were bottled up in Hampton Roads. The British landed 2500 infantry and Marines against Craney Island on 22 June 1813. The American garrison of 750 (including the *Constellation*'s 50 Marines under Lieutenant Henry B. Breckinridge) held them off. The British did take Hampton, defended by a few hundred militia stiffened by a handful of Marines.

On 27 June 1814 an expedition of some 4000 British

troops sortied from the Gironde under the command of Major General Robert Ross, a distinguished veteran of the Spanish Peninsular campaign against Bonaparte. Point of attack was to be decided by Vice Admiral Alexander Cochrane. The admiral and the general rendezvoused in Bermuda and on 3 August sailed for the Chesapeake. Ross landed his troops at Benedict, Maryland. Impeded by nothing more than the blazing August sun, he marched to Marlboro, arriving there on 23 August and meeting with Cockburn's force, which included two battalions of Royal Marines.

Bladensburg

On the American side, the defense of Washington had been entrusted to the uncertain hands of Brigadier General Henry Winder, USA. There were no prepared defenses, but on paper he had about 10,000 troops available, mostly militia. Commodore Joshua Barney, who had earlier burned his flotilla of useless gunboats, had about 400 seamen and five guns with which to cover the bridge over the Eastern Branch (now called the Anacostia River) which led to the Navy Yard. He was joined there by Captain Samuel Miller, Marine Corps adjutant, and 103 Marines from the Washington Barracks.

On 24 August the British committed themselves to the easier crossing at Bladensburg, farther up the Eastern Branch, and some five miles from the Capitol. On the west side of the river, Winder with six or seven thousand men, of whom not more than three hundred were regulars, had thrown a line. Barney, not under Army orders and with no intention of putting himself under Winder's immediate command, moved to a position on a commanding piece of ground astride the road to Washington and about a mile behind the American line.

The British advance, led by the Light Brigade, under Colonel Thornton of the 85th Regiment, came across

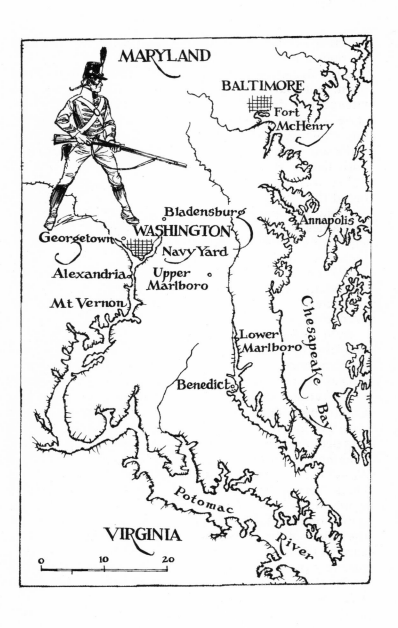

MARYLAND

BALTIMORE

Fort
McHenry

Bladensburg

WASHINGTON

Annapolis

Georgetown

Navy Yard

Alexandria

Upper
Marlboro

Mt Vernon

Lower
Marlboro

Chesapeake Bay

Benedict

Potomac

VIRGINIA

River

0   10   20

the river—some by the bridge, some wading—behind a barrage of Congreve rockets. Winder's militia scattered and the British assumed the road to Washington to be open, but Barney's force handed them a rude and unexpected shock. The five guns, served man-of-war style, cleared the advance from the road with grape and canister. After a third charge failed to budge the sailors and Marines, the English began to work around both flanks. Barney was shot through the thigh and Miller was also wounded. Almost encircled, they ordered their troops to retire. Both were then captured. The Marines had lost 8 killed and 14 wounded. British casualties were 64 killed, 185 wounded. Meanwhile, Madison's government was fleeing Washington. Lieutenant Colonel Commandant Wharton, having sent Miller off to battle with every available man, now loaded the Marine pay chest into a commandeered wagon and headed, in company with the paymaster, for Frederick, Maryland.

By nightfall, the British were in the capital. As Ross and Cockburn rode into Capitol Square they received some rounds of small-arms fire from the Gallatin House. Ross's horse was killed and he ordered the house burned and the occupants put to the sword. The Capitol building was then set afire. Ross and Cockburn, with two hundred men, marched on to the White House and personally put it to the torch. Elsewhere in the city, Commodore Thomas Tingey, superintendent of the Navy Yard, ordered it burned to keep its works and ships from falling into British hands. Next morning, while Ross went about the business of destroying public buildings, Cockburn amused himself by sacking the offices of the newspaper *National Intelligencer*. "Be sure all the C's are destroyed," he ordered, "so that the rascals cannot any longer abuse my name."

The Commandant's House and the Marine Barracks were left untouched. There are several legends to explain the omission: Cockburn and Ross are supposed to have used the House as their headquarters; or they left the House and Barracks unmolested as a mark of their esteem for the stand the Marines had made at Bladensburg; or, as professional officers, they would not burn married officers' quarters. However, there is no evidence to support any of these explanations, and perhaps the Barracks and House went unburned simply because they escaped the incendiaries' attention.

The British marched out that night, leaving their dead unburied at Bladensburg and their wounded in American hands, retiring swiftly and in good order to the Chesapeake. Re-embarked, they moved next against Baltimore. Aghast at the fate of Washington, the Americans undertook the defenses of Baltimore with more determination. Among the defenders was a naval brigade which included the Marine survivors of Bladensburg. Ross landed fourteen miles from the city, his advance was checked, and he himself killed. There was then some effort at a night attack on 13 September. The British fleet bombarded the defensive works, primarily Fort McHenry, all day and on up until midnight, but when dawn came, as a young American, Francis Scott Key, held by the British saw it, ". . . our Flag was still there."

New Orleans

On 19 September Admiral Cochrane sailed for Halifax and there were no more raiding expeditions in the Chesapeake. The British landing force, after Baltimore, went to Jamaica where they were joined in November by Major General Sir Edward Pakenham, Wellington's brother-in-law, sent out to take Ross's place.

At New Orleans, Major Daniel Carmick's Marines, now up to about 300 in strength, had been fighting Creole pirates under Jean Lafitte. On 14 September 1814 Carmick put the pirate stronghold at Barataria to the torch. Admiral Cochrane is supposed to have offered Lafitte 30,000 pounds sterling and a commission in the Royal Navy to join the British. Lafitte refused, volunteering himself and his men for the defense of New Orleans in exchange for an American pardon. Major General Andrew Jackson, now on the scene as the American commander, accepted.

The British plan was to move against New Orleans through Lake Borgne. For once, Jefferson's gunboats gave good service. Lieutenant Thomas ap Catesby Jones's lake force of five gunboats and 182 men, including 35 Marines, was attacked on 14 December by nearly 1000 English embarked in forty-seven barges. One by one the gunboats were captured but the attack cost the British 300 killed and wounded.

When Jackson took up his famous defensive line behind the Rodriguez Canal, one flank on the Mississippi, the other secured by a cypress swamp, Carmick's Marines were in the center and Lafitte's buccaneers were manning much of the artillery. Pakenham ordered an attack on 28 December, but after feeling out the strength of Jackson's defense, broke it off. Carmick, leading a countercharge, fell with wounds that would eventually cost him his life. Pakenham's main attack came on 8 January 1815. He sent 1200 troops across the river while the main body, 5300 strong, advanced in a frontal assault. Waiting behind the breastworks were some 3500 Americans with another 1000 in reserve. In twenty minutes, the British had lost 2036 killed and wounded. Pakenham, hit three times, was dead. American casualties, by some accounts, were as few as 8 killed, 13 wounded. Jackson let the British bury their dead, about 700 of them, and go back to their ships unmolested. Pakenham's body went home to Ireland in a cask of rum.

Ironically, the war was officially over before the battle was fought; the Treaty of Ghent had been signed on Christmas Eve, 1814. Even so, New Orleans was not the last engagement of the war. Ships at sea could not be informed of the peace and isolated actions continued for another six months. On 20 February 1814 the *Constitution*, already known as "Old Ironsides," with

Captain Archibald Henderson on board as senior Marine, engaged and captured the miniature frigate *Cyane*, 34, and the sloop-of-war *Levant*, 20, in a four-hour battle.

So ended the second war with Britain. The muster rolls of the Corps for 30 June 1814, at the peak of hostilities, show only 11 officers and 579 enlisted men, although actual strength may have been somewhat higher. First priority had been to provide detachments to the ships of the blue-water Navy. There were never enough Marines to do even this, let alone provide Marines for the equally critical Lake squadrons. Company-sized units under Miller and Carmick had fought heroically at Bladensburg and New Orleans but apparently no thought was given to forming an expeditionary force or even a permanent battalion structure. Nor indeed, did the nature of the war offer any particularly inviting amphibious targets. As the nation turned from war to peace, the future of the Marine Corps was ambiguous.

1816–1844
"...insult to the Flag reveng'd."

Courts-Martial for Commandants

Archibald Henderson (brevetted a major for gallant
service in the *Constitution*) and others thought Wharton's failure to take the field at Bladensburg disgrace-
ful. Henderson, born in 1783 at Colchester, Virginia,
almost within the boundaries of the present-day base at
Quantico, charged the Commandant with neglect of
duty and conduct unbecoming an officer and gentleman. There was an Army general court-martial
(ashore, remember, the Marine Corps was subject to
the Articles of War and Army jurisdiction) in September 1817, but to Henderson's intense disgust Wharton
was acquitted. The new President, James Monroe,
urged Wharton to resign, but he doggedly continued in
office until his death the following year, 1 September
1818.

By the workings of the iron rules of seniority,
Irish-born Anthony Gale, duelist of the *Ganges*, was
appointed Lieutenant Colonel Commandant on 3
March 1819. Gale's hot temper and dubious personal
habits soon put him at cross purposes with the Secretary of the Navy. Again there was an Army general

court-martial. Among the charges was one of
". . . being intoxicated in common dram shops and
other places of low repute in the City of Washington."
Gale pleaded not guilty by reason of temporary insan-
ity, but the court found him guilty as charged. President Monroe approved the sentence, which was dis-
missal from the service, and it was put into execution
on 16 October 1820.

Henderson, who was commanding at Carmick's old
post in New Orleans, was now named Commandant.
The Peace Establishment Act of 1817 had put the
authorized strength of the Corps at 50 officers and 942
enlisted Marines. The Act had also created the posts of
Adjutant and Inspector, Quartermaster, and Paymaster; a staff structure which would continue until
World War II. Actually on board on 30 June 1820,
according to official returns, were 19 officers and 552
enlisted men. Henderson decreed that all newly commissioned officers would come to duty at Headquarters
for training, the beginning of what is now called The
Basic School. Also at Headquarters a skeleton battalion was to be maintained both for training and expeditionary uses.

In the Caribbean and along the Gulf of Mexico, there
was a plethora of revolutionary governments all issuing letters of marque and the line between privateering
and outright piracy was indistinguishable. In 1822 a
West India Squadron was created and a year later,
Commodore David Porter, the Marines' old friend, was
given command. He built a base at mosquito-infested
Key West, got the shallow-draft boats he needed for
in-shore work and some three hundred Marines for
expeditionary use. Constrained by orders from the
Secretary of the Navy which urged harmony with local
Spanish officials and cautioned against overzealous-
ness, Porter found it advantageous to operate in concert with the British Navy. American courts showed a
tendency to release prisoners for lack of evidence.
British captains were less squeamish and inclined to

hang pirates without judicial ceremony. With sometimes the cooperation, sometimes the opposition of the
Spanish governors, Porter's squadron swept the coasts
of Santo Domingo, Cuba, and part of Yucatán. Then, on
14 November 1824, he landed two hundred sailors and
Marines at Fajardo, Puerto Rico. This went beyond his
orders and was an embarrassment to Washington.
Porter was recalled and court-martialed. Given six
months' suspension, he resigned from the United
States Service and went off to be Commander-in-Chief
of the Mexican Navy.

In these years there were other expeditions and
actions in more faraway places, against pirates, slav-
ers, and sundry unenlightened heathen. They were of
the kind where the after-action report almost invari-
ably concluded with the words ". . . insult to the Flag
reveng'd." Some examples follow:

In April 1820, Marines on board the *Cyane*, now
under the American flag and refitted as a 24-gun sloop,
helped in the taking of seven slaving schooners off the
coast of West Africa. In the summer and fall of 1827,
Marines in the sloop *Warren*, 18, and schooner *Por-
poise*, 12, searched out pirates in the Greek archipelago. A landing party from the *Lexington*, 18, went
ashore in the Falkland Islands on 1 January 1832,
impressed the Argentines with a fanfaronade of musk-
etry, and shook loose three impounded American
schooners. On the other side of the world, pirates had
seized the merchantman *Friendship*, loading pepper in
the harbor of Kuala Batu, Sumatra, and had killed
several members of the crew. The *Potomac*, 44, put 250
Marines and sailors ashore on 7 February 1832, and in
two bloody days they killed the local sultan, captured
four pirate forts, and burned the town.

At home there were troubles of a different kind.
Andrew Jackson was now President. Like many other
Army generals and several Presidents since, he saw no
reason for a separate corps of Marines and, in December 1829, recommended to the Congress "that the

Marine Corps be merged in the artillery or infantry, as the best mode of curing the many defects in its organization. . . . Details for Marine service could well be made from the artillery or infantry, there being no peculiar training required for it."

There was serious confusion as to the legal and administrative status of the Corps stemming from the ambiguous nature of the 1798 Act: Was the Corps part of the Army or Navy, or was it something of unique nature? Hearings were held by both Houses of Congress. In 1831 Secretary of the Navy John Branch recommended the "discontinuance of the Marine Corps or its transfer entirely" to either the Army or Navy. There were supporters of the Corps, though, among the public and in the Congress and on 30 June 1834, "An Act for the Better Organization of the Marine Corps" was passed. It established that afloat or ashore, the Marine Corps was part of the Department of the Navy, a separate service, sister to but not part of the U. S. Navy, but that the President could direct the Marines to perform such duties as his judgment dictated, including service with the Army. (The distinctions made were exceedingly fine and successive Army and Navy generations have not always completely understood them so that they have required constant reassertion.) The Act of 1834 additionally raised the rank of the Commandant to colonel and the authorized strength of the Corps to 63 officers and 1224 enlisted (actual strength was a third less). Also in 1834, President Jackson took the Marines out of their blue uniforms and put them into a grass-green coat with buff facings and gray trousers.

Seminole War (1836–1842)

Next year there was trouble in Florida. The government had decided to relocate the Seminoles to what is now Arkansas and sent troops to Florida to enforce the move. The Seminoles under their principal chief Osceola, who was half-English, half-Creek, withdrew to the almost inaccessible depths of the Everglades and by spring of 1836, with a thousand soldiers trying to round up three thousand Indians, the Army was in difficulty. The Creek Indians, parent nation to the Seminoles, now elected to go on the warpath in southern Georgia and Alabama. Colonel Henderson volunteered a regiment of Marines and on 23 May 1836 Andrew Jackson, using the authority of the Act of 1834, ordered all available Marines to service with the Army.

By stripping down all shore stations, Henderson was able to field half the strength of the Corps in a two-battalion regiment commanded by himself. He left Sergeant Major Triguet behind at Headquarters to do the administration ("He is a respectable old man, and has no other failing than that which too often attends an old soldier"), and the Marine Band to flesh out the guard at the Marine Barracks and Navy Yard.

Lieutenant Colonel Samuel Miller, late of Bladensburg, assembled the 1st Battalion at Fortress Monroe, Virginia, where Henderson joined them, and on 2 June they left in the chartered steamer *Columbus* for Charleston, South Carolina, and then went by "steam car" to Augusta, Georgia. From there it was a thirty-four-day foot march to Columbus, Georgia, where Henderson reported to Major General Winfield Scott. The 2d Battalion, formed at New York, arrived a few days later. Scott was planning a careful, deliberate campaign. Jackson, who disliked Scott in any case, grew impatient and replaced him with Major General Thomas S. Jesup.

Some of the Marines were armed with Samuel Colt's new revolving cylinder rifles, but these proved to have the distressing habit of going off on their own accord, so the Marines went back to their muskets. By the end of the summer, the Creeks were on their way to the Oklahoma Territory and attention could be returned to the Seminoles in Florida. Jesup divided his forces into two brigades. Henderson was given command of the 2d Brigade and it included, in addition to his Marine Regiment, a battalion of friendly Creeks officered by Marines, the 4th Infantry Regiment, an artillery regiment, and some Georgia volunteers. Henderson's brigade pushed the Seminoles back to the Hatchee-Lustee River northeast of Tampa. On 27 January 1837, in a long day's confused fight, the Americans crossed the river. Only one dead Indian and two dead Negroes were counted, but it was a victory, and four days later a Seminole chief, Abraham, offered to parley. The chiefs agreed to move their people to a reservation and a peace treaty was signed on 6 March 1837.

On 22 May, Henderson, thinking the war was over, started back for Washington, leaving behind a two-company battalion of 189 officers and men under the command of Samuel Miller. On 2 June, 700 Seminoles waiting at Tampa for transportation were spirited away by a war party headed by Osceola himself, and the war was on again. In September, Osceola asked for a meeting with Jesup. Jesup ignored the truce, arrested Osceola, and had him carried off to Fort Moultrie in South Carolina, where he died in January 1838. By the summer of 1842 the war had worn itself out and the Marine battalion returned north. In addition, some 130 Marines had served in the "Mosquito Fleet," a shallow-draft division of the West India Squadron that patrolled the coast and probed the watery reaches of the Everglades. Sixty-one Marines had died in the six long years. Archibald Henderson was brevetted a brigadier general, the first Marine to hold that rank, for his victory at Hatchee-Lustee. As for the Seminoles, there never was a formal treaty, and while some 4000 were moved to Oklahoma, many slipped away and, as every tourist in Florida knows, they are still in the Everglades.

Jackson's grass-green uniform did not outlast the war. The green faded badly in field service; a return to the blue uniform was authorized in 1839, and executed in 1841. The new uniform had a dark blue coat and light blue trousers (with a scarlet stripe down the seam for the officers and NCOs). For dress, there was still a tall leather shako. For undress use, there was a dark blue cloth cap with a patent leather visor. The cap device was a fouled anchor encircled by a wreath done in gold embroidery.

5

1845–1859
"…to the Halls of the Montezumas."

Filibustering in California

At eight in the evening of 30 October 1845, First Lieutenant Archibald H. Gillespie met secretly with President James K. Polk. Before seeing the President, the thirty-three-year-old Gillespie had been questioned by the Secretary of the Navy as to his proficiency in Spanish and told that he was to carry dispatches to California, going by way of Mexico and observing conditions there. He was also to deliver a packet of personal letters to Captain John C. Frémont, then on his third exploration of the West.

Gillespie, thinly disguised as a Scotch-whisky salesman, sailed to Veracruz, proceeded overland to Mexico City, found the country torn by revolution but anti-Yankee, and formed a low opinion of its soldiery. It was February before he emerged on the west coast at Mazatlán and reported to the elderly Commodore John D. Sloat, commander of the Pacific Squadron, who sent him on to Honolulu in the 18-gun sloop *Cyane* (namesake of the War of 1812 capture) ostensibly as a merchant bound for China. *Cyane* then doubled back to Monterey, California. Here, on 17 April 1846, Gillespie delivered his memorized dispatches to the American consul. California was already in a state of insurrection, but it appeared the Californians would accept a British protectorate rather than ask for annexation by the United States. The British Pacific Fleet flagship, *Collingwood*, was off the California coast and outgunned the American Pacific Squadron several times over.

First leg in Gillespie's search for Frémont was to go up the Sacramento to Sutter's Fort. There, Gillespie recruited a couple of local Americans as guides and with a total party of five men started north through Indian country. Frémont, who had left St. Louis in June 1845 with sixty mountain men, including the already legendary Kit Carson, had broken a trail across the Salt Desert, made a winter crossing of the High Sierras, and since December had been oscillating between Oregon and California, fighting Indians when the need arose and brushing with the Californian authorities.

Gillespie and Frémont met on the banks of the Klamath the night of 9 May 1846. There were, Frémont estimated, about eight hundred Americans in northern California, all good citizens, armed and equipped for service. That night, an Indian raiding party caught them in their blankets and Frémont lost three men before the raiders were beaten off. The next morning, Frémont marched to the nearest Indian village, burned it, killed fourteen or fifteen braves and perhaps a squaw or two, and then headed for the California settlements.

Mexican War (1846–1848)

On the very day that Frémont and Gillespie met in Oregon, the battle of Resaca de la Palma had been fought in Texas and a state of war existed between the United States and Mexico. In California, oblivious to these events, Gillespie had been sent ahead by Frémont to Yerba Buena (present-day San Francisco) to get supplies. By the time he got back up to the Sacramento, in mid-June, the Bear Flag had been run up at Sonoma and California declared a republic. A California Battalion was formed, four companies, totaling 224 rifles, with Frémont as commander and Gillespie as his adjutant.

On the coast, dispatches as to the official state of war reached Commodore Sloat and on 7 July 1846 the U. S. flag was raised over Monterey. Frémont's assortment of mountain men, traders, horse thieves, Indians, and sailors had by this time assumed the approximate status of a battalion of irregular mounted Naval infantry. He reached Monterey on 19 July, where Commodore Robert F. Stockton had replaced the lethargic Sloat. The California Battalion was crowded on board the *Cyane*, sailed for San Diego, and took it without a fight on 29 July. Stockton then issued a proclamation naming Gillespie Military Commandant of the South and left him with about fifty men to hold the City of the Angels. Gillespie's position was almost immediately invested by an enemy force he generously estimated at six hundred. He elected to march out with full military honors rather than fight, and at the end of September was picked up at San Pedro by the 18-gun sloop-of-war *Vandalia*.

Stockton now made a couple of tries at recapturing Los Angeles with the help of a landing force of some three hundred sailors and Marines. These operations were interrupted by news that Brigadier General Stephen W. Kearny, USA, with an advance party of his Army of the West was just east of San Diego. Stockton dispatched Gillespie with a detachment of the California Battalion to find Kearny. He did, and found that Kearny, who had already been met by Kit Carson, had no army with him, but only about a hundred dragoons on worn-out horses.

A fairly good-size force of Mexicans was at Rancho Santa Margarita (site of present-day Camp Pendleton), and on 6 December 1846 the Battle of San Pascual was

fought, American dragoons and riflemen against Californian lancers. Although the Mexicans left the field to
the Americans, Kearny had suffered 19 killed and 30
wounded (including Gillespie and himself) out of a total
of 153 Americans. His force too weakened to move,
Kearny took up a hilltop position near San Bernardo
which was quickly surrounded by the Californians. Kit
Carson slipped through the Mexican lines and on 11
December brought back a relief column that included
Lieutenant Jacob Zeilin, who had the Marine detachment in the frigate *Congress*.

When they all got together at San Diego, the combined American strength was about six hundred. With
the dual American commanders, Stockton and Kearny,
eyeing each other suspiciously, the column started
north on 29 December. There was a last fight on 8
January 1847 at the crossing of the San Gabriel, and
two days later Stockton reoccupied Los Angeles.

With Scott at Veracruz

While these heady events were taking place in California, more conventional operations were being pursued along the rim of the Gulf of Mexico. Having fought and won the battles of Palo Alto and Resaca de la Palma on 8 and 9 May 1846 against the gorgeously uniformed but poorly armed Mexican army, Brigadier General Zachary Taylor crossed the Rio Grande into Mexico on 18 May, a historic moment somewhat marred by a Marine landing party having gone ashore at Burrita on the Mexican side of the river some hours earlier.

The problem facing Commodore David Conner's Gulf Squadron was twofold: the blockade of the Mexican Gulf ports and the support of Taylor's army as it moved south into Mexico. By combining all the Marine detachments in the squadron, a two-hundred-man provisional battalion was formed under Captain Alvin Edson. There were raids against Frontera and Tampico in October; Tampico was secured in November; and two unsuccessful attempts were made at taking Alvarado. By then it had been recognized that no matter what success Taylor might continue to have, it was a long, perhaps impossible, march from the Rio Grande to Mexico City. Accordingly, half his army was detached for service with Major General Winfield Scott, who was to land at Veracruz.

Scott landed on 9 March 1847. He put 12,000 men ashore on an undefended beach some three miles south of the city, then in an attack coordinated with Commodore Conner's squadron, brought Veracruz under siege. Edson's battalion, numbering some 180 Marines, went ashore with Worth's division and gave good service. On 21 March Commodore Matthew C. Perry, who had been the naval second-in-command and acting as what we would now call the amphibious force commander, succeeded Conner in command of the Gulf Squadron. There was a strenuous bombardment of the city, the

walls were breached, and Veracruz capitulated on 29 March 1847.

Perry, the younger brother of Oliver Hazard Perry, had had landing force experience before coming to the Gulf when he commanded the Africa Squadron. Under the Webster–Ashburton Treaty the United States had been cooperating with the British in the suppression of the slave trade. In November 1843 Perry had landed with a party of Marines and sailors in Liberia to investigate the reported murder of some Americans. Perry got into a scuffle with the native chief, one King Ben Crack-O. A Marine sergeant shot Crack-O. Some other Marines pinned the chief to the ground with their bayonets until he could be tied up and carted off. In the general melee that followed, Crack-O's village and several others were burned.

With Veracruz captured, Commodore Perry went back to the neutralization of the remaining Gulf ports.

More aggressive and imaginative than Conner, he formed a landing force brigade, about 1500 strong, with Edson's battalion serving as a nucleus. Alvarado was captured on 1 April and Tuxpan on 18 April. This left Frontera, at the mouth of the Tabasco River, the one port of consequence still to be won. Perry put his landing force ashore at Frontera on 15 May 1847. He then sent a column of shallow-draft steamers, gunboats, and barges up the river toward San Juan Bautista. On 14 June, there was a final fight for the town: 400 Mexican defenders were chased away and 12 guns and 600 muskets captured. Perry elected to hold the town until 22 July, when the approach of the yellow fever season made it wise to withdraw.

On to Mexico City

In Washington, Archibald Henderson was set upon repeating his performance in the Seminole wars. On 3 March he had gotten approval from President Polk to form a Marine regiment for service with Scott. The regimental headquarters and 1st Battalion were formed at Fort Hamilton, New York, under command of Lieutenant Colonel Samuel E. Watson, and arrived at Veracruz on 1 July 1847. Captain Edson's Marines were supposed to form the 2d Battalion, but Commodore Perry, busy with his Tabasco expedition, was not about to release them, so the regiment had to be reorganized into a single battalion.

Scott had moved out of Veracruz on 8 April. In front of him were three hundred miles, all uphill, to the Mexican capital. Dictator Antonio Lopez de Santa Ana, after being defeated at Buena Vista in February by "Old Rough and Ready" Taylor, had hurried south and was in good position to stop Scott, all advantages as to terrain, numbers, and logistics being in the defenders' favor. But Scott beat him in a series of battles beginning with Cerro Gordo and the American army had now paused at Puebla to bring up supplies and rein-

forcements for the final drive against Mexico City. The
Marine Battalion arrived at Puebla on 6 August and
was brigaded with Brigadier General John A. Quitman's division. Lieutenant Colonel Watson, who had
served under Scott in the War of 1812, was given
command of the 2d Brigade and Major Levi Twiggs,
also an elderly veteran of the War of 1812, moved up to
command of the Marine Battalion. Two days later,
Scott, with 11,000 men, cut his lines of communications and marched out of Puebla.

The Mexican army in front of him now numbered
32,000. A month's hard fighting, in which the Marine
Battalion did little except protect the baggage trains,
brought Scott within assaulting distance of Mexico
City. Key to the city was Chapultepec Castle, protecting the two causeways which led to San Cosme and
Belen gates. Scott planned to attack the Castle with
Pillow's division coming against the west face and
Quitman's division against the southern face. Major
Twiggs was to lead the assault in Quitman's attack,
with Captain John G. Reynolds heading the "pioneer
storming party" made up of forty volunteer soldiers
and Marines. At 0800, 13 September, following two
hours of bombardment, the attack began. Major
Twiggs, wearing an India rubber coat and carrying a
favorite double-barreled fowling piece, stepped out in
front. Immediately behind came Captain Reynolds, his
pioneers carrying scaling ladders, pickaxes, and wreck-
ing bars. Unexpected fire from five Mexican guns to
their right rear caused them to take cover in a ditch.
Quitman told them to hold at that point. Twiggs got
tired of waiting, climbed out into the open, and was
shot dead by a volley from the Castle. Reynolds now
urged Watson to get things moving but the old man
was waiting for orders from Quitman. Captain George
C. Terrett went off on his own with his company and
captured the troublesome battery. Terrett then started
across the causeway with sixty-seven men and two
sections of Army light artillery. A troop of Mexican

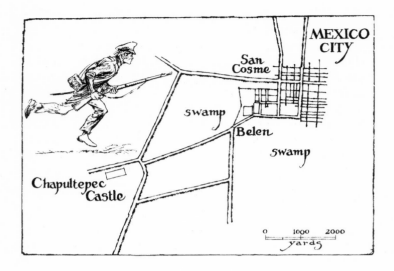

lancers clattered out but failed to stop Terrett. He was now providentially joined by Second Lieutenant Ulysses S. Grant and twenty-six soldiers from the 4th Infantry. Together they carried the San Cosme Gate.

To their rear both Pillow's and Quitman's divisions had gotten over the walls and into Chapultepec. By nightfall Quitman had taken the Belen Gate. During the night the Mexican army, except for some irregulars, evacuated the city. Quitman marched in the next morning. The Marines were given the job of clearing the Palacio Nacional. A Marine lieutenant cut down the Mexican colors and ran up the Stars and Stripes. General Scott ("Old Fuss and Feathers" to distinguish him from "Old Rough and Ready" Taylor), a man of immense girth, heavily climbed the stairs of the "Halls of Montezuma" to write his victory dispatch.

In the West, the conquest of California completed, the Pacific Squadron turned its attention to Mexico's west coast ports. Mazatlán, Guaymas, Muleje, San Blas, and San José were quickly, and, for the most part, uneventfully, taken. The landing at Mazatlán was on 10

November 1847, the Corps' 72d Birthday. A force of 730 sailors and Marines went ashore, covered by the frigates *Congress* and *Independence* and the ubiquitous *Cyane*. Jacob Zeilin, now a captain, was ensconced in the Presidio as military governor, where he remained until 17 June 1848.

By that time, the Marine Battalion from Scott's army had returned to the capital. The citizens of Washington gave the Commandant a new set of colors emblazoned with a new motto: "From Tripoli to the Halls of the Montezumas."

Panama, Japan, China, and Elsewhere

Gold was discovered near Sutter's Fort in January 1848. There were three routes to California: across the plains, around Cape Horn, or, quickest of all, across the Isthmus of Panama. In 1846 the United States had concluded a treaty with New Grenada (now Colombia) giving the United States "the right of way or transit across the Isthmus of Panama upon any modes of communication that now exist or that may be hereafter constructed."

In 1855, after seven years' work and a high death rate from fever, the American-owned Panama Railroad was opened across the narrow neck. To protect it, Marines made landings at Panama City in 1856 and again in 1860. In neighboring Nicaragua there had been three landings in the years 1852 to 1854, the last on 12 July 1854 when Greytown was bombarded and burned. Much farther south, landings were made at Montevideo, Uruguay, in November 1855 and January 1858; the second landing being in company with the British, John Reynolds, now a brevet major, leading the U. S. Marines. That same year, three hundred Marines, the combined detachments of the Brazil Squadron, went up the Paraná River to Asunción, Paraguay, in a show of force.

In July 1853 Commodore Matthew Perry took the

East India Squadron on its historic visit to Japan, stopping en route at Okinawa and in the Bonins. In the squadron, now-Major Jacob Zeilin had six officers and two hundred enlisted Marines. You can see them in contemporary Japanese woodprints; blue jackets, white trousers and cross-belts, and tall black shakos. There was a second, even more elaborate, visit in February 1854. On 31 March the first treaty between Japan and the United States was concluded; two ports, Shimoda and Hakodate, were opened to trade. The modernization of Japan had begun.

China was in the grip of the Taiping Rebellion. The East India Squadron was based at Hong Kong. On 4 April 1854 the sloop *Plymouth* put her sergeant's guard ashore in company with Royal Marines to protect foreign concessions at Shanghai. The performance was repeated by the steam frigate *Powhattan* on 19 May 1855, and on 4 August Marines from the *Powhattan* again joined the British, this time in an action against a pirate base near Hong Kong.

Canton was a treaty port and in the fall of 1856 there was trouble. Main contestants were the British and French against the Cantonese but a small Marine guard had been put into the city to look after U. S. interests (consuls, missionaries, and traders). About the time that Captain Andrew H. Foote, commanding the sloop *Portsmouth*, accepted the Cantonese governor's assurances of protection and agreed to withdraw the landing party, his boats were fired upon by the so-called "Barrier Forts." There were four of these forts in the Pearl River, European-engineered and armed with a profusion of heavy guns behind seven-foot breastworks faced with granite. On 16 November 1856 the East India, or Asiatic, Squadron, moved against the offending forts with the steam frigate *San Jacinto* and the two sloops *Portsmouth* and *Levant*. On the twentieth, Captain Foote went ashore at the head of 287 sailors and Marines (the Marines being under command of Captain John D. Simms, who had been among those present at Chapultepec). The first fort was taken from the rear, the remaining three systematically reduced. Some 170 cannon were captured—up to 8- and 10-inch caliber—and either spiked or rolled into the river. Of the 5000 (by U. S. estimate) Chinese defenders, at least 250 and perhaps 500 were dead. American losses were 7 killed and 20 wounded.

In these years the Home Squadron cruised from Newfoundland to the mouth of the Amazon, with special attention given the Caribbean. Cuba was in revolution and part of the Squadron's mission was enforcing U. S. neutrality. The Mediterranean Squadron had had a quiet time since the affairs with the Barbary pirates. The African Squadron continued its antislave trade patrols. The remaining squadron, the Pacific Squadron, usually based at Valparaiso, had a wide expanse of water to cruise. There were punitive landings in the Fiji Islands in 1855 and 1858. The sloop-of-war *Decatur* was kept on station at the village of Seattle in the Oregon Territory to keep the Puget Indians in check, and one sharp action occurred there on 26 January 1856. Duties afloat had not changed much since the days of the Continental Navy. There were still landing parties, still sharpshooters in the fighting tops, still practice at repelling boarders, but internal discipline was easier. There were new uniform regulations in 1859. The dress uniform had a French-style shako with a pompom which was not popular; but the rakish fatigue cap, copied after the French *képi*, would stay in style for fifty years.

Archibald Henderson died in office on 6 January 1859 at age seventy-six, having been Commandant for thirty-nine years. The next senior officer, Lieutenant Colonel John Harris, was named Colonel-Commandant. In his forty-five years of service Harris had seen three wars and he was already sixty-six years old.

6

1859–1865
"–this Negro question..."

Harpers Ferry

On a Sunday night, 16 October 1859, a man with a long gray beard and a fierce eye who called himself Isaac Smith came into Harpers Ferry, where the Shenandoah joins the Potomac, with some eighteen armed men, white and black. They took possession of the U. S. Arsenal—no soldiers were in garrison there—and rounded up some hostages. By now "Smith" had been recognized as the abolitionist John Brown, last heard from in bloody Kansas. The local militia came gingerly onto the scene, there was some shooting, and Brown took his men and hostages into a brick building on the Arsenal grounds where the fire engines were kept.

In Washington after the first confused reports came clacking in by telegraph, the Secretary of War ordered Lieutenant Colonel Robert E. Lee, who was at Arlington (home on leave from Texas), to put down the insurrection. A cavalry lieutenant, J. E. B. Stuart by name, volunteered to go along as his aide. They left that afternoon for Harpers Ferry on the five-o'clock train.

There were no Federal soldiers immediately available, but a detachment of eighty-six Marines from the Washington Barracks had already gone forward, under Lieutenant Israel Greene, their officer-of-the-day, who had orders to report to the senior Army officer present. By ten o'clock Lee and Stuart had joined up with them. They marched together onto the Arsenal grounds and relieved the militia who showed no disposition to close with the fanatic in the firehouse. At daybreak, Lee told Greene to form two storming parties and have them ready. Stuart was sent forward with a note demanding surrender. There was to be no parley. If the answer from Brown was no, Stuart was to wave his hat and get out of the way, and Greene and his men would go forward.

That's the way it worked out. Jeb Stuart waved his plumed hat, of a kind that would later become famous, and the Marines went forward in two squads of twelve men each: blue frockcoats, sky-blue trousers, and white cross-belts. They hammered at the double doors of the engine house with sledges, made no impression; they found a ladder and used it as a battering ram. Greene led the way through the opened door. The second and third Marines behind him were hit. Greene saw a bearded man down on one knee reloading his carbine. Greene slashed down on him with his dress sword, cut him deep in the neck, then bent his sword double in a thrust that caught on a leather strap. The wounded Brown was hauled out on the grass and put on a mattress, his men all dead or captured, and the hostages freed.

Next day Brown talked to his captors: ". . . You may dispose of me very easily. I am very nearly disposed of now; but this question is still to be settled —this Negro question, I mean. The end is not yet."

The Union Divides

Lincoln was elected President on 6 November 1860. On 20 December, the South Carolina legislature voted

unanimously to take South Carolina out of the Union. Out-going President James Buchanan took some half-hearted measures to preserve the Union. On 5 January, forty Marines were sent to man the moldering ruins of Fort Washington across from Mount Vernon. Thirty more were dispatched to Baltimore to garrison Fort McHenry. In Florida, several hundred Alabama militia marched against the Pensacola Navy Yard. It fell without opposition on 16 January, the Marine detachment accepting a parole.

On 1 January 1861 the strength of the Marine Corps had stood at 1892 officers and men. Half the captains in the Corps and two-thirds of the lieutenants resigned to take commissions under the Confederacy. Among those who went south were some of the best, including

Terrett of Mexico City, Simms of the Barrier Forts, and Greene of Harpers Ferry. John Harris himself wavered —to the extent of giving a letter of recommendation to an officer going south. All the field-grade officers stood firm (or perhaps, considering their age, infirm), except Major Henry B. Tyler, the Adjutant and Inspector, who, with his second lieutenant son, joined the Rebellion. Lincoln, inaugurated 4 March, put an abrupt end to the resignations. Officers so requesting found their names stricken from the list and themselves summarily dismissed.

When Major General Irving McDowell's 35,000-man half-trained army of volunteers moved out of Washington on 16 July 1861, there was in the line of march a hastily put together Marine battalion of 13 officers and 336 men, mostly recruits. Hard-fighting, sometimes hard-drinking Major John Reynolds was in command. Major Jacob Zeilin had a company.

On 21 July, the Union right wing, in the opening moves of the First Battle of Manassas, crossed Bull Run at Sudley Springs and turned left against the Confederate flank. Reynolds' battalion was ordered to support Captain Charles Griffin's West Point Battery, a Regular Army unit. Griffin lost one gun but got five to the top of Henry House Hill, where he was joined by another battery of six guns. On the right of the two Union batteries, a blue-clad regiment emerged from the woods. The blue line was almost onto the guns before the regiment was recognized as the 33d Virginia. About this time, "Jeb" Stuart, now a colonel of Virginia cavalry, came riding out of the woods. The guns were lost, then recaptured. Three times the Marine battalion threatened to break, with Reynolds holding them together. Then the whole Union line began to waver. At first the disengagement was handled in good order, then it gained momentum. There was a disorganized retreat back to Washington. A grim-faced Reynolds posted himself at the Long Bridge leading over the Potomac, sorted out his Marines from the formless blue column, and marched them back to the Barracks. The Marine battalion had taken forty-four casualties. Among the seriously wounded was Jacob Zeilin. Colonel Commandant Harris reported sadly to Secretary of the Navy Gideon Welles that this was "the first instance in Marine history where any portion of its members turned their backs to the enemy."

With the Blockaders

A month later, on 28 August 1861, two hundred fifty Marines and soldiers, landing in surfboats, took Fort Clark on the eastern side of Hatteras Inlet and three days later took Fort Hatteras on the other side of the inlet. These forts were held by the Union for the remainder of the war and gave a foothold for further operations against the Carolina coastline.

Flag Officer Samuel F. DuPont, who had the South Atlantic Blockading Squadron, saw the need for a special landing force separate from the ships' Marine detachments. Major Reynolds joined him with a 300-man battalion. It was to spearhead the landing of 13,000 Army troops at Port Royal, South Carolina. Unfortunately, for transport, the Marines were given the *Governor*, a fragile, side-wheeler river steamer. In the rough weather off Hatteras the *Governor* began to break up. Before she went down on 3 November 1861, there was a successful transfer of the battalion to the steam frigate *Sabine*; only 7 Marines were lost but the delay made them miss the assault.

Reynolds' battalion continued to serve with DuPont's squadron, pecking around at the Carolinas and Georgia in a minor way, until it was landed against Saint Augustine, Florida, in March 1862. There was no fight, Saint Augustine had been abandoned, and DuPont reluctantly decided there was no further mission for Reynolds' battalion and returned it to Washington.

The restive Reynolds, now a lieutenant colonel, managed to get in trouble with the lethargic Harris.

Gideon Welles confided to his *Diary* that "almost all the elder officers of the Marine Corps are at logger-heads and should be retired." In May 1862 Harris brought Reynolds up before a court-martial on charges of drunkenness and contempt for a superior officer. The Court acquitted Reynolds, who immediately retaliated by preferring charges against Harris. Gideon Welles cut short the business of charge and counter-charge by issuing a letter of reproof to both Harris and Reynolds.

Flag Officer David G. Farragut, with the Western Gulf Blockading Squadron, had meanwhile forced the mouth of the Mississippi and had proceeded against New Orleans. The three hundred Marines in the squadron were formed into a four-company battalion under command of Captain John L. Broome. On 29 April 1862 they went ashore at New Orleans, ran up the Union flag over the customhouse and city hall, and held the city until the Army arrived two days later.

The sea gates to Charleston, South Carolina, were defended by nine major works, including Fort Sumter. There was a joint attack in July 1863, the naval forces under Rear Admiral John A. Dahlgren, the gun expert. This failed. In August, Major Jacob Zeilin was sent down with a fresh battalion of three hundred Marines. It was inflated into a regiment and training in landing operations began. Zeilin was dissatisfied with what he had to work with, and he was sick besides. He was replaced by Reynolds, who reduced the regiment back to a battalion and turned it over to Captain Charles G. McCawley. Fort Wagner, pounded to rubble by naval gunfire, was taken by the Army on 7 September 1863 and this was to be followed, next day, by a Marine assault against Fort Sumter. It was to be a night landing to be made from strings of small boats towed inshore by tugs. Control was bad and the boats went off in every direction. Only a hundred and fifty Marines and sailors landed on the proper beach and these were beaten back by Rebel rifle fire, the Marines taking forty-four casualties. After this fiasco, the Marine battalion went into camp on Folly Island where they endured much sickness. They continued under these unhappy circumstances until early 1864, when the battalion was finally broken up and its pieces parceled out to other duties.

On 12 May 1864, Colonel Commandant John Harris died, old and wornout by wartime demands that exceeded his capabilities. Gideon Welles attended Harris's funeral, then confided to his *Diary*: "His death gives embarrassment as to a successor." A month passed while Welles wrestled with the problem; then on 9 June, he pithily observed in his *Diary*: "Concluded to retire the Marine officers who are past legal age, and to bring in Zeilin as Commandant of the Corps. There seems no alternative." Major Zeilin was then serving, remote from the war, as commanding officer of the Marine Barracks at Portsmouth, New Hampshire. Next day, President Lincoln named him the seventh Commandant of the Marine Corps.

Confederate Marines

On the other side of the lines, the Confederacy's seagoing Navy was limited by geography and resources to blockade runners and raiders. There was no great role to be played by the Confederate States Marine Corps. The Confederate Congress on 20 May 1861 had authorized a Marine Corps of ten companies. The Colonel Commandant was Lloyd J. Beall. He did his best with a near-impossible situation. One of his last reports is dated 30 October 1864:

> . . . *By this return it will be seen that the aggregate strength of the Corps amounts to 539. Of this number, 2 captains, 3 lieutenants, and 62 enlisted men are prisoners of war in the hands of the enemy.*
>
> *Not included in this return are 32 recruits*

received at the naval station, Charleston, from the conscript camp near Raleigh, N.C.

The Marine Corps is distributed at the following naval stations: Mobile, Savannah, Charleston, Wilmington, and on Drewry's Bluff; also on board the three ironclad steamers in the James River, and as guards at the Richmond Navy Yards. Marine Guards have been assigned to the armed steamers Tallahassee *and* Chickamauga, *destined to operate against the enemy's commerce at sea.*

Since my last report the Marines have been under the enemy's fire at Drewry's Bluff near Richmond and on the James River; also in the naval and land engagements near Mobile on the 5th and 6th of August last. A Marine guard under Lt. Crenshaw was attached to the Confederate steamship Tallahassee *during the late cruise, when much damage was inflicted upon the enemy's shipping at sea.*

Upon all occasions when the Marines have been called upon for active service they have displayed the promptness and efficiency of well-disciplined soldiers.

There had been a long-standing order in England for parchment commissions, suitably engraved. These finally arrived by blockade runner in November 1864. By that time engraved commissions were the least of the Confederacy's needs.

Fort Fisher

By the end of 1864, the only Atlantic port remaining reasonably open to Confederate blockade runners was Wilmington, North Carolina, defended at Cape Fear by the formidable Fort Fisher. The assault of Fort Fisher turned into a curious affair, fought twice, because the Federals tried once, failed, and then tried again. Landing force commander for the first attack was the

Massachusetts politician Major General Benjamin F. Butler, who had an amateur's notion that if an explosive-filled ship were moved close inshore and then blown up, the earthen walls of the fort would tumble down. This was tried on 24 December 1864. It didn't work and next day, Christmas, while Rear Admiral Porter's big guns pounded the fort, Butler with 3000 men went ashore north of the main work, made a hesitant approach, observed a mine field with alarm, and after two days' fumbling, gave up and went back aboard ship.

Command of the expedition now passed to the more resolute Major General Alfred H. Terry. Porter promised him two days' bombardment with a total weight of 600 guns, followed by an attack against the seaward face of the fort. Meantime, Terry, his force now up to a strength of 8500, was to come in from the land side.

The assault was executed on 15 January 1865. The Marines of Porter's Squadron, about 400 of them, organized into a provisional battalion, were to land, dig in, and then cover with rifle fire the 1600 sailors who were to "board" Fort Fisher with cutlass and pistol. This hare-brained plan of attack went all wrong. The sailors were shot to pieces before the Marines could get into position, but, even badly executed, the diversion served its purpose. Terry's soldiers got through the mine field and over the breastworks and the fort was taken before the day was done.

The Navy was quick to blame the failure of its assault on the Marines. If the time spent in charges and countercharges had been used instead for careful analysis, Fort Fisher might have yielded all the lessons, negative and positive, required as a basis for a modern amphibious doctrine. The requirement for a single, not divided, command; the folly of last-minute "provisional" landing-force organizations; the need for adequate ship-to-shore communications; and the value of naval gunfire, properly applied, were all demonstrated if the quarreling participants had only taken time to look at them.

Within months of Fort Fisher, the United States' worst war was over. The Corps had expanded modestly to a peak strength of 4167 officers and men, and had lost 148 killed and 312 dead of other causes. There had been grave moments and the glimmerings of proper amphibious usage, but overall the Corps had gained little in the way of reputation. In 1864, there was a Congressional resolution introduced to transfer the Marine Corps to the Army. After debate, the resolution was tabled, but the thought did not go away.

7

1865–1898
"...as a separate Corps be preserved..."

The Gilded Age

The next thirty years, from the close of the Civil War until the Spanish American War, was a time of shrinking strength, an aging officer corps, and a questioning of the Corps' status and future useful purpose. The Navy was in a slow, sometimes reluctant, transition from sail to steam. The traditional duties of seagoing Marines seemed questionable in the new iron ships. The need for the seizure and defense of advance bases was only dimly foreseen. The state of the amphibious art stayed at the level of ships' landing parties and provisional battalions. These improvisations were good enough for the landings that had to be made "to protect American lives and property": China (1866, 1894, 1895), Formosa (1867), Japan (1867, 1868), Nicaragua (1867, 1894, 1896, 1898), Uruguay (1868), Mexico (1870, 1876), Korea (1871, 1888, 1894), Panama (1873, 1885), Hawaii (1874, 1889, 1893), Egypt (1882), Haiti (1888, 1891), Samoa (1888), Argentina (1890), Chile (1891), and Colombia (1895). Sometime during this period, the archetypal war correspondent Richard Harding Davis coined the much-used phrase: "The Marines have landed and have the situation well in hand." Internally the Marines also had their uses in the sometimes strident political and labor unrest in the cities. They were called out on occasion for riots and affrays in Baltimore, Boston, Philadelphia, and New York.

The new Commandant, Jacob Zeilin, was another Philadelphian, born there in 1806, and with his square-cut beard and clean upper lip he looked like a Pennsylvania Dutch farmer. On 18 June 1866, with the Civil War over only a year, the House of Representatives directed its Committee on Naval Affairs to consider abolishing the Marine Corps and transferring its functions to the Army. The Committee listened to a long line of witnesses and on 21 February 1867 reported:

> . . . *no good reason appears either for abolishing it, the Marine Corps, or transferring it to the Army; on the contrary, the Committee recommends that its organization as a separate Corps be preserved and strengthened . . .*

For good measure, Zeilin was promoted to brigadier general. He now set about quietly to strengthen the fabric and institutions of the Corps. In 1867 he adopted the Army's new system of infantry tactics, developed by Major General Emory Upton, USA, and approved for the Army by a board headed by U. S. Grant. All that a lieutenant or brigadier general needed to know about infantry tactics, even the startling effects of the new breech-loading rifles, had been reduced to a little blue-bound book that could be carried in a tunic pocket.

It was about this time that the "Marine Hymn" was first being heard. Curiously, not much is known about its origins. Apparently not able to rhyme "Montezuma," the unknown poet inverted his chronology and came out with the familiar, "From the Halls of Montezuma to the Shores of Tripoli." The verse has an easy meter and can be fitted to many tunes. The melody which was used, and which has become world-famous, is unmistakably the same as a marching song in Offenbach's operetta *Geneviève de Brabant*.

On 19 November 1868, the Marine Corps emblem in essentially its present form was adopted. There was a borrowing from the Royal Marines in that the globe (Western hemisphere, to be sure) was used as the center of the device. A fouled anchor was put behind it and an American bald eagle perched on top. Next year, 1869, the Corps adopted a blue-black shell jacket and trousers, both liberally encrusted with gold braid, as officers' evening dress. The uniform survives today, almost unchanged, except for slightly less ornamentation. As was said before, the Mameluke sword came back in 1875 for officers with the Army foot officer's saber continuing as the Marine NCO sword. A new set of uniform regulations also came out in 1875. The French influence continued strong despite the disastrous Franco–Prussian War. The undress uniform got a shorter jacket and the *képi*-style forage cap was a little flatter. The full-dress shako was shortened. For a time, company grade officers were supposed to wear an English model "pillbox" or "round cap" for fatigue duty but it was never popular. The leather stocks which had been on the uniform list for a hundred years now disappeared forever.

Korea (1871)

On 30 May 1871, Rear Admiral John Rodgers with five ships of the Asiatic Squadron was attempting to convey the American Minister to Seoul when the defenders of the Hermit Kingdom had the bad manners to fire upon him from the forts guarding the Han River approaches. Rodgers put a landing force ashore on 10 June 1871. A two-company Marine "battalion" under Captain McLane Tilton was out in front. Tilton had been on the board that in 1869 had adopted the

Remington .50-caliber "rolling-block" breech-loader for Navy use, and he was unhappy about going ashore with "muzzle fuzzels" as he called the .58-caliber muzzle-loading rifled muskets which were the standard Civil War arm. Muzzle fuzzels or not, the Marines got ashore, 4 officers and 105 men, and across the mud. An improvised brigade of bluejackets followed the Marines, the forts were carried, and when the day was done 481 cannon (numerous but antique) had been captured, along with 40 or 50 impressively large battle standards. The landing force had only 11 casualties, 2 of them Marines, and counted 243 Korean dead. Six Marines got Medals of Honor. In those days this was the only medal for gallantry in action and it was rather freely given. It also was limited to enlisted men. Officers' valor was still recognized by brevet promotions.

In 1874 there was another Congressional crisis as to the future of the Corps. Once again the Corps survived, although the new act did require that the rank of the Commandant be reduced to colonel on Zeilin's retirement. As the next senior Marine, Charles Grymes McCawley was his obvious successor, and Zeilin in 1871 had brought him to Washington for duty with that in mind. McCawley, the son of a Marine captain, was another Philadelphian, born there in 1827. He had been commissioned in 1847, barely in time to join Watson's regiment as it sailed for Veracruz, and was brevetted a first lieutenant for Chapultepec and a major for the aborted assault on Fort Sumter.

Having provided for his orderly succession, Brigadier General Jacob Zeilin, age seventy and with forty-five years' service, retired voluntarily on 1 November 1876. Colonel McCawley, white-haired, mustached, and of impressive girth, was a methodical man. Before assuming office he had prepared a series of careful memoranda on his objectives and intentions. Most of these centered on higher enlistment standards, better training, better officer selection and instruction, enforcement of uniform regulations, standard tables of organization, and regularizing of staff and command procedures. It was under McCawley that the ubiquitous typewriter entered the service.

Until now Marine officers had been drawn by direct appointment from civilian life. In 1882 McCawley succeeded in getting a quota of graduates from the Naval Academy assigned to the Marine Corps. This would be the sole source of Marine officers until the Spanish-American War.

Colonel McCawley also succeeded in getting started a clothing factory for Marine uniforms in Philadelphia, and it would survive until gobbled up in the McNamara consolidations of the 1960s. McCawley did not tinker much with the uniform regulations themselves, except to authorize in 1880 a cork sun helmet, covered with white duck and complete with a detachable Prussian-style spike and brass chin strap. Two years later a less fortunate winter service version in black was adopted. It was never popular. It was poor aboard ship for the same reasons that the tar-bucket shakos of the first half of the nineteenth century had been awkward and disliked.

Music and Mottoes

On 9 June 1868, John Philip Sousa was enlisted in the Marine Corps as a music boy. His enlistment contract shows him to be "13 years 6 months 3 days of age" and the term of enlistment was for "7 years 5 months 27 days." His father, Antonio Sousa, worked at the Marine Barracks, Washington, as a carpenter and some-time member of the Marine Band. The boy, who was musical, had shown an inclination to run off and join a circus, so his father had marched him over to the Barracks and signed him up.

At twenty-one, having served out his enlistment, John Philip Sousa left the Corps for the civilian world of music. By 1880 the Marine Band was in the doldrums. The leader was dismissed as "unfit for the Service," and Sousa, with a little prodding of the Commandant by his father, was appointed band leader with a stipend of $94.00 a month. The prolific and inventive Sousa then proceeded to turn out marches, change instrumentation, recruit musicians, and perform with increasing aplomb and virtuosity that commanded first national and then international attention.

Of Sousa's many marches, none is more stirring than "Semper Fidelis," the only march officially authorized for a Service by the Congress and habitually used by the Marines for the march-past in parades and reviews. *Semper Fidelis* had been adopted as the Corps motto in 1883, succeeding the various other tentative mottoes, including *Fortitudine* used in the early 1800s, and a most blatant borrowing from the Royal Marines in 1876 of *Per Mare, Per Terram*, sometimes used in its English form, "By Sea and by Land." The new motto (not completely unique, it is shared with the Devonshire Regiment) was put on a ribbon placed in the beak of the eagle on the Marine Corps emblem and thus, firmly fixed, it has endured.

There is a tradition that the Marine Band may not leave the Capital without Presidential permission. In 1891 Sousa asked President Benjamin Harrison if he could take the Band on tour. Permission was granted and the tour was a great success; so much so that Sousa could not resist the blandishments of the commercial theater and he left the Marine Corps on 30 July 1892 to go on to become the international March King.

At Alexandria, Panama, and the Bering Sea

In 1882 the combined British and French protectorate of the Khedive in Egypt was threatened by the nationalist Arabi Pasha. The British Mediterranean Fleet converged on Alexandria in June, and the microscopic U. S. European Squadron, three ships with the flag in the screw sloop *Lancaster*, went along. On 11 July the

British bombarded the city. The Americans put a landing party ashore on the fourteenth under command of Marine Captain Henry Clay Cochrane, who had been Lincoln's aide at Gettysburg the day the President made his speech. Cochrane announced that his landing party would ". . . stick by the British and take their chances." The risk was not all that great. By that time the British had four thousand troops, including four hundred fifty Royal Marines, ashore. Among the American Marines was a new second lieutenant, a Virginian named somewhat redundantly Littleton Waller Tazewell Waller, who would bear watching.

In 1884 the Marines got a new rifle, the celebrated Springfield .45–70 single-shot breech-loader (a few were still extant in 1942 and used for bayonet training at Quantico), and a year later in Panama there was an opportunity to try it out. French efforts to build a canal across the Isthmus had collapsed. The Colombian government had withdrawn its troops to combat revolution elsewhere. USS *Alliance*, a rebuilt wooden gunboat, arrived on the Atlantic side on 18 January 1885 and put its Marine detachment ashore to guard the property of the American-owned Panama Railroad. By March a loose coalition of rebels had control of the railroad right-of-way and the cities of Panama and Colón. Another gunboat, the *Galena*, took station off Colón, a good portion of which was burning, and landed its Marines under Second Lieutenant Charles A. Doyen to guard the U. S. consulate.

On the first of April, Colonel McCawley telegraphed Lieutenant Colonel Charles Heywood at Brooklyn Navy Yard to have two hundred fifty Marines ready for service in Panama in twenty-four hours. Heywood, a native of Maine, had been commissioned in the Corps in 1858 and in the Civil War had made his reputation at the captures of Forts Clark and Hatteras and at sea with Farragut. He sailed for Panama with a battalion on 3 April. Four days later, a second battalion of Marines and one of bluejackets also left New York.

Meanwhile, the Gulf Squadron had converged on Panama and its Marines landed in a provisional battalion. Heywood arrived on 11 April, crossed the Isthmus with his brigade, securing the railroad as he went, and established himself at Panama City on the Pacific side. By the thirtieth, Colombian troops were back and policing the city. The Marines began to thin out their forces and on 25 May the last of the brigade embarked for home.

Colonel McCawley retired on 29 January 1891 and Charles Heywood became the Colonel Commandant next day. Despite McCawley's best efforts, the Marine Corps was stagnant. Promotions were glacially slow. The Military Retirement Act of 1885 had nudged only a few of the officers of Civil War vintage into retirement. Heywood instituted fitness reports and promotion examinations. He began, on 1 May 1891, the School of Application at the Marine Barracks, Washington, for newly commissioned officers. The standard text was still Upton's *Tactics*. His older officers, who regarded themselves as "practical" men, were skeptical of these academic affectations.

The first half of the decade was very quiet. Some slight titillation was caused by a foray into the Bering Sea in 1891. For some years there had been a wholesale killing of fur seals at their breeding grounds by poachers, mostly British. England and the United States agreed to police the area jointly. Great Britain sent three ships. The United States sent four Navy ships and two revenue cutters, and chartered a small steamer to be used as a prison ship. The Marines involved were under Henry Clay Cochrane, still a captain. The breeding grounds were patrolled, suspicious ships were boarded and searched, and seal poaching was suppressed, but as an expedition it didn't amount to much. As cold weather set in, the exercise was closed out and in October the little fleet sailed for home.

The next year, 1892, there were some exceedingly practical changes to the field uniforms—apparently inspired by the dress habits of the Indian-fighting Regular Army. A broad-brimmed "campaign" or "field" hat, creased "fore and aft" with a large Marine Corps emblem on the left side, was adopted along with high canvas leggings. The leggings would last, growing increasingly shorter, until the middle of the Korean War. Also, sensibly, a blue flannel shirt usually was substituted for a coat in the field.

Revolution in Cuba, always endemic, broke out afresh in 1895. Spain sent 120,000 soldiers under General ("the Butcher") Weyler to put it down. Congress passed resolutions recognizing the Cubans as belligerents. President Grover Cleveland held back on putting the resolutions into effect, choosing to recognize the Cuban revolutionaries as *insurgents* rather than *belligerents*—thus creating a new status in international law which would have interesting applications in subsequent twentieth-century happenings. President Cleveland was succeeded by William McKinley. The Marine Band played at the inauguration on 4 March 1897. During the drive from the Capitol to the White House, Cleveland remarked to McKinley, "I am deeply sorry, Mr. President, to pass on to you a war with Spain. It will come within two years. Nothing can stop it."

1898–1902
"Civilize 'em with a Krag!"

The Spanish-American War

There was a sharp report and then a heavier explosion deep in the bowels of the armored cruiser *Maine* as she rode at anchor in Havana's harbor on the night of 15 February 1898. Captain Charles Sigsbee, interrupted in the writing of a letter to his wife, left his cabin, went out into the smoke-filled passageway, and stumbled into his Marine orderly.

"Sir," said Private William Anthony, drawing himself up to attention and saluting, "I beg to report that the Captain's ship is sinking."

The *Maine* had come into the harbor on 25 January. Spanish reception had been cool but correct. Now 232 seamen and 28 Marines were dead. First Lieutenant Albertus W. Catlin, the senior Marine, was unharmed. Like his captain, he had been in his stateroom writing a letter home when the explosion occurred. Although no definitive evidence, then or now, connected the Spanish with the sinking, the cry went up, "Remember the Maine!" On 19 April, Congress passed a resolution of intervention. Three days later, President McKinley informed the neutral nations that a state of war existed between the United States and Spain.

On 27 April Colonel Commandant Heywood ordered a Marine battalion formed, and five days later it sailed from Brooklyn for Key West aboard the ex-banana boat USS *Panther*. The five rifle companies had the new Lee rifle, a bolt-action .236-caliber weapon using smokeless powder. There was also an artillery company equipped with a battery of four 3-inch landing guns. The commanding officer was Lieutenant Colonel Robert W. Huntington, who had been with Reynolds as a lieutenant at First Manassas and in the Carolinas.

In the Pacific, Commodore George Dewey, commanding the Asiatic Squadron, caught Admiral Patricio Montojo's elegant but antique squadron at anchor off Sangley Point, the southwestern lip of Manila Bay, as dawn broke 1 May. He gave his famous order to the captain of his flagship *Olympia*, "You may fire when you are ready, Gridley." Battle stations for the Marines in Dewey's five cruisers were the rapid-fire guns of the secondary batteries. For two hours the Americans blazed away, retired for breakfast, then came back and finished the job. Seven Spanish ships were destroyed, three land batteries silenced, 381 Spanish sailors were dead and many wounded. Dewey had had 2 officers and 6 men, none of them Marines, slightly hurt. Two days later, on 3 May, the Marine detachment from the protected cruiser *Baltimore*, under First Lieutenant Dion Williams, landed and raised the flag over Cavite naval station. But there were still 13,000 Spanish troops in Manila itself and a kind of uneasy standoff was maintained until sufficient Army troops could arrive to take the city.

In Washington, on 4 May, the Naval Appropriation Act raised the Commandant's rank once again to brigadier general, and brought the Marine Corps up to a permanent authorized strength of 3073 men, plus a wartime augmentation of 43 lieutenants and 1580 men. One of the new lieutenants, commissioned on 20 May, was a Philadelphia Quaker named Smedley D. Butler, age eighteen (or maybe sixteen—there is a suspicion that he added two years to his age). He had an inside track to the new commissions. His father was a member, and later chairman, of the House Naval Affairs Committee.

Guantanamo

In the Caribbean, by the end of May, Rear Admiral William T. Sampson had bottled up the Spanish Fleet under Admiral Pascual Cervera in Santiago de Cuba, but he needed an advance base close by from which to coal his blockaders. "Can you not take possession of Guantanamo, occupy as a coaling station?" asked the Secretary of the Navy. "Yes," said Sampson. "Send me Huntington's Marine battalion."

On 7 June the *Panther* chugged out of Key West with Huntington's battalion on board. Meanwhile, the protected cruiser *Marblehead* was shelling Guantanamo, defended by a single decrepit gunboat and a reported seven to nine thousand Spaniards. Some of Sampson's fleet Marines had gone ashore to reconnoiter. On 10 June, Huntington's battalion landed inside Guantanamo Bay, forty miles from Santiago. There was no opposition at the beach. First Spanish reaction came at midnight and for the next three days Huntington was sniped at and harassed, losing his men by ones and twos. Crux of the matter seemed to be Cuzco Well, the Spanish water supply (water supply at semiarid Guantanamo has always been a consideration).

On 14 June, Huntington sent out two companies of Marines, along with 60 to 70 Cuban guerrillas, to take the well. The dispatch boat *Dolphin* was to provide naval gunfire support. Sun and heat caused more casualties than Spanish bullets and command eventually developed upon Captain George F. Elliott. The *Dolphin*'s shells began dropping on the Marines' position. Lean, cadaverous Sergeant John H. Quick went

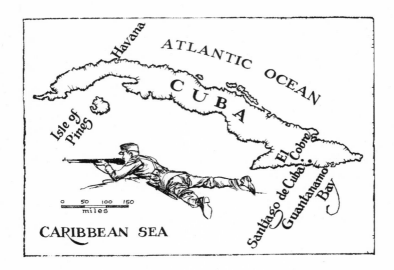

up on a ridge line to wigwag an adjustment. The estimated 500 Spanish defenders were routed. The Marines counted up and found their own casualties to be 6 killed, 16 wounded.

There was no further fighting of consequence at Guantanamo. On 3 July, Admiral Cervera elected to come out of Santiago. The victory was even more lopsided than Manila Bay. Cervera's four armored cruisers and three destroyers were no match for Commodore Winfield Scott Schley's five battleships and armored cruiser. Every Spanish ship was sunk or surrendered.

In the Pacific, on 21 June, the protected cruiser *Charleston* had approached Guam and fired twelve rounds with its 3-pounders at old (and abandoned) Fort Santa Cruz. A Spanish officer came out in a small boat with apologies; he had no powder with which to return the "salute," and had to be informed that a state of war existed between Spain and the United States. First Lieutenant John Twiggs ("Handsome Jack") Myers took the *Charleston*'s Marines ashore and the amenities of surrender were observed.

Hostilities ceased on 12 August. On 13 August (the apparent extra day was the consequence of a cut cable and the international date line) the American Army came out of the trenches it had thrown around Manila and entered the city. Years later, in testifying before the House Naval Affairs Committee, Admiral Dewey said that if he had had five thousand Marines embarked with his squadron at Manila Bay he could have taken Manila on 1 May and the Philippine Insurrection might have been avoided.

In the Philippines

There had been a revolt against the Spaniards, led by twenty-seven-year-old Emilio Aguinaldo, in 1896. Directly after the Battle of Manila Bay, Dewey brought the half-Tagalog, half-Chinese Aguinaldo back by gunboat from exile in Hong Kong. On 12 June 1898 Aguinaldo had declared an independent Philippine Republic with himself as President and commander-in-chief. He cooperated with the Americans in the languid siege of Manila and on 13 August entered the city with the U. S. Army fully expecting the government to be turned over to him. Instead, he was told to march himself and his "army" out of the city. On 4 February 1899 actual hostilities began with an abortive attack against Manila.

"Civilize 'em with a Krag!" was the American battle cry for the nasty little war that followed. (In 1900, the Marine Corps, which was beginning to learn that its weapons had to be the same as the U. S. Army's, would abandon its straight-pull Lee rifle in favor of the Army's .30-caliber Krag-Jorgensen. The Marine Corps had also gotten its first machine gun, the high-wheeled Colt-Browning "potato digger.")

On 9 March 1899 Dewey cabled for a Marine battal-

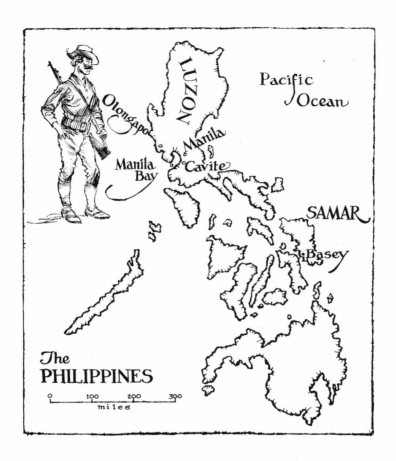

Olongapo

LUZON

Pacific Ocean

Manila

Cavite

Manila Bay

SAMAR

Basey

The PHILIPPINES

0 100 200 300
miles

ion to reinforce the naval station at Cavite. The "First Battalion of Marines," 15 officers and 260 enlisted men, under command of Colonel Percival C. Pope, arrived on 23 May. This was not considered enough and a 2d Battalion, under George Elliott (last heard from at Cuzco Well and now a major), came out on 21 September and had almost immediate employment.

In concert with larger U. S. Army operations, Elliott (about this time elevated to lieutenant colonel) made a frontal assault on 8 October against the fortified town of Novaleta, southwest of Cavite. The attack, divided into two columns, sloshed through swamp and rice paddy, and with the help of a little naval gunfire from the gunboat *Petrel* drove the insurgents from the town at a cost of one Marine killed, ten wounded.

A 3d Battalion, under the pugnacious Major L. W. T. ("Tony") Waller, a thick-legged little man with a large mustache and a larger ego, arrived on 15 December 1899. A reinforced company under Captain Henry L. Draper was sent to Subic Bay, above the northern edge of Manila Bay, to begin the pacification of the area around Olongapo. Draper set himself energetically to the task (including the burning of the town of Benectian on 16 February 1900). Operations in the Philippines were then interrupted by events in China.

The Boxer Rebellion

Secretly supported by the Dowager Empress, the "Righteous Fists of Harmony" (the Europeans called them the "Boxers") were raging across North China determined to expunge the "foreign devils." The legations in Peking, dubious of the protection of the Imperial Chinese government, had sent out a call for help.

On 24 May 1900, Captain John Myers landed at Taku from the USS *Oregon* with twenty-eight Marines and five seamen with orders to get to Peking and establish a legation guard. (After his adventure at Guam, Myers, on 23 September 1899, had landed at Olongapo with a detachment from the USS *Baltimore* and captured a threatening rifled gun from the Philippine insurgents.) On 29 May "Handsome Jack" was joined by Captain Newt H. Hall with twenty-six more Marines from the USS *Newark*. Under command of the more senior Myers, the combined detachments commandeered a tug to haul them forty miles upstream to Tientsin. On 31 May, two trains were made up (after a threat to hang the stationmaster) and loaded with an unlikely

mélange of American, French, Russian, German, Aus-
trian, Italian, and Japanese sailors and Marines. The
trains got to Peking that night. The American Marines
marched off to the U. S. Legation through a dense-
packed, muttering mass of Chinese, the five sailors
dragging behind them their high-wheeled Colt machine
gun (which would prove invaluable in days to come).
On 6 June the rail line to Tientsin was cut by the Boxers
—the track torn up, bridges blown, stations burned.

Boxers in full ceremonial regalia were now circulat-
ing through Peking working up the Chinese into a
xenophobic fury. Demonstrations began in earnest on
13 June. Captain Hall went out from the Legation
compound and cleared the street at bayonet point.
Chinese Christians, many of them horribly burned or
wounded, began coming into the Legation Quarter.

Meanwhile, an eight-nation 2500-man relief column
had been organized in Tientsin under Vice Admiral Sir
Edward Seymour, RN. The U. S. contingent were
mostly bluejackets, stiffened by a couple of squads of
Marines under a first sergeant, all commanded by
Captain Bowman H. McCalla, USN, of the *Newark*.
McCalla was no stranger to expeditionary service. He
had commanded the naval forces ashore at Panama in
1885 and had been senior officer present at the Guantanamo landing.

On the morning of 10 June, the whole force moved
out, repairing the railroad as they went, and harried by
both the Boxers and Imperial troops. After a week they
had gotten as far as An Ping, sixty-five miles up the line
(and where the U. S. Marines would have another
"incident" in 1946), and still twenty-five miles short of
Peking. At An Ping, Seymour's column was stopped
cold by the Chinese on 18 June and began a retreat
back to Tientsin.

More help was on the way. The navies of Europe and
Japan were converging on Taku. At Cavite, on 14 June,
Major Waller mounted out a bobtailed battalion, 7
officers (including First Lieutenant Smedley Butler as

one of his company commanders) and 131 men. They landed at Taku on 19 June, coaxed an old locomotive and a string of flat cars into life, and started for Tientsin. En route they joined forces with a battalion of 440 white-bloused Russian infantry, continuing along the railroad until stopped by a blown bridge twelve miles short of Tientsin. The Russian colonel argued for an attack beyond the bridgehead, first thing in the morning. Waller, no shrinking violet when it came to combat, agreed. The Russians and Americans moved out in the last hours of darkness and in the bright light of morning found that they had moved into a sleeve with Imperial troops on their front and right, Boxers on their left, perhaps 1500 or more in all. The Russians withdrew leaving the Marines alone, with 3 dead and 9 wounded. They carried out their wounded, got back to the bridgehead, found an Allied force building up there and attached themselves to the 600-man British naval contingent under Commander Christopher Cradock, RN.

This was on the twenty-first of June. By the next day, Seymour's column had worked its way back to the Hsi-ku arsenal six miles north of Tientsin. Seymour's Royal Marines, supported by the Germans and the Americans, captured the arsenal and Seymour led his weary column inside its walls to await help. Of McCalla's 112 sailors and Marines, 32 had been killed or wounded.

Two days later, on the twenty-fourth, the international force which had built up south of Tientsin drove into the foreign quarter against not very much resistance and next day reached Seymour at Hsi-ku arsenal. McCalla, himself three times wounded, turned over the residue of his command to Waller.

In Peking there had been heavy fighting. The Legation Quarter was roughly a square, cut from east to west by Legation Street and from north to south by a canal. At the southwest corner was the American Legation backed up against the Tartar Wall, sixty feet high and forty feet wide. The U. S. Marines threw a barricade across the Wall facing west toward Chien Men gate. The Germans had a comparable position facing east toward Hata Men gate. The British Legation, where the foreign women and children had been concentrated, was at the northwest corner of the Quarter. The British minister, Claude MacDonald, was chosen to be commander-in-chief of the mixed defense force.

On 23 June the Chinese set fire to Hanlin Yuan Academy, just outside the British compound. In an effort to save it, Royal and U. S. Marines sallied forth to drive off the Boxers. On the next night the Chinese attacked the British compound itself. On the twenty-seventh the Chinese made a daylight attack against Myers' position. His Colt machine gun cut them down. On 1 July the Germans gave way after receiving a heavy shelling and the American rear was left exposed. The U. S. Marines momentarily fell back, then, with the help of the British Marines, counterattacked and regained their position on the Wall.

Next day, 2 July, the Chinese pushed a fifteen-foot tower in place on the Wall overlooking Myers' strongpoint. That night, in a blinding rainstorm, he got off a raid with thirty U. S. Marines, twenty-six Royal Marines, and fifteen Russian sailors. The signal was "Go!" and they moved out at 0130. They overran the Boxer barricade, killed thirty-six, and took two flags. Myers tripped over a Chinese spear and got the head of it through his calf. Two U. S. Marines were killed, an English Marine and Russian sailor were wounded. "Captain Myers's post on the wall," wrote MacDonald, "is the peg which holds the whole thing together."

After the night attack the Chinese showed more caution. Fighting slowed to desultory sniping by both sides. Myers' leg became badly infected (later, he would get typhoid) and command devolved on Captain Hall. There was a flareup on 15 July. Private Daniel Daly held an advanced post on the Wall alone until Hall could bring up reinforcements. Next day, the sixteenth, a kind of truce was agreed upon.

The event which caused the Imperial government to desist in its support of the attacks against the Legation Quarter was the fall of Tientsin's native city. There were now close to six thousand foreign troops in Tientsin. The headquarters of the 1st Marine Regiment, along with its commander, Civil War veteran Colonel Robert L. Meade, and another battalion had arrived at Taku from Cavite on 10 July. Two battalions of the U. S. 9th Infantry had come in four days earlier and these were brigaded with the Marines under Meade's command, about a thousand Americans altogether.

With these forces in place, the attack against Tientsin's native quarter began 13 July. The Russians and the French were acting independently. The British, Americans, and Japanese were loosely grouped under Brigadier General A. R. F. Dorward, British Army. For the attack the U. S. Marines had the left flank of Dorward's group. The 2d Battalion, Royal Welch Fusiliers, were on their right. (And since then on Saint David's Day, 1 March, and the Marine Corps Birthday, 10 November, the Commandant of the Marine Corps and the Colonel of the Royal Welch exchange the watchword, ". . . and Saint David.")

The native city had two walls around it. The outer wall was pounded earth. Dorward's attack went over the outer wall at seven in the morning and then through the muck of flooded rice paddies to the second wall which was of stone. A Marine artillery company that had arrived with Meade banged away with its battery of 3-inch landing guns. The battery commander was Captain Ben H. Fuller, a future Commandant. Lieutenant Butler went down with a bullet through his thigh. There was no getting over the wall and at nightfall the attack pulled back. Next morning, before dawn, the Japanese blew in the south gate and by daylight the Allies were in the city in mass. There was much burning and looting, all of which the Marines virtuously ascribed to someone else.

Fresh foreign troops were arriving in a steady stream. On 30 July Major General Adna R. Chaffee, USA, arrived to take command of all U. S. forces which now numbered about 3000. On 3 August a new Marine battalion, designated the 4th, came into Tientsin, under Major William P. Biddle. Colonel Meade at this point was invalided home and Biddle, who was senior to Waller, moved up to command of the 1st Marine Regiment. The international force now numbered 18,600. One Marine battalion was left behind in Tientsin. The regiment with two battalions and its artillery company, 482 Marines, was to make the march to Peking. Butler, who had just reached nineteen, argued his way out of the hospital and rejoined his company as it prepared to move out.

By 13 August the outskirts of Peking had been reached, the heat and dust of the march proving more of an affliction than the Chinese. The Allies had agreed to a day of rest but on the fourteenth the Russians went charging into the city, and this brought along everyone else. Waller's 1st Battalion was assigned to cover a battery of the 5th Artillery in breaching the Chien Men gate. Butler got his second wound entering the Chinese City, a bullet excising "South America" from a Marine emblem tattooed on his chest. There was some slimy work going through the Water Gate from the Chinese City into the Legation Quarter but resistance was not great. By late afternoon the foreign legations were reached. They found that of the Legation Quarter's defenders, totaling something less than 500, 65 had been killed and 135 wounded. Of the 56 U. S. Marines and sailors, 17 were casualties.

Back to the Philippines

On 28 September the Secretary of the Navy ordered the 1st Marine Regiment returned to Cavite. The regiment marched out of Peking on 3 October and on 10 October sailed from Taku for the Philippines. Once back in the Philippines, the Marines were able to reorganize into a proper brigade, two regiments of two battalions each: aggregate strength 1678. The 1st Regiment went to Olongapo; Brigade headquarters and the 2d Regiment stayed at Cavite. The insurrection on the main island of Luzon had been fairly well put down. But while the Christian Tagalogs had come to accept American rule, the Muslim Moros of the southern islands were not yet mollified. The island of Samar was most troublesome. On 28 September 1901, Company C, 9th Infantry, was caught at evening mess at Balangiga and massacred. Waller was sent with his battalion, 14 officers and 300 men including Gunnery Sergeant John Quick, to help. On 24 October he landed with two companies at Basey. His other two companies went in at Balangiga.

Brigadier General Jacob M. ("Hell-Roaring Jake") Smith, USA, reportedly told Waller, "I want no prisoners. I wish you to burn and kill. The more you burn and kill, the better it will please me."

Operating against some three thousand Moros, Waller's two columns "burned and killed" through the first two weeks of November. The hard-core Moros withdrew to a jungle stronghold in the cliffs above the Sojoton River, an area never penetrated by the Spaniards. Waller went after them on 15 November, three columns converging in a hair-raising night attack that finished off organized Moro resistance, or so it seemed.

General Smith now ordered Waller to reconnoiter a telegraph route from the east coast of Samar to Basey. Waller decided to start from Lanang, work up the Lanang River as far as he could go, find a trail to the Sojoton River, and then down the Sojoton to Basey. The maps were no good but it looked to be about fifty-two miles. They started off three days after Christmas 1901, five Marine officers, fifty Marines, two Philippine guides, and thirty-three native bearers. The trails they followed made no sense. Rations ran short.

Waller began suspecting the loyalty of the guides. Fever was weakening his men. He decided to push on to Basey with the strongest men and leave the rest to follow at a more leisurely pace. He arrived at Basey on 6 January, picked up help and supplies, and started back the next morning. For nine days he searched without luck, getting back to Basey, sick and exhausted, on 17 January.

Captain David D. Porter, namesake of the Civil War admiral, left behind with the main body, had decided to go back to Lanang going off with seven Marines (including Gunnery Sergeant Quick) and six natives. The remainder were left behind to follow along as best they could. In all, ten Marines were lost.

Convinced that the disaster had been caused by treachery, Waller held a drumhead court-martial on 20 January 1902 in the plaza of Basey and shot eleven of the natives. His battalion then embarked for Cavite, where, to Waller's surprise, he was brought up before an Army general court-martial on 17 March on charge of murder. He was acquitted and eventually the whole proceedings were thrown out on a technicality, but the shadow of the incident hung on and may well have kept Waller from becoming Commandant.

1899–1916
"...a pacific effect upon the Oriental mind."

Panama and the Canal

On 1 April 1899, Marines from the protected cruiser *Philadelphia* went ashore in Samoa, in a combined landing party with Royal Marines from two British ships, to intercede in an argument between two chiefs as to the succession to the Samoan throne. They burned a village, managed to get themselves ambushed, and withdrew ignominiously. Samoa was eventually partitioned among Great Britain, Germany, and the United States. A naval station was set up at Tutuila in American Samoa in 1904 and the Fita-Fita guard, trained and commanded by Marine NCOs, established. There were also landings in Nicaragua (1899), Panama (1901, 1902, 1903), Honduras (1903), Dominican Republic (1903), Beirut, Syria (1903), Tangier (1904), and a minor expedition to Abyssinia (1903).

The Commandant, Charles Heywood, was promoted to major general, the first in the Corps' history, in July 1902 (but with the proviso that his successor be a brigadier general). He retired on 3 October 1903 at age sixty-four, and in his final report noted that the Corps' strength was 278 officers and 7532 men, an all-time

high. The new Commandant was Alabama-born
George F. Elliott, already fifty-seven years old.

The Spanish-American War had revived American
interest in a canal across the Isthmus. The rights and
property of the moribund French Panama Company
had been acquired for $40 million. Colombia, proprietor
of the Isthmus, was offered $10 million in gold and
$250,000 a year in exchange for absolute U. S. sover-
eignty over a ten-mile-wide strip. Colombia asked for
$25 million. President Theodore Roosevelt said not one
dollar more, and the Colombian Congress adjourned on
31 October 1903 without taking action. Three days
later, in a bloodless coup, revolutionaries seized control
of Panama City. Numbers of U. S. Marines were conveniently close. A landing party from the USS *Nash-
ville* went ashore at Colón (on the Atlantic side) with
orders to keep the Colombian garrison from crossing
the Isthmus to Panama City. A battalion of Marines
under Major John A. Lejeune, embarked in the USS
Dixie, was ordered forward from Jamaica. It came into
Colón on 5 November and Lejeune promptly landed
two companies. The Colombian garrison was persuaded to depart aboard a Royal Mail steamer for
Cartagena, and next day President Roosevelt recognized the independence of the new Republic of Panama. On 9 November a second Marine battalion put out
from Philadelphia for Panama aboard the USS *Prairie*.
Then, on 3 January 1904, Brigadier General Elliott
himself arrived in the USS *Dixie* with two more
battalions, one of them commanded by Lieutenant
Colonel "Tony" Waller. (That same day the Marine
detachment from the USS *Detroit* was landing at
Puerto Plata in the Dominican Republic. Two days
later, three officers and a hundred Marines would
arrive in Seoul from the Philippines to protect American lives and property endangered by the Russo–
Japanese War. In Africa, Captain George C. Thorpe
and nineteen Marines were wending their way back to
Djibouti, after having escorted a diplomatic mission to

the court of Emperor **Menelik** in mysterious Addis Ababa.)

In Panama, Elliott collected his battalions into a provisional brigade of two regiments and stayed on until 16 February, by which time the new regime was firmly in place. On 4 January, President Roosevelt had explained the occupation to the Congress in a special message: "No one connected with this government had any part in preparing, inciting or encouraging the late revolution of the Isthmus of Panama." Digging on the canal got started in May. At least one Marine battalion would remain in Panama until 1914.

In North Africa, in a pale repetition of the days of the Barbary pirates, a bandit named Raisouli had kidnaped a U. S. citizen, one Ion Perdicaris, and was holding him for ransom. Roosevelt sent a cable: "Perdicaris alive, or Raisouli dead." The Marine detachment from the armored cruiser *Brooklyn* under "Handsome Jack" Myers of Peking went ashore at Tangier on 30 May 1904 to insure the message was understood. Perdicaris was returned alive.

Next year, on 12 September 1905, a detachment of a hundred Marines from the Philippines under Captain Harry Lee relieved a company of the 9th Infantry as Legation Guard in Peking, beginning the era of "China duty" which would continue until interrupted by World War II. In December of the same year, Marines were also assigned to guard the U. S. Embassy in troubled Saint Petersburg.

Cuban Pacification (1906–1909)

The Spanish-American War had also left the United States with the problem of what to do with Cuba. The Cubans were encouraged to hold a constitutional convention and the result was almost a carbon copy of the U. S. Constitution and government with one interesting exception, the so-called "Platt Amendment," which gave the United States "the right to intervene for the preservation of Cuban independence, the maintenance of a government adequate for the protection of life, property and individual liberty, and for discharging the obligations with respect to Cuba imposed by the Treaty of Paris. . . ." Such intervention by U. S. Marines would be required eight times between 1906 and 1917.

In August 1906 the Liberal party, defeated in a somewhat fuzzy election, went into open revolt and President Tomás Estrada Palma, head of the incumbent Moderate party, asked for U. S. help. On 13 September an improvised battalion of one hundred thirty Marines and sailors from the USS *Denver* went ashore at Havana and camped in front of the President's palace. Another battalion under Major Albertus W. Catlin came into the harbor in the *Dixie* on 16 September. Ships' detachments were landing along the north coast to protect American-owned sugar plantations and railroad property. A special commission under William H. Taft, then Secretary of War, arrived on 19 September to help and advise. An anguished President Palma resigned, effective 28 September; virtually his last official act was to ask for a guard on the Cuban treasury (which was provided by a platoon of thirty Marines). Roosevelt told Taft to form a provisional government with himself as governor. Two more Marine battalions had arrived in Havana harbor from Norfolk and Philadelphia. These were combined with Catlin's battalion into the 1st Regiment under Lieutenant Colonel George Barnett.

A 2d Marine Regiment was formed under Lieutenant Colonel Franklin J. Moses, a veteran of the march to Peking, two of its battalions being shaken out of the Atlantic Fleet. The ubiquitous L. W. T. Waller, promoted to colonel the previous year, arrived on 1 October to take command of the two regiments combined into a brigade. By then Barnett was ashore and had occupied Cienfuegos.

The U. S. Army of Cuban Occupation began arriving 10 October. The Marine brigade was disbanded (after reaching a peak strength of 97 officers and 2795 men) and Waller left for Norfolk on 1 November. But the 1st Marine Regiment stayed on under Army command. There was no fighting for them to do but a good deal of guard duty—and that *sine qua non* of pacification, collection of illicit weapons. The last Marine elements sailed for home on 23 January 1909.

The Great White Fleet

All was not in complete harmony in Washington. A clique in the Navy was urging the President to take the Marines off the Navy's capital ships. The Army had revived the old proposition that the Corps, or at least its functions, be transferred to the Army. While these interesting proposals were being argued, sixteen battleships, painted white and as beautiful as gigantic yachts, put out from Hampton Roads, Virginia, 16 December 1907. The cruise of the Great White Fleet was under way. The Russo-Japanese War was over, thanks to the mediation of President Roosevelt, but the Japanese were restive. So the Fleet was to go to Japan on a friendly visit, the President, in the words of naval historian Commodore Dudley W. Knox, "correctly believing that a display of overpowering force would have a pacific effect upon the Oriental mind."

In Washington, Elliott continued to battle for the status of the Corps. Twice he was offered personal advancement to major general but he held out for the rank to go to the office, not the man. This was finally done. Congress created the permanent rank of Major General Commandant and he was promoted in May 1908. On 12 November of that year President Roosevelt was persuaded to sign Executive Order 969, which spelled out the duties of the U. S. Marines:

> *(1) To garrison the different navy yards and naval stations, both within and beyond the continental limits of the United States.*

(2) To furnish the first line of the mobile defense of naval bases and naval stations beyond the continental limits of the United States.

(3) To man such naval defenses, and to aid in manning, if necessary, such other defenses, as may be erected for the defense of naval bases and naval stations beyond the continental limits of the United States.

(4) To garrison the Isthmian Canal Zone, Panama.

(5) To furnish such garrisons and expeditionary forces for duties beyond the seas as may be necessary in time of peace.

No mention of duties afloat! Withdrawal of the Marines from combatant ships had already begun in October. Elliott, Waller, and others sought help in Congress. There was a strong friend in the person of Congressman Thomas Butler, father of Smedley Butler, and now Chairman of the House Naval Affairs Committee. On 22 February, Washington's Birthday, the Great White Fleet steamed back into Hampton Roads, the 40,000-mile cruise a fitting climax to Roosevelt's spectacular Administration, having been received enthusiastically everywhere and nowhere more so than in Japan. On 3 March, as Roosevelt's protégé, William H. Taft, was about to begin his Presidency, a rider was tacked on to the Naval Appropriations Bill:

Provided, that no part of the appropriations herein made for the Marine Corps shall be expended for the purposes for which said appropriations are made unless officers and men shall serve as heretofore on board all battleships and armored cruisers and also on such other vessels of the Navy as the President may direct. . . .

So the Marines stayed on the battleships and those who had come off prematurely were put back on with a few extra added.

Advance Base Studies

In 1901 a detachment of four officers and forty enlisted Marines under Major Henry C. Haines at Newport, Rhode Island, had been directed to begin a study of advance-base operations, building on Spanish-American War experience. They tested their findings with small-scale exercises at Newport and Nantucket, and the following year there was a regimental-size landing problem at Culebra, a small island east of Puerto Rico.

The Marines began to think about the uses of keeping a battalion or regiment afloat in transports. Such a force in the Caribbean, for example, would be conveniently at hand to half a dozen potential trouble spots. In these years a number of small liners brought into the Navy during the Spanish-American War as auxiliary cruisers were increasingly used as transports. Closest to an assault transport was the much-used 6100-ton *Dixie* which carried ten 6-inch guns and could make 16 knots flank speed. There were also the larger but slower *Prairie* and *Buffalo*—6900 tons and 14.5 knots. Pondering these matters, General Elliott in 1908 recommended "transports for the sole and exclusive use of the Marine Corps."

That it was a time of change was apparent even in the uniforms. Khaki had come into use for tropical field service during the Spanish-American War. (Heywood had sent "campaign suits of brown linen" to Huntington at Guantanamo; Huntington had replied that the "lightweight underclothes would be much better if they were lighter in weight.") A mustard-colored flannel shirt replaced the blue shirt of the Philippine Insurrection and Boxer Relief. In 1901 the Marine Corps emblem moved from the side to the front of the field hat. In 1903, a standing-collar khaki blouse was added.

Next year the spiked helmet disappeared without lament and a bell-crowned visored cap came in. In 1912 a new model field hat was introduced, stiffer, with a narrower brim, and a four-dent "Montana peak" to replace the fore-and-aft crease. In the same year it was decided to adopt a forest-green winter service uniform, with dull bronze ornaments and buttons.

General Heywood had been dismayed at Marine marksmanship in the 1890s, and had gotten the Corps into competition shooting. At the Sea Girt matches in 1901, the Marine Corps team managed only sixth place, but a new second lieutenant from Delaware, Thomas Holcomb, won a gold medal for highest individual score and by the next year he was world's champion. In 1906, the Mauser-type bolt-action Springfield M1903s began replacing the Krag-Jorgensen. In the same year Congress authorized monthly pay of $1.00 for marksman, $2.00 for sharpshooter, and $3.00 for expert. With "beer money" to shoot for, Marine marksmanship improved dramatically and a forty-year love affair with the "Oh-Three" began.

Congress was also fairly liberal with construction money. The Marine Barracks at Eighth and Eye was overcrowded and worn out with use. Various Victorian excrescences had gone onto the Commandant's House in the 1840s, along with a bathroom. In the 1890s a mansard roof was added. In 1903 the enlisted and bachelor quarters were condemned by a Navy medical board and pulled down. By 1910 the quadrangle had been rebuilt, essentially in its present form, with hard burnt brick.

Nicaragua (1909–1913)

In November 1909 Major Butler was sent down to the Isthmus to take command of the Panama battalion. A month later he and his battalion were off to Corinto on the west coast of Nicaragua. Dictator José Santos Zelaya, an anticlerical "Liberal," had a bad reputation for stirring up trouble. Besides, he was heavily in debt—both to the United States and Europe. The staunchly Catholic "Conservatives" under Juan J. Estrada made a revolution against him. The United States, deciding that the Conservatives more nearly represented the Nicaraguan people, broke diplomatic relations with Zelaya's government. A provisional regiment of seven hundred fifty Marines under Colonel James E. Mahoney came down from Philadelphia. Most of the force stayed in Corinto, but Butler reconnoitered the full length of the railroad to Granada and came to certain conclusions as to what he would do if he had to fight along that line. In March, Mahoney went home to Philadelphia and Butler returned to Panama.

But on the east coast, by late spring, the Conservatives were pushed back into Bluefields. So, on 19 May 1918, the USS *Paducah*, a new 1000-ton gunboat, put its landing force ashore, and on 30 May Major Butler arrived with fifteen officers and four hundred fifty men. General Estrada, much encouraged, now moved west and triumphantly marched into the capital at Managua. By September, Butler and his battalion were out of the country and back in Panama.

Major General Commandant Elliott retired on 30 November 1910 at the age of sixty-four, and for a while there was no Commandant (and there were pressures from some segments of the Army and Navy to keep it that way). Acting Commandant was rotund William P. Biddle, who had come up from Panama the previous April. The Corps thought that "Tony" Waller would be the new Commandant, but there was the matter of his smudged record in the Philippines. The Pennsylvania Republicans closed in on President Taft and persuaded him that Biddle of the Philadelphia Biddles should be named. Accordingly, on 3 February 1911, Biddle became the eleventh Commandant of the Marine Corps.

Slavery had ended in Cuba in 1886, but race problems had continued and in 1912 the blacks erupted in the Negro Rebellion. On 22 May the 1st Provisional

Marine Regiment came together with practiced ease at
Philadelphia, this time commanded by Colonel Lincoln
Karmany, and next day was on its way to Guantanamo
aboard the *Prairie.* A 2d Regiment was assembled at
Key West under Colonel Mahoney. Its 1st Battalion
was sent to Guantanamo, its 2d Battalion went into
Havana. Both regiments were combined into the 1st
Provisional Marine Brigade under Karmany. Of great
concern were the American-owned sugar plantations
and mines near El Cobre and Siboney. The Marines
fanned out into Oriente Province, put companies or
platoons into twenty-six towns and rode all the trains.
The Cuban government got things under control. The
Marines pulled back into Guantanamo and in late July
came home.

While those events were taking place in Cuba, things
were going badly for the incumbent Conservative
government in Nicaragua. Cries for help came out of
the U. S. Legation at Managua. Butler's battalion was
again summoned and arrived at Corinto, 354 officers
and men, on 14 August. He worked his way up the
ninety miles of railway to Managua, half by bluff, half
by force, finding bits and pieces of U. S. landing parties
along the way. While Butler was setting things to right
in Managua, Colonel Joseph H. ("Uncle Joe") Pendleton arrived at Corinto on 4 September with the 1st
Provisional Marine Regiment, 780 men in the USS
Buffalo. Pendleton, who had come into the Marine
Corps from the Naval Academy in 1884, was then
fifty-two years old, a portly, pleasant man with a loose
mustache and steel-rimmed glasses. Butler was told to
open the rail line from Managua southeast to Grenada
on the edge of Lake Nicaragua. About halfway, near
Masaya, his train had to run the gauntlet of shelling
from two hilltop forts, called Coyotepe and Barranca.
He marked their position for further attention and shot
his way through. The last fifteen miles to Granada took
five days. Butler was running hot from fever and

temper and his men began to call him "Old Gimlet Eye."

There were still the two bypassed forts outside of Masaya to be attended to. Butler backtracked to meet with Pendleton, who was coming up the railroad with the main body. The rebel position stretched from hill to hill and they seemed to have about a thousand men up there. Pendleton began banging away with three field pieces on 2 October. Before daylight on 4 October, eight hundred fifty Marines and sailors moved out, holding hands so as to keep contact in the darkness. At 0515, the assault began and in forty minutes it was all over. Twenty-seven rebels were dead (they shot their general) and nine captured. Government cavalry went off in pursuit of the rest. There had been eighteen Marine casualties. In November Pendleton left with most of his regiment and Butler returned to Panama. By January 1913 all Marines were out except for a hundred left behind at Managua as a legation guard.

General Biddle was tiring of the job as Commandant. In Washington, there was always the chronic hostility of the Army and some parts of the Navy to combat and the chilly Wilson was even less friendly to the Corps than Roosevelt or Taft had been. There was also a residual coolness between Biddle and the pro-Waller faction of his own officer corps. He retired voluntarily on 24 February 1914. Under Biddle the Corps had grown to a strength of ten thousand. He had worked hard on training and organization, insisting on three months of recruit training, and dividing each Marine post and station into a barracks detachment of nondeployables and one or more numbered companies, each with two officers and a hundred men, ready for instant expeditionary service. Recruit depots were set up at Philadelphia, Port Royal, Mare Island, and Puget Sound. In 1912 he argued prophetically for "one large post on each coast, eventually to be capable of housing a brigade of two regiments at war strength." Perhaps

most important of all, on 23 December 1913, he
activated the Marine Advance Base Force under command of Colonel George Barnett. It was to be a small
brigade of two regiments. The 1st Regiment was also
called the "Fixed Defense Regiment" and was the
forerunner of the defense battalions of World War II.
The 2d Regiment was organized along infantry lines
with four rifle companies, a machine-gun company,
and a battery of landing guns and was a prototype of
the battalion landing teams of World War II and later.
(Somewhat confusingly, the regiments later exchanged
numbers so that the 1st Regiment is in fact the
ancestor of the 2d Marines and the 2d Regiment the
ancestor of the 1st Marines.) The Advance Base Brigade also had an aviation detachment, activated on 27
December 1913, with two officers, seven enlisted men,
and two Navy flying boats.

The Marine Corps was just getting into the "aeroplane" business. In 1911, First Lieutenant Alfred A.
Cunningham, while stationed at Marine Barracks, Philadelphia, had rented a pusher-type contraption for
$25.00 a month from a Philadelphia inventor and
thrashed around the half-mile field inside the Navy
Yard. He never succeeded in getting "Noisy Nan" off
the ground, but his enthusiasm was rewarded with
orders in May 1912 to the new aviation camp at
Annapolis. From here he was sent off to Marblehead,
Massachusetts, where, on 1 August 1912, after two
hours and forty minutes of instruction, he soloed in a
Curtiss seaplane, and became the first Marine pilot
(and the fifth naval aviator). Next to qualify was First
Lieutenant Bernard L. Smith and it was Smith who was
given command of the new Aviation Detachment in the
Advance Base Force.

Veracruz (1914)

On Biddle's retirement, Colonel Barnett was ordered to
Washington, and on 25 February 1914 he was named

Major General Commandant for a four-year term, this fixed tenure with the possibility of a four-year extension having been legislated the year before by Congress. Barnett was the first graduate of the Naval Academy (class of 1881) to become Commandant.

Almost immediately his Marine Advance Base Force got its first expeditionary testing. In Mexico, Francisco Madero had been assassinated and General Victoriano Huerta had made himself dictator-president. On 9 April 1914 the paymaster and boat crew from the dispatch boat *Dolphin* went ashore at Tampico to buy gasoline and were thrown in jail. General Huerta, as soon as he was informed, ordered their release and sent a note of apology and regret, but Rear Admiral Henry T. Mayo was not satisfied. He asked for a twenty-one-gun salute to the American flag, and this Huerta refused. The Navy now moved into a kind of loose blockade of Mexico's Gulf ports.

The Marine Advance Base Force was poised at New Orleans and Pensacola, with leathery John Archer Lejeune, now a colonel, in momentary command. A "Cajun" from Pointe Coupée Parish in southern Louisiana, Lejeune had been born on his family's cotton plantation in 1867, had graduated from the Naval Academy in 1888, and had been the Marine officer in the USS *Cincinnati* during the Spanish-American War. His brigade was now called forward to Veracruz.

On 20 April, President Wilson received word that a German merchant ship was coming into Veracruz with a cargo of arms for Huerta. A message was sent crackling to the Fleet: "Take Veracruz at once." The 2d Marine Regiment led by Lieutenant Colonel Wendell C. ("Buck") Neville was first ashore next morning, 21 April. They landed against no resistance, took the cable station and power plant, and by noon developed a hot fire fight in the railroad yards. In support Neville had a provisional 3d Regiment scoffed up from the Fleet and under Lieutenant Colonel Albertus Catlin. On the Marines' left were several Navy battalions in coffee-dyed whites. At nightfall Neville was joined by Butler, who had come charging onto the scene with his Panama battalion in the scout cruiser *Chester*. Next morning Neville resumed the attack and it turned out to be a house-to-house proposition, going over the roofs and through the walls.

Lejeune was now in the harbor with the rest of the Marine Brigade. He came ashore mid-morning on the 22d (falling overboard between ship's boat and seawall in the process) and that afternoon the 1st Marine Regiment under Lieutenant Colonel Charles G. Long began to land. The Naval Brigade was also building up so that the landing force, under overall command of Rear Admiral Frank F. Fletcher, had a total of about 7,000 men ashore. By 24 April Veracruz was pacified; American casualties had been about 135. On 29 April Brigadier General Frederick Funston, USA, arrived with an Army brigade and assumed command of operations ashore. Two days later Colonel "Tony" Waller came in and relieved Lejeune of the Marine Brigade; no reflection on Lejeune, but Waller was senior. The Brigade strength stood at about 3100. Huerta was persuaded to leave Mexico on 15 July and the Carranza government took over. Some Marines stayed on at Veracruz until 23 November 1914.

Haiti (1915)

Haiti's finances had collapsed and the foreign banks were anxious to get their money. Germany, France, Great Britain, and the United States all found reason to put Marines ashore in 1914.

In 1902, Germany, Britain, and Italy in pursuing claims against Venezuela for damages sustained during a revolution as well as a bond default, had blockaded that hapless republic, captured its fleet, and bombarded the coast in three places. After a year of this, Roosevelt had advised Kaiser Wilhelm (whom he mistook for the ringleader) that if the three powers did not

submit their claims to The Hague for arbitration, he would send down Admiral Dewey with the Atlantic Fleet to break the blockade. Roosevelt told the Congress that the United States would not go to war to prevent a European nation from collecting its just debts providing the European action did "not take the form of acquisition of territory." However, in what would come to be called the Roosevelt Corollary, he went on to say that in case of "chronic wrongdoing or impotence" on the part of a Latin American state, the United States was bound by the Monroe Doctrine "however reluctantly" to intervene and to "exercise an international police power."

This was the case with the Dominican Republic. By 1904, debts owed European banks had reached $32 million and the interested powers, in light of the Venezuelan incident, were asking Roosevelt what he intended to do about it. His solution was to indemnify the debt, appoint a financial receiver for the bankrupt government, and take over the customhouses, import duties being the one sure form of taxation.

The United States offered the Haitian government an

indemnification and financial receivership similar to the Dominican formula but this was refused. In December 1914 the Marine detachment from the gunboat *Machias* landed at Port-au-Prince and carted off for safekeeping the last $500,000 in Haiti's treasury.

In March 1915 a revolution put Vilbrun Guillaume Sam into the presidency. On 27 July, there was a bloody uprising in Port-au-Prince. Losing control, President Sam gave orders for the slaughter of 167 political prisoners and then took refuge in the French Legation. The crowd sought him out, pulled him apart, and ate his heart. Next day, Rear Admiral William B. Caperton, with his flag in the armored cruiser *Washington*, landed an improvised "regiment" under his senior Marine, Captain George Van Orden, one battalion of bluejackets and two companies of Fleet Marines. They went into Port-au-Prince against sniper fire and restored order. The 2d Marine Regiment, under Colonel Eli K. Cole, came down from Philadelphia in the battleship *Connecticut*, arriving 4 August. The 1st Marine Regiment and Headquarters, 1st Marine Brigade, under Colonel Waller came in on 15 August on board the *Tennessee*. Waller, with 2000 Marines to work with, took over ten customhouses and garrisoned the more important towns. He himself went north to Cap Haitien, where most of the problem seemed to be, taking the 1st Battalion, 1st Marines, and Major Butler as a kind of roving battalion commander and executive officer.

The insurgents in the north called themselves "Cacos," after a red-plumed bird of prey, and they managed to wear something red on their ragged clothing as a badge. "General" Rameau and his particular band of Cacos had been harassing the Marine detachment at Gonaïves. Butler came storming over the mountains, caught up with Rameau on 18 September, literally yanked him off his horse, and sent him into Port-au-Prince as a prisoner. In this exercise he was helped by a young lieutenant from Virginia named Alexander A. Vandegrift.

Butler next volunteered to reconnoiter Fort Capois, reputedly the Caco mountain stronghold. For his patrol he took twenty-six Marines on local ponies. They got themselves ambushed at a stream crossing after dark on 24 October. The animal carrying the patrol's only machine gun was killed in mid-stream and the rest of the pack train was scattered. Gunnery Sergeant Dan Daly volunteered to go back and get the machine gun, which he did, adding a second Medal of Honor to the one he had gotten on the Wall at Peking. There was an all-night fight that cost the Cacos seventy-five dead, by Butler's count, to one Marine wounded. Waller then gave Butler five companies of Marines and two of sailors to clean out Fort Capois, which he did on 5 November.

The Cacos's last fixed bastion, which they thought impregnable, was the ruins of an eighteenth-century French fort eight miles south of Grande Rivière and on top of 4000-foot Montagne Noire. Butler was given three companies of Marines and one company of sailors in Marine uniforms to do the job. They began the climb the night of 17 November 1915, Butler moving at the front of the 13th Company. Butler got to the wall with two lieutenants and twenty-four Marines, found the sally port bricked up, located an open drain with Caco bullets *whanging* through it. "Oh, hell," said a sergeant. "I'm going through." He went, followed by Butler and his orderly, with the rest of the 13th Company close behind. There was a wild hand-to-hand fight, Marine bayonets against Caco swords and clubs, called *cocomacaques*. The Cacos who didn't die went over the wall into the bush. "General" Josefette's body was found in its frock coat, with a large brass chain adorning his chest, and his high hat lying near by.

Major Butler was given a second Medal of Honor for Fort Rivière to add to one he had tried to refuse for

Veracruz. (He thought that Medals of Honor were much too freely handed out for the Mexican intervention.) In Port-au-Prince there was a new government (friendly to the United States) which agreed to the creation of a Haitian constabulary officered by Americans. First commandant of the Gendarmerie d'Haiti was Butler, promoted to lieutenant colonel and grandly fleeted up to major general in the Haitian service. With the field grades being filled with Marine officers and the company grades with Marine NCOs, the Gendarmerie went up to a hundred and twenty Americans and twenty-five hundred Haitians. They were clothed in surplus Marine uniforms, armed with Krags, and drilled in English. With occasional Marine help, they maintained the government, kept law and order, and outdid themselves in what another generation would call "civic action." They built roads, overhauled the telegraph system, put in a postal system, improved the water supply and general sanitation, took an interest in the schools, refurbished the lighthouses and navigational aids, and provided fire-fighting services to the principal towns.

Santo Domingo (1916)

Across the border separating the third of Hispaniola that is black and French-speaking from the two-thirds that is predominantly mulatto and Spanish-speaking, there was new trouble. Marine landing parties had been bobbing in and out of the Dominican Republic since the turn of the century, but the civil war of 1916 would require a more prolonged stay.

By April things were out of control and, on 5 May 1916, Captain Frederic M. ("Dopey") Wise came over from Port-au-Prince in the *Prairie* with the 6th and 9th Companies. He moved into Fort Geronimo outside Santo Domingo. By the fifteenth, a hefty battalion of 375 Marines and 225 bluejackets had been lined up under command of Major Newt Hall (second-in-command at Peking) for an assault against the ancient walls of the oldest city in the New World. Wise remarked later that it was like Veracruz but without the fighting; not a shot was fired, not a weapon found. On 26 May, Wise went around the island in the old *Panther* to the northwest corner of the Republic, landed at Monte Cristi (important then for cowhides, tallow, and logwood), ran into 150 ragged rebels and chopped them down with his single machine gun. On 1 June, Fleet Marines came ashore against stiff rifle fire at Puerto Plata, the north coast's most important port and very European, and pushed the rebels up into the hills.

Something more substantial in the way of a Marine force was required and on 4 June, the 4th Marine Regiment, commanded by "Uncle Joe" Pendleton, was moved by rail from San Diego (where it formed the West Coast Expeditionary Force) to New Orleans whence it outloaded for the Dominican Republic. Pendleton landed at Monte Cristi on 18 June. He was nominally in command of the 2d Marine Brigade (all the Marines in the Republic, nose count: 47 officers and 1728 enlisted men), but at Monte Cristi he had only a few more than 1000. Leaving 235 Marines to garrison the place, he started down the road with 833 officers and men toward Santiago de los Caballeros, some one hundred kilometers away. That part of Hispaniola is semiarid, rough *bosque* with cactus and thorn bushes and not much grass. Thirty kilometers down the road was Las Trencheras, a ridgeline crossing the road at right angles, where the Dominicans had beaten the Spanish in 1864. Pendleton pummeled the ridge with his artillery, got his machine guns into an enfilade position, and on 27 June the Marines made a stand-up bayonet attack that cleared the ridge. The Dominicans counterattacked the night of the twenty-eighth under the mistaken notion that "Uncle Joe" Pendleton's machine guns wouldn't function at night. The final fight on the road to Santiago was at Guayacanes, another ridgeline position. On 3 July, the artillery and machine guns again did their work. Meanwhile, a battalion had landed at Puerto Plata under Major H. I. ("Hiking Hiram") Bearss. The two columns met at Navarrete on 4 July, and marched into Santiago two days later without further resistance.

On 29 November 1916, Captain (soon to be Rear Admiral) Harry S. Knapp became Military Governor (in a combination of a Cuban and Haitian pacification formulae). Ten towns were garrisoned and the 2d Marine Brigade settled down to an eight-year stay. The Guardia Nacional Dominicana, patterned on the Gendarmerie d'Haiti, was activated on 7 April 1917. It was authorized a strength of 1234 officers and men and its first commandant was Lieutenant Colonel George Thorpe, the same Thorpe who made the march to Addis Ababa. The officer ranks were open to Dominicans but not many members of the better families cared to join. One of the brightest and best was a young sugar-plantation policeman named Rafael Leonidas Trujillo.

Back in Washington

Barnett was proving to be exactly the right Commandant for the Corps of that time, fully qualified for the home-guard wars of Washington. Deftly, unobtrusively but firmly, he set about improving relationships with the Navy. The old Naval Station at Port Royal, South Carolina, was now called Parris Island and receiving all recruits from east of the Mississippi. Recruits from west of the Mississippi were sent to Mare Island in California. San Diego, home of the West Coast Expeditionary Force, was developing into a major base. An embryonic Marine Corps Reserve was started. The National Defense Act of August 1916 entitled the Marine Corps to seven brigadier generals. Three went to the Staff: the Adjutant and Inspector, the Quartermaster General, and the Paymaster General. There were four promotions in the Line: Waller, Lejeune, Pendleton, and Cole.

Ex-President Theodore Roosevelt, mellowed by the years or perhaps just pleased by the workings of the Roosevelt Corollary, remarked that the three most efficient military-constabulary organizations in the world were the French Foreign Legion, the Canadian Mounted Police, and the U. S. Marines, each supreme in its own sphere of operations.

10

1917–1918

"The whole nation
has reason to be proud...."

Over There

War against Germany and the Central Powers was
declared on 6 April 1917. Spurred by the slogan "First
to Fight" there was a rush of recruits into the Marine
Corps. The newborn Marine Corps Reserve, mobilized
on 16 April, contributed three officers and thirty-three
enlisted men. The recruit depots at Parris Island and
Mare Island were soon swamped, and temporary recruit centers had to be opened at Philadelphia, Brooklyn, and Norfolk Navy Yards. On 14 May, six thousand
acres were leased at Quantico, south of Washington, as
the beginnings of a major new base.

Major General Commandant George Barnett was
determined that a Marine expeditionary force would be
on board the first convoy to sail for France. The War
Department was not particularly receptive: the thought
being that the Army had soldiers enough of its own.
But on 29 May, President Wilson approved the sending
of the 5th Marine Regiment. Commanded by Colonel
Charles A. Doyen, the regiment sailed on 14 June in the
Navy transport USS *Henderson*, and arrived at Saint
Nazaire on 27 June 1917. Pershing parceled out the

regiment as line-of-communication troops, mostly as military police. The 6th Marines under Albertus Catlin, now a colonel, and the 6th Machine Gun Battalion came over in late 1917. The Marines were brought together in early 1918 as the 4th Brigade, 2d U. S. Division, commanded by Doyen, promoted to brigadier general. It was a big brigade, 280 officers and 9164 enlisted Marines, as big as most of the understrength French and British divisions of the time. There was some winter training under the Chasseurs Alpins, whose disdain for the rifle except as a place to put the bayonet was in sharp conflict with Marine traditions. On Saint Patrick's Day, the Brigade went into a quiet bit of trenches southeast of Verdun. Four days later the Germans began their Amiens offensive. Foch, reconstituting his reserve, pulled out the French division and left the Marine Brigade with a division front. Here they learned the realities of trench warfare: cooties, rats, wire parties, raids, and gas. They were relieved on 9 May and rejoined the 2d U. S. Division northwest of Paris. In addition to the Marine Brigade, the big 28,000-man Division had the 3d Infantry Brigade, three field artillery regiments, an engineer regiment, and a field signal battalion. By late May the Brigade was in reserve positions between Paris and Beauvais, with every expectation of following the 1st U. S. Division into the Cantigny offensive. Doyen had been invalided home and command of the Brigade had gone to Army Brigadier General James G. Harbord, who had been Pershing's chief of staff.

On 31 May, the 75th Company, 1st Battalion, 6th Marines, was billeted at a French farm with a stone barn so vast that it could sleep the entire war-strength company of two hundred fifty Marines. Platoon Sergeant Gerald C. Thomas and several buddies had gone to regimental headquarters about five kilometers away for Memorial Day services. A company runner found them and told them to get back to the company area; they were moving out. The company got into heavy marching order and out onto the road. French *camions* came along and they were on their way, not to Cantigny, but to the Paris-Meaux sector, up near a place called Château-Thierry.

Château-Thierry and Belleau Wood

On 27 May 1918, Ludendorff, with forty-odd divisions, had launched his Chemin des Dames offensive, the northern front had been sliced in two, and the Germans were coming through a four-kilometer gap left by the wreckage of the French 43d Division. The Division commander thought he still had some *poilus* fighting in Bois de Belleau west of Château-Thierry and asked for a counterattack. A French colonel, less sanguine, gave a Gallic shrug and advised Colonel Wendell Neville, commanding the 5th Marines, to retreat. "Whispering Buck" Neville (his Marines were fond of saying that he could make himself heard at GHQ Chaumont—without benefit of telephone—by sticking his head out of a dugout doorway) is supposed to have looked at the Frenchman coldly and roared: "Retreat, hell. We just got here."

A half-dozen others, Marine and Army, subsequently claimed the quotation, but Neville himself later attributed it to Captain Lloyd Williams, commanding the 51st Company, 2d Battalion, 5th Marines, in response to a French major of the 49th Chasseurs à Pied who had penned a note, "Retreat, the Germans are coming."

Whoever said it, it reflected the mood of the U. S. 2d Division. On 1 June 1918 they formed a line astride the Paris-Metz road, 23d Infantry on the left flank, 6th and 5th Marines in the center, 9th Infantry on the right. At dawn on 2 June, the German 28th Division, a good one much admired by the Kaiser's wife, attacked along the axis of the road, destination Paris, and hit the Marine center. The German veterans got a lesson in rifle fire that began to kill at eight hundred yards. A French aviator thought he saw the American line falling back

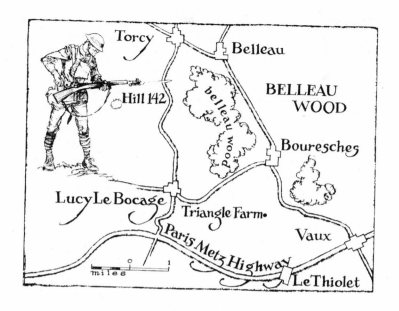

and so reported to his corps commander. An inquiry came down through channels; Harbord in turn asked Major Thomas Holcomb, commander of the 2d Battalion, 6th Marines. "When I do my running," said Holcomb flatly, "It will be in the opposite direction."

The Germans attacked again on the 4th and 5th of June, then sullenly took up defensive positions. Belleau Wood, in front of the Marines, was a natural fortress, a square mile of woods and tumbled boulders. Behind it were the villages of Torcy, Belleau, and Bouresches. In the woods were two battalions of the 461st Imperial German Infantry liberally augmented with Maxim machine gunners.

The French general, Jean Degoutte, ordered an attack by the Americans. It began on the morning of 6 June, the 1st Battalion, 5th Marines, going forward in four waves, lines neatly dressed—tactics preached by the French but not practiced by them since 1915. Across the wheat fields, dotted with blood-red poppies, the German machine gunners waited for them, let them get close before opening fire. By noon the 1st Battalion, 5th Marines, had taken Hill 142 west of the wood. Now came the second phase of the attack. The 2d Battalion, 5th Marines, and the 2d and 3d Battalions, 6th Marines, went into the wood itself. War correspondent Floyd Gibbons, before he himself was wounded, heard Gunnery Sergeant Daniel Daly (of Peking and Haiti) yell to his platoon, "Come on, you sons of bitches. Do you want to live forever?" Colonel Catlin went down, shot through the right lung. Two platoons of the 6th Marines, one of them under a young Tennessee law graduate, Lieutenant Clifton B. Cates, got into the village of Bouresches and held it against repeated counterattacks. Sergeant Major John Quick (he of Guantanamo and Samar) brought up the ammunition to Cates in a Ford truck and won the DSC.

The Marines were working with Springfield rifles and bayonets, Chauchat automatic rifles, and Hotchkiss machine guns. They had no trench mortars, no signal flares or Very pistols, and there was a shortage of grenades. The Marines had to either shoot the German machine gunners or crawl up and bayonet them. They took two-thirds of the woods by nightfall and the price was high. At the day's end there were 1087 Marine casualties, dead and wounded.

They consolidated on the seventh, digging a line of shallow rifle pits. Someone called them "foxholes" and the name stuck. The Germans tried a counterattack on the eighth. The Marines went forward again next day and by the night of 12 June had all the northern tip of the woods. The attack was costly and among the Marine dead was Captain Williams of the 51st Company, he who had best claim to "Retreat, hell." The German IV Corps counterattacked in strength on 13 June behind a cloud of mustard gas. The Marines held their ground, but by the fifteenth Harbord was demanding that his brigade be relieved. The 7th U. S. Infantry, half-trained, came up on the night of 16 June, and filed into the random line of foxholes. The Marine Brigade, some of its battalions down to one-third strength, went into Division reserve. The 7th Infantry lasted three days before it was used up. The Marines went back in the attack on 23 June, and on the twenty-sixth, Harbord could send the signal: "Woods now U. S. Marine Corps entirely." General Degoutte, commanding the French Sixth Army, on 30 June decreed, "Henceforth in all official papers, Belleau Wood shall bear the name, 'Bois de la Brigade de Marine.' "

The Germans made their own sober assessment and begrudgingly allowed that the Marines, with more experience, might be considered to be of storm-trooper quality. There was also a less formal assessment being made in the *feldgrau* ranks. *"Teufelhunden,"* or "Devil-dogs," they called their new enemy, an appellation the Marines accepted as a compliment.

Meanwhile, Brigadier General Lejeune had arrived in France with Barnett's offer of another Marine brigade for the AEF and the personal expectation of becoming the Marine Division commander. Pershing tartly reported to the Secretary of War that "While Marines are splendid troops, their use as a separate division is inadvisable." He was, however, willing to take another Marine infantry brigade. An offer of a Marine artillery regiment, the 10th Marines, was turned down—although individual Marine artillery officers would be acceptable as replacement officers. Lejeune was ordered to the command of a National Guard brigade.

Soissons and Saint Mihiel

On 14 July, Harbord, now a major general and a jaunty hybrid in his *poilu*'s helmet and Marine emblems, moved up to command of the 2d Division, and "Buck" Neville was promoted to brigadier general and given the Marine Brigade. Next day, Ludendorff launched the last German offensive of the war. The 2d Division was attached to the French XX Corps for a counterattack near Soissons. The 5th Marines were to be in the initial assault; 6th Marines were to follow in reserve. On the night of the seventeenth, they moved through mud and rain into their attack positions in the Forest of Retz. Next morning, at dawn's first gray light, the 5th Marines jumped off and by noon had advanced two miles. Next day, the 6th Marines passed through the 5th Marines, went a mile and a half, and ran headlong into a corps-size German counterattack. "Cliff" Cates, now a company commander, found himself in an abandoned trench and sent back a scribbled message: ". . . I have only two men left out of my company and 20 out of other companies. . . . I have no one on my left, and only a few on my right. I will hold."

That night a fresh division came up and the Marine Brigade came out of the line, 1972 casualties for two days of work. By now German intelligence was reporting, "The Marines are considered a sort of elite Corps. . . ."

After Soissons, the Marine Brigade got ten quiet days on the Moselle near Nancy. There they were visited by Franklin D. Roosevelt, then the young Assistant Secretary of the Navy. Roosevelt had just toured Belleau Wood and authorized the enlisted Marines to wear the Marine Corps emblem on the collars of their Army issue uniforms (until then an officer's privilege) "in recognition of the splendid work of the Marine Brigade."

The Marines had worn their "greens" to France but in January 1918 Pershing had ordered them into Army olive drab to simplify the problems of supply and, also, it was said, to make unit identification by the enemy more difficult. Doyen had acceded to the order reluctantly. Except in rear areas, the beloved field hat also had to be given up and the soft "overseas" cap substituted. In the line the flat British-style trench helmet was worn, sometimes dressed up with the addition of a Marine Corps emblem.

On 29 July 1918 Harbord was detached to take over

the AEF's burgeoning Service of Supply, and Lejeune, in an Army concession to Marine sensibilities, was given the 2d Division. Coming up next was the first big all-American push, two U. S. corps to pinch out the Saint Mihiel salient. Colonel Harry Lee now had the 6th Marines and Colonel Logan Feland the 5th Marines. The 3d Infantry Brigade led off at dawn on 12 September, following behind a four-hour artillery preparation. As always, there was mud and rain. The Marines passed through next day and by nightfall on the fifteenth, both regiments had their objectives. It was an easy fight compared to Belleau and Soissons but nevertheless there were 706 fresh Marine casualties to be added to the bill.

Brigadier General Eli Cole brought over the 5th Marine Brigade in September. The War Department told Pershing to use it as he saw fit. Command was passed from Cole to Smedley Butler, a brigadier general at thirty-seven, youngest in Corps history. To "Old Gimlet Eye" Butler's intense disgust the Brigade was assigned to guard duty with the Service of Supply with headquarters at Brest.

In the Air

On the day war was declared there were six officers, headed by Alfred Cunningham, one warrant officer, and forty-three enlisted men in the Marine Aeronautical Section at Naval Aeronautic Station, Pensacola. Soon afterward the detachment was transferred to the Navy Yard at Philadelphia. There, a hangar was built on the river with openings at both ends—one for seaplanes, and the other for land planes. Total flying inventory consisted of "two land aeroplanes, two sea aeroplanes, one school land aeroplane, and two kite balloons."

In October 1917 the detachment was split into the 1st Marine Aviation Squadron (land planes)—which was moved to Mineola, Long Island—and the 1st

Marine Aeronautic Company (seaplanes). The latter company, under command of Major Francis T. ("Cocky") Evans (first pilot to loop a seaplane), sailed from Philadelphia on 9 January 1918 with ten Curtiss R-6 seaplanes and two Curtiss N-9s for Ponta Delgada in the Azores. From then until the Armistice they assiduously would fly antisubmarine patrols without ever sighting a U-boat.

In early 1918 the 1st Marine Aviation Squadron had moved from Mineola to Gerstner Field in Louisiana. About this time, Cunningham (now a captain) returned from France, where he had been exploring opportunities for employment. His recommendation was that four Marine squadrons be sent to form the Day Wing of a proposed Navy Northern Bombing Group to be based near Calais. Accordingly, the 1st Marine Aviation Squadron was transferred from Louisiana to Curtiss Field (redesignated "Marine Flying Field") in Miami in April 1918 and expanded into the 1st Marine Aviation Force, with four squadrons—A, B, C, and D. Senior squadron commander was thirty-three-year-old Captain Roy S. Geiger. Captain Cunningham, as commander, 1st Marine Aviation Force, arrived at Brest on 30 July with Squadrons A, B, and C (Squadron D would not arrive until October). Room was found for them on fields near Calais. They (redesignated Squadrons 7, 8, and 9) were to receive the first seventy-two American-built De Havilland-4 bombers to arrive in France, but the DH-4s when they got there were so badly put together that they had to be rebuilt. Meanwhile, the Marine pilots were assigned to RAF Squadrons 217 and 218, which had the British De Havilland, and a lucky few to RAF Squadron 213, which had the Sopwith Camel.

Meuse-Argonne and Blanc Mont

On the ground, the 2d Division had moved over to General Henri Gouraud's Fourth Army for the Meuse-

Argonne offensive. The Allies were now up against the Hindenburg Line. By the end of September the French had been stopped near Somm-Py in the Champagne Sector. Key terrain was Blanc Mont—the "White Mountain"—held by the Germans since 1914. Lejeune told Gouraud the 2d Division could take Blanc Mont. The Marines would attack frontally against the ridge. The 3d Infantry Brigade would come in from the right. The French would advance on the left against a projection called the Essen Hook.

On 3 October 1918 the 6th Marines jumped off at 0555 hours on the heels of a thunderous five-minute preparation by two hundred guns and had its objective before noon. Meanwhile, the French were lagging two miles behind, stopped by the Essen Hook. The 5th Marines took it for them in a right angle attack. (". . . remarkable," said Gouraud's operations summary.)

Next day, 5th Marines changed direction once again, passed through the 6th Marines on the ridge, and drove to Saint Etienne, three miles away. The Germans counterattacked in regimental strength but failed to halt the advance. On 6 October, the Marines entered Saint Etienne and their part of the battle was over. It had cost them 2,538 casualties and brought a third citation in French Army orders. This entitled the two regiments to the streamer of the Croix de Guerre and to this day the 5th and 6th Marines wear the red-and-green *fourragère*.

After Blanc Mont the 2d Division moved back to the American First Army and was assigned to the V Corps for the final drive of the war. The Division was assigned a narrow, two-kilometer front in the center of the First Army line and given the mission of driving a wedge into the German defenses. Facing the Marines was the German 61st Division, in process of being relieved by the 52d Division, supported by the Bavarian 15th Division whom the Leathernecks had previously met on Blanc Mont.

Supported by three hundred guns and a company of fifteen light tanks, the 2d Division jumped off on 1 November with the Marine Brigade out front in the assault, the 5th Marines on the right, 6th Marines on the left; the regiments themselves deployed in column of battalions. The attack went through the German defenders like a knife. The battalions leapfrogged forward and by the end of the first day, the advance had moved nine kilometers and taken seventeen hundred prisoners. The Germans withdrew behind the Meuse. Elsewhere along the Western Front the German Army was in general retreat but against the American First Army they showed a streak of stubbornness. On 10 November, the 143d Birthday of the Corps, the 5th Marines made a night crossing of the Meuse and next morning resumed the attack. Then, at eleven o'clock, the shooting stopped and the war was over.

In the air, Major Cunningham (he had been promoted in August) had not been able to get his squadrons into action in their own equipment until October and then only by some shrewd trading of new Liberty engines for British fuselages. By this time the original targets of the Northern Bombing Group, the submarine pens at Ostend, Zeebrugge, and Bruges had been abandoned by the Germans. Pershing assigned the Group to support the British and it was given the general mission of attacking any rear-area targets which might hinder the retreat of the German Army. When it was over on 11 November, 1st Marine Aviation Force in its brief period of action had lost 4 dead, shot down 12 Germans, and flown 57 bombing missions. In the nineteen months the United States was in the war, Marine aviation had expanded to 280 officers, 2,200 men, and 340 aircraft.

After an uneventful tour of duty along the Rhine in the Army of Occupation, the Marine Brigade came home to Quantico; and on 12 August 1919, there was a march past the White House. During the war the strength of the Corps had gone to about 76,000. Some

32,000 had served in France. There had been 11,366 casualties of whom 2,459 were killed or missing in action. Only 25 Marines were taken prisoner. ("Surrendering wasn't popular . . ." said Colonel Catlin.) Woodrow Wilson took the last review, then wrote the Commandant a brief note: "The whole nation has reason to be proud of them."

11

1917–1941
"...if attacked, shoot and shoot to kill."

West Indies and Siberia (1917–1920)

There had been an excursion to Siberia, beginning on 29 June 1918, when the veteran USS *Brooklyn* put her Marines ashore in Vladivostok. The Japanese, British, and French were also there and the Marines were given the old Imperial Navy Yard to patrol.

In the Caribbean, while larger events were taking place in Europe, revolt had flamed up again in Cuba. The Platt Amendment was invoked and Marines from the Atlantic Fleet were landed in eastern Cuba in February 1917. They came out in May—the declaration of war with Germany causing higher priorities for their employment. Then in August 1917 the new 7th Marines were landed. (Sugar was a strategic material and this was the Sugar Intervention.) The 9th Marines followed in December, along with the 3d Marine Brigade headquarters. In July 1918 the Brigade headquarters and the 9th Marines went to Texas to join the 8th Marines who were already there, watching the border in the belief that German agents were somehow fomenting a Mexican reconquest of the Southwest. In December the

1st Marines came down from Philadelphia to join the 7th Marines in Cuba and both the regiments were put under 6th Brigade command. By the end of August 1919 all Marines were gone from Cuba except for one battalion which remained in Camaguey, near Guantanamo, until 1922.

Across the Windward Passage, a new Caco chieftain had emerged in Haiti, one Charlemagne Masséna Peralte. In March 1919 the Commandant of the Gendarmerie asked for the help of the 1st Marine Brigade, which had been standing on the sidelines. The Brigade was essentially the light-weight 2d Marine Regiment, less than a thousand men, but reinforcements began to arrive, including Squadron E with seven Curtiss HS-2 flying boats and six Curtiss "Jennies."

From April to September the Marines and *gendarmes* fought 131 actions against the Cacos. By then the old campaigner, Colonel Frederic Wise, had come down to take command of the Gendarmerie and on 2 October Colonel John H. Russell took over the Brigade. Four days later Charlemagne sent 300 men on a raid into Port-au-Prince. Thirty Cacos were killed but it was now obvious that the rebellion would not be put down until Charlemagne himself had been dealt with.

On the night of 30 October 1919, Captain Herman H. Hanneken (permanent rank, Sergeant, USMC) started out with First Lieutenant (Corporal, USMC) William R. Button (faces blackened) and led by Private François, a *gendarme* "deserter," to get Charlemagne personally. The bait was a Browning automatic rifle Button was carrying, ostensibly captured from the *blancs*. This plus François's persuasiveness got them past the challenges of six Caco outposts and into Charlemagne's camp in the hills above Grande Rivière. François pointed out the Caco chief in the firelight. Hanneken put two .45-caliber slugs into Charlemagne while Button chopped away at his bodyguard with the BAR. Charlemagne's body was lashed across a mule and packed down to Cap Haitien where, after a proper Christian service, it was buried in a block of concrete so the Cacos wouldn't dig it up and perhaps resurrect Charlemagne as a *zombie.*

Another Caco leader, Benoît Batraville, rose to take Charlemagne's place. Colonel Russell, reinforced by the 8th Marines who arrived in December 1919, worked out a plan to comb the bandit-infested country with relays of fresh patrols, never letting up the pressure. First move, though, came from Batraville. On the night of 14 January 1920 he infiltrated three hundred men into Port-au-Prince. Marine and *gendarme* patrols searched them out during the early morning hours on the 15th and there was a good deal of shooting. By daylight, sixty-six Cacos were dead and twice that number wounded.

Some 3200 real or professed Cacos surrendered during January and February. But Batraville himself fought on. Marine fliers had been experimenting with bombs dropped out of mail sacks tied to the landing gear spreaders of their Jennies and DH-4s. Then some proper bomb racks had arrived from the States and they found that if they dived at a target at a 45° angle they got good accuracy. In March, two Marine aircraft caught Batraville on a hilltop near his native Mirebalais and drove him into the rifle and machine-gun fire of converging Marine patrols. In the slaughter that followed, Batraville lost 200 more Cacos killed and wounded.

On 4 April 1920 Batraville ambushed a small patrol and ritualistically ate the roasted heart and liver of the Marine lieutenant, but the magic did him little good. On 19 May another Marine patrol found him, a Marine sergeant knocked him down with a burst from his BAR, and a second sergeant finished him with a bullet through the head. There would now be a long period of peace in Haiti under the firm hand of newly promoted Brigadier General Russell, U. S. High Commissioner.

Santo Domingo

Across the frontier (marked in the north by the well-named Rio Massacre) the neighboring Dominicans were not all submitting meekly to Rear Admiral Knapp's military government, a government in which "Uncle Joe" Pendleton held the portfolios of War and Navy, Interior, and Police. On 29 November 1916, First Lieutenant E. C. Williams had shot his way into the *fortaleza* at San Francisco de Macorís. Governor Pérez took umbrage at Williams' action and went off into the bush with two hundred followers. Converging Marine columns from La Vega and Sanchez drove Pérez south and his band was gradually worn away. After Pérez there were other smaller *grupos* to be hunted down. One of the stiffest actions of 1917 was that fought against a bandit called "Chacha" at Consuelo sugar plantation near San Pedro de Macorís by another old campaigner, Lieutenant Colonel "Hiking Hiram" Bearss. That was in January. There was also Vincentico Evangelista who was holding out farther north near El Seibo. "Chacha" gave himself up and Evangelista was eventually killed.

A system of provost courts was set up. In 1917 and the first half of 1918, some 53,000 firearms were collected. More than 100 skirmishes were fought in 1918. The most difficult operation of the year was the two-hundred-fifty-mile pursuit of one Dios Olivorio into the western mountains. Brigadier General Ben Fuller relieved "Uncle Joe" Pendleton on 21 October 1918 as commander of the 2d Brigade which now had the 3d Marines as well as the 4th Marines. In February 1919 Fuller got another regiment, the 15th Marines, added to his Brigade and Squadron D arrived with six DH-4s. There were 200 fire fights that year.

In December 1920 President Wilson announced that the Marines were going to be withdrawn. Strength of the Brigade, now under Brigadier General Logan Feland, stood at about 120 officers and 2000 men. There was a systematic series of cordons-and-searches and in the eastern provinces virtually every male Dominican was picked up for screening. By the spring of 1922 banditry was almost at a halt. Command of the Brigade now rotated to Brigadier General Harry Lee, and in December he also became the military governor. During the year the 3d and 15th Regiments were disbanded and their assets absorbed by the 4th Marines and the reactivated 1st Marines.

The Guardia, never popular with the Dominicans, had gotten up to 1200 in 1918 then had sagged as low as 350 in 1921. It was now renamed the Policía Nacional Dominicana, built back up to 1200, and began taking over the garrisoning of the *fortalezas* and *puestos*. By 1923 the shrinking Brigade was acting mainly as a reserve for the National Police. A new constitutional government was sworn in on 12 July 1924. In August the 4th Marines started back to San Diego from whence they had come eight years earlier, and on 16 September 1924 the last Marine company left Santo Domingo. Said General Lee in his final report: "We left a state enjoying peace, and with a loyal and well-developed military force, with fine roads, many schools, a fine military hospital, and, in short, with every promise for a future of stable government under Dominican rule."

Lejeune Becomes Commandant

On 12 February 1918 General Barnett had been appointed to a second term as Commandant, but in the years following the end of the war he had trouble with the Secretary of the Navy, abstemious Josephus Daniels. On 18 June 1920 he received a sealed letter from the Secretary demanding that he retire immediately or accept a reduction to brigadier general and reassignment. Barnett bit the bullet and was sent to the Department of the Pacific in San Francisco, a newly created kind of West Coast Marine Corps headquarters. The new Commandant, as of 30 June 1920, was the leathery Cajun and 2d Division Commander, John Lejeune.

Lejeune understood that readiness was the hallmark of the Marine Corps and specifically, although it had been obscured by the events of World War I, amphibious readiness. In 1921, the Marine Corps Schools at Quantico were consolidated. Three courses were offered: The Basic Course (in 1924 it moved to Philadelphia, where it would remain until World War II), the Company Officers' Course, and the Field Officers' Course. The Advance Base Force headquarters (which during the war years had been under tough old "Tony" Waller) was also moved to Quantico and in 1922 it was redesignated the East Coast Expeditionary Force.

One of Lejeune's planners was Lieutenant Colonel Earl H. ("Pete") Ellis who had been adjutant of the 4th Marine Brigade in France. In 1923 Ellis took a year's leave to tour Micronesia and died in the Japanese-held Palau Islands under circumstances still not fully explained. But before that, in 1921, he had developed the 50,000-word Operation Plan 712, "Advanced Base Operations in Micronesia" in which, predicting that Japan would strike first, he had written: ". . . it will be necessary for us to project our fleet and landing forces across the Pacific and wage war in Japanese waters. To effect this requires that we have sufficient bases to support the fleet, both during its projection and afterwards."

In the early 1920s the Marines from Quantico under Smedley Butler (their dress uniforms were a convenient blue for the Union and cadets from the Virginia military schools wore the Confederate gray) amused themselves and official Washington with re-enactments of some of the Civil War battles: Wilderness, Gettysburg, New Market, and Antietam. There was also strenuous athletic competition—boxing, football, and baseball.

On Broadway, *What Price Glory?* coauthored by

Maxwell Anderson and Lawrence T. Stallings was a great hit. As a new lieutenant, Stallings had joined the 3d Battalion, 5th Marines, at Belleau Wood and commanded a platoon at Bouresches. Going against a machine-gun nest on 25 June 1918 got him wounds that eventually cost him a leg and caused his retirement as a captain in 1920. There was also his friend Captain John W. Thomason, Jr., of the 49th Company, 1st Battalion, 5th Marines, whose book *Fix Bayonets!* came out in 1926 and was followed by a long series of articles and stories in *The Saturday Evening Post.* Thomason's florid Kiplingesque prose was illustrated with his own lean, pungent, pen-and-ink sketches. The tough, wise-cracking, hard-as-nails, heart-of-gold Marine sergeant, as played by Edmund Lowe, Victor McLaglen, and Wallace Beery, began to appear on the American movie screen. The public image of the United States Marine was taking shape: lean, sunburnt, in faded khaki and rakish field hat, rattling through some jungled banana republic on board a narrow-gauge railroad, an '03 rifle in one hand and a bottle in the other, or in olive drab with a tin helmet and heavy marching order, shouldering arms and starting down a shell-rutted road for the Western Front murky with gray-green fog, turning to grin and wave good-by to Mademoiselle, the innkeeper's gallant if naughty daughter.

Meanwhile less colorful Marines were analyzing the mistakes of Gallipoli and identifying the bare bones of a viable amphibious doctrine. In 1922 and 1923, there were exploratory battalion-size landing exercises at Guantanamo, Panama, and Cape Cod. In 1924, there was a brigade-size maneuver that established an advance base at Culebra Island off Puerto Rico in concert with an assault against the Panama Canal. The next year, there was a joint Army-Navy problem at Oahu with 1500 Marines simulating a 42,000-man landing force. There would be no more exercises for the next seven years but the lessons learned began to get down on paper. The crux of the matter was getting from ship to shore with the necessary men and materiel. A good deal of attention was focused on landing craft and the possibility of amphibian vehicles.

In 1921, there was a rash of mail robberies. On 11 November, Secretary of the Navy Edwin Denby (himself a World War I Marine) put Marines to watching post offices and riding the mail trains and postal trucks with orders ". . . if attacked, shoot and shoot to kill." The mail robberies came to a sudden halt. (In October 1926 the robberies began again. Twenty-five hundred Marines were detailed to guard the mails and once more the robberies stopped abruptly.)

Second Nicaraguan Campaign (1926–1933)

In Nicaragua the seesaw between the Conservatives and Liberals had continued. The presence of a company-size Marine Legation Guard in Managua cooled off a Liberal revolt in 1922. A partially U. S.-supervised and almost-honest election in 1924 chose a coalition government: Conservative Carlos Solarzano as President, Liberal Juan Sacasa as Vice President. The Legation Guard packed up and left on 4 August 1925.

With the Marines gone, a coalition government was more than Conservative General Emiliano Chamorro Vargas could stomach. Open revolt began in October, Solarzano and Sacasa fled the country, and in January 1926 Chamorro made himself President. In May, the *Cleveland* briefly put a landing party ashore at Bluefields. By August, a Liberal army under José María Moncado had pushed the Conservatives back into Bluefields, and the Marines and seamen came ashore once again (this time from the *Galveston*), declaring Bluefields and its environs a neutral zone. The Liberals and Conservatives were persuaded to accept a truce and promised to attend a peace conference at Corinto on the opposite coast. A landing party was put ashore from the *Denver* at Corinto (which was also declared a neutral zone). Chamorro viewed the whole proceedings

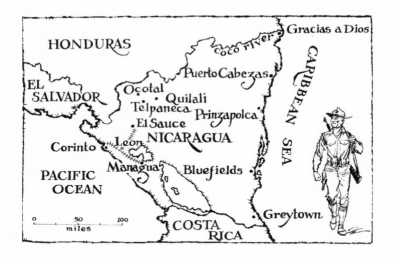

with growing suspicion and on 30 October resigned as
President and withdrew. Adolfo Díaz, who had been a
pliant President during the intervention of 1912, was
elected Chief Executive by the rump conference. His
government was promptly recognized by the United
States, and he equally promptly asked for help in
protecting American lives and property. Meanwhile,
Mexico was insisting that Sacasa, somewhere in Gua-
temala, was the legitimate President. Also, General
Moncado was still in the field in eastern Nicaragua and
proving resistant to Díaz's offers of honors and money.
With Mexican help, Sacasa came back into the country
in early December 1926 and joined up with Moncado.
Together they came storming down the Mosquito
Coast, helping themselves to American-owned supplies
and equipment as needed. An American was killed at
Puerto Cabeza and Marines went ashore from the
Special Services Squadron to establish neutral zones
there and also at Prinzapolca and Río Grande. On 10
January 1927 the 2d Battalion, 5th Marines, under
Lieutenant Colonel James J. Meade, arrived from
Guantanamo and landed at Bluefields.

Blocked by the Americans, Moncado marched west toward Managua. Meade, leaving one company in position on the Escondito River west of Bluefields, re-embarked the rest of his battalion, took them through the Canal, and landed them at Corinto. He then took his bobtailed battalion up the old familiar ninety miles of railroad to Managua, relieved the Legation Guard, and assumed responsibility for the defense of the capital from a completely willing President Díaz.

Marine Observation Squadron One under Major Ross E. ("Rusty") Rowell arrived on 26 February with six vintage De Havillands. The USS *Henderson* came down from Quantico with the rest of the 5th Marines. President Coolidge had also hurriedly authorized the sale of three thousand Krag rifles, two hundred Browning machine guns, and three million rounds of ammunition to the Díaz government. On 26 March the 2d Marine Brigade was reactivated under command of Logan Feland. The Conservatives and Liberals were now facing each other at Matagalpa, up in the hills north of Managua. The Marines slid in between them and established another "neutral zone" on 17 April. About this time Henry L. Stimson arrived on the scene to arbitrate. The Stimson-Díaz plan offered general amnesty with a restoration of property and both sides turning in their weapons. There was a thirty-minute conference on the banks of the Tipitapa River the afternoon of 4 May and a deal was struck whereby the Conservatives were to stay in office until 1928 when there were to be U. S. supervised elections. Meanwhile, the Marine brigade would guarantee law and order, disarm both sides, and create a Guardia Nacional. Disarmament was sweetened by a U. S. offer of $10.00 for every firearm relinquished. One Liberal not acceding to the order to stack arms was Augusto César Sandino, who took off with a hundred and fifty men up into the mountains of Nuevo Segovia, near the Honduran border. A Marine detachment was sent after him and set itself up in garrison at Ocotal.

The new Guardia, patterned on the Haitian and Dominican models, was supposed to have sixty officers (thirty-five of them Marines) and a thousand men but it was having trouble getting started. One of the new Guardia companies with forty-eight men joined the thirty-eight-man Marine detachment at Ocotal on 5 July. Sandino slipped into Ocotal the night of 15 July. The fire fight began about one o'clock in the morning and went on until eight, when Sandino sent in a demand for surrender under a flag of truce. The Marines refused and the battle started again. Two DH-4s came over on morning patrol, saw something was wrong, and while one strafed the attackers, the other landed outside the town to interrogate some of the locals. "Rusty" Rowell came on station at two-thirty with four De Havillands, each armed to the teeth with four twenty-five-pound bombs and all the machine-gun ammunition it could carry. There was a dive-bombing attack which would later interest certain German students of air warfare and fifty-six Sandinistas were killed and about twice that number wounded. Altogether the Marines claimed, perhaps with a degree of enlargement, to have killed nearly three hundred bandits. Their own losses were one dead and five wounded.

Sandino's stronghold was reported to be a place called El Chipote, but no one was quite sure where that was. Some two hundred and twenty-five Marines and *guardias* were sent into Nuevo Segovia to look for it. On 19 September, a fair-sized battle was fought at Telpaneca, ten miles from Ocotal. Then, on 8 October, a Marine plane was shot down on razor-backed Sapotillal ridge, a few miles north of Telpaneca. A patrol sent out to rescue the pilot and observer walked into an ambush but fought its way clear. Two larger patrols then converged on the ridge, fighting an estimated two hundred and fifty Sandinistas and killing or wounding sixty, but the downed plane was not reached until 30

October and then it was too late. Sandino had already captured and hanged the two fliers.

On 23 November Rowell's observers finally pinpointed El Chipote northeast of Sapotillal ridge. In early December, two columns of Marines and *guardias,* about two hundred men altogether, were sent forward to set up a base at Quilali before moving against El Chipote. And on 30 December, there was a hard fight on the banks of the Jicaro River outside Quilali. The Marines pushed through, were hit again, then pushed through a second time. The second column was intercepted at Sapotillal, lost both its officers, but managed to hold a piece of high ground until the first column could reach it. Once joined, they beat their way back to Quilali, where they were promptly besieged by Sandino.

Tied down by thirty wounded, there appeared to be no way to break out. The town's main street was turned into an improvised airstrip and on 6 January, First Lieutenant Christian F. Schilt came in with an O2U-1 biplane, the original Vought Corsair. The plane had no brakes and the Marines had to halt it as it went careening down the street by grabbing at its wings, but in three days Schilt made ten round trips, brought in 1400 pounds of supplies, and took out eighteen of the more critically wounded.

Reinforcements arrived on 10 January 1928 and the Marines started north again from Quilali. On 14 January, Major Rowell worked over El Chipote with a four-plane flight. The patrols cautiously probed toward the crest, got there on the 26th of January, and found it deserted. Sandino had ducked across the Honduran border. He came back into the high coffee country with six hundred men and on 27 February, near a place called Bromaderos, attacked a pack train escorted by a platoon of Marines. The mules were driven off but the Marines got to a ridgeline where they held out until a company could come to their rescue.

The Coco River, which begins at Cabo Gracias a Dios on the Mosquito Coast, forms two-thirds of Nicaragua's border with Honduras and reaches as far west as Quilali and Ocotal. The Marines working along the east coast were mostly from the ships of the Atlantic Fleet. Captain Merritt A. Edson, a remote cousin of Alvin Edson of the Mexican War, had the detachment from the *Denver*. Edson, red-haired, wiry, pale-skinned, and with ice-blue eyes, had left the University of Vermont at the beginning of World War I to go into the Marine Corps and had served variously as aviator, ordnance officer, and match shot. In April 1928 he moved up the Coco with a strong patrol but missed Sandino. He went out on a second patrol on 26 July. The Coco, never pleasant in its upper reaches, turned wild under torrential rains. Battling the elements and malaria and resupplied by air drop, Edson made his first contact with the bandits on 4 August. There was a second fight on 6 August, a third skirmish on 14 August, and three days later he reached his destination at Poteca, some four hundred miles upstream from Cabo Gracias a Dios. But Sandino himself once again eluded the Marines.

Elections were held, as promised, on 4 November 1928 with some nine hundred Marines and sailors acting as poll-watchers. Voters had their fingers dipped in red ink to prevent absent-minded repeat voting. General Moncado, running on the Liberal ticket, won the presidency by a narrow but honest plurality. By the first of the year the bandits were hard at it again in the northern mountains. Sandino lost a chief lieutenant, one Manuel Jirón, captured by none other than Herman Hanneken, executioner of Charlemagne and now a first lieutenant. Sandino himself slipped off to Mexico to raise funds. While he was gone, there was a corresponding reduction in banditry and in August 1929 the 11th Regiment went home to be deactivated. The Guardia Nacional was by now up to a strength of about two thousand but was still shaky and in the next two years there would be at least nine mutinies.

In May 1930 Sandino came back into northern Nicaragua. Three strong Marine columns went looking for him in the familiar hill country between the Coco and Bocay but he was as elusive as ever, although he was wounded in the leg on 19 June by an air strike. He was still at large in February 1931 when Secretary of State Stimson announced that the Marines would be reduced by 1 June to a battalion, plus supporting aviation, and confined to the Managua area. All were to be out by the inauguration of the next President.

One of Sandino's hardest-driving pursuers was Guardia Captain (First Lieutenant, USMC) Lewis B. ("Chesty") Puller. One forty-man patrol led by "Chesty" Puller fought four battles in ten days and killed thirty bandits. Another fight by Puller's company came the day after Christmas 1932. Puller was riding shotgun on the new El Sauce-León rail line when the bandits tried to take the train. Rebel losses were thirty-one killed.

Liberal Juan Sacasa was inaugurated on 1 January 1933. Next day the last elements of the Marine Brigade sailed in the old *Henderson* from Corinto for home. In six years of campaigning, forty-seven Marines had been killed, sixty-seven more wounded. A year later Sandino returned once again to Nicaragua. He was captured and shot on order of the new Jefe Director of the Guardia Nacional, Marine-trained Colonel Anastasio ("Tacho") Somoza.

China Service (1927–1938)

More pleasant than the Second Nicaraguan Campaign was the 1927 expedition to China. With the Kuomintang on the march in the south and the warlords contesting for control in the north, there had been reason for reinforcement of the Legation Guard and intermittent landings at Shanghai throughout the 1920s. In February 1927 Chiang Kai-shek marched on Shanghai. A provisional Marine battalion was hurriedly put together from the Asiatic Fleet and detachments in the Philippines, and landed to help protect the International Settlement. Two weeks later, the 4th Marines arrived from San Diego, and along with the other foreign troops was put under the coordinate control (but not command) of Major General John Duncan, British Army.

General Lejeune designated the skinny old warhorse, Smedley Butler, to command all U. S. Marines in China. The 6th Marines, disbanded in 1925, were hurriedly reorganized at Philadelphia and sent by rail to San Diego, where Butler set up the 3d Brigade headquarters and together the regiment and brigade headquarters sailed for Shanghai, arriving there 2 May 1927. In his brigade, Butler had the 4th and 6th Regiments; 1st Battalion, 10th Marines (armed with French 75-mm field guns); some engineers and light tanks; and a Marine squadron rescued from a lonely vigil on Guam.

The war was now raging in the north. Butler left the 4th Marines in Shanghai (continuing a tenure which would last until Pearl Harbor) and went north with the rest of the 3d Brigade to Tientsin, piously explaining his mission as "solely for the defense of life and property." With his old companions, the 15th U. S. Infantry in Tientsin and the Legation Guard at Peking, there were about 5,200 Americans in the north. Chiang Kai-shek had Peking by mid-summer 1928 and there was no real fighting for the Marines, neither for the Brigade nor the 4th Marines in Shanghai. The 3d Brigade, less the 4th Marines, was pulled out in January 1929 and returned to San Diego. The Legation Guard in Peking was kept at about 500 strength, including the famous troop of "Horse Marines" mounted on sturdy Mongolian ponies and armed, along with their '03s, with heavy, straight-bladed swords designed by a U. S. Army cavalryman named George S. Patton.

In 1932 the clash between the Japanese and Nationalists in Shanghai occasioned the 4th Marines to be joined briefly by the 31st U. S. Infantry from the Philippines, and in September 1937 the 2d Marine Brigade, under handsome Brigadier General John C. ("Johnny Beau") Beaumont, came out from San Diego with the 6th Marines. Brigade headquarters and the Sixth stayed on until February 1938 and then went home again. The 15th U. S. Infantry also departed, ending their long-term stay in Tientsin, and a detachment of the Legation Guard fell heir to their soot-gray barracks.

The uniform regulations of 1928 copied the British roll-collar coat with shirt and tie ("field scarf") for the green and khaki uniform, but the standing collar persisted for the blue uniforms and the officers' white uniforms. The officers had also brought back from France pegged riding breeches, field boots, and the Sam Browne belt.

Lejeune and Butler Depart the Scene

Major General Lejeune was reappointed, first by Harding and then by Coolidge, for a total of nine years as Commandant. He retired in 1929, at age sixty-two, and became Superintendent of the Virginia Military Institute. His successor was his long-time friend and World War I comrade Wendell Neville, but big, robust "Buck" Neville served little more than a year as Major General Commandant before dying in office on 8 July 1930.

Smedley Butler, the senior general in the Corps, was a strong contender for next Commandant, but Ben H. Fuller was less controversial and had more years commissioned service, so, a safe choice, Fuller was named Commandant in August 1930. A year later Butler went roaring off into noisy retirement. "Uncle Ben" Fuller served competently but quietly and for the last half-year before his retirement for age on 1 March 1934, he was off inspecting posts and stations, foreign and domestic, and the real hands holding the reins of the Corps were those of John H. Russell, the Assistant Commandant.

Russell had come up from Haiti in 1930 after nine years as High Commissioner. (On 21 August 1934 the last remnant of the 1st Marine Brigade marched out of the Casernes Dessalines in Port-au-Prince and sailed for Quantico.)

In 1933 Russell had persuaded the Secretary of the Navy that the Expeditionary Force should be redesignated the Fleet Marine Force and made an integral part of the U. S. Fleet. The 1st Marine Brigade was to be home-ported at Quantico and the 2d Brigade at San Diego, and each was to have an infantry regiment; an artillery battalion (75-mm pack howitzers); an antiaircraft battalion; companies of engineers, light tanks, and chemical troops; and an aviation group.

General Russell served only two years as Commandant before reaching the statutory age limit; but before retiring in December 1936 he also instituted selection boards for officer promotions. President Roosevelt went much deeper for the next Commandant, picking the relatively junior Brigadier General Thomas Holcomb, who, as a young officer, had distinguished himself first as a team shot and later as a battalion commander in France.

At Quantico an Equipment Board was established in 1933 and together with the Marine Corps Schools continued to test doctrine and materiel. The thinkers had collected their findings into a *Tentative Manual for Landing Operations*, published in 1934. The Navy issued the revised manual in 1938 as *FTP-167, Landing Operations Doctrine, U. S. Navy*, and in 1941 the U. S. Army brought out its own edition, almost identical, as *FM 31-5, Landing Operations on Hostile Shores*. From 1935 on, there were annual Fleet Landing Exercises. By 1938 all the basic types of landing craft used in World War II were well along in their development. The Roebling "Alligator," invented for rescue work in the

Florida Everglades, was adopted by the Marine Corps in 1940 and became the progenitor of the LVT family of amphibian tractors. The problem of getting from ship to shore was well on its way to solution. And so were the related problems of command relationships, ship-to-shore communications, naval gunfire support, combat loading, and air cover.

After World War I, General Barnett had tried to return to the policy that all appointments to the rank of second lieutenant would be made from Naval Academy graduates or the enlisted ranks, but there were many vacancies to be filled and in May 1921 Lejeune arranged with the War Department to commission twelve graduates from "Distinguished Military Colleges" having Reserve Officer Training Corps. One of the dozen commissioned that year was Randolph McCall Pate who would one day be Commandant. In 1927 a stocky farm boy from Battle Ground, Indiana, named David M. Shoup, was commissioned from the DePauw University ROTC. His year at the Basic School was interrupted by a tour with the 6th Marines in Tientsin, Butler needing junior officers to fill out the Brigade. In 1930 a short, trim, black-haired Vermonter, Wallace M. Greene, Jr., whose ancestor Nathaniel Greene had done so well against Cornwallis, came into the Corps from the Naval Academy. He was followed four years later by the diminutive Victor H. Krulak, nicknamed "the Brute," who had been coxswain of the Annapolis crew. Next year among the lieutenants from the Naval Academy was burly Robert E. Cushman, Jr., of Minnesota, and also in 1935 Leonard F. Chapman, Jr., who was commissioned from the University of Florida. In those Depression years, the prospect of $125-a-month second-lieutenant's pay and the promise of sea duty and China service attracted the best the country had to offer. In 1936 barrel-chested Lewis W. Walt, a great football player and wrestler at Colorado State University, came into the Corps and a year later was looking across the sandbagged barricades of the

International Settlement in Shanghai in company with "Wally" Greene. In 1937 the taciturn and brilliant Keith B. McCutcheon took his commission in the Corps after graduating from Carnegie Institute of Technology. The next year would see Raymond G. Davis coming in from Georgia School of Technology and tall, good-looking Donn J. Robertson commissioned from the University of North Dakota.

Beginning in 1935, there was another source of Marine officers, called the Platoon Leaders Class. In the PLC a college student spent two six-week periods in summer training as a private first class in the Reserve and on graduation was commissioned a Second Lieutenant, U. S. Marine Corps Reserve. William K. Jones of Joplin, Missouri, was commissioned in 1938 after two summers in the PLC and graduation from the University of Kansas. That same year, Marion E. Carl, who had graduated from Oregon State College, resigned an Army Reserve commission to become a Marine aviation cadet.

American Defense Service (1939–1941)

On 30 June 1939, there were 18,052 active-duty Marines, which made the Corps about the same size as the New York City police force. On 8 September, seven days after Germany marched into Poland, Roosevelt proclaimed a "limited national emergency." For the Marine Corps this meant an increase in enlisted strength of 25,000 and authority to recall volunteer officers and men from the retired list. A year later, on 5 October 1940, the Secretary of the Navy ordered the Organized Marine Corps Reserve to active duty. There were 23 Reserve battalions totaling 232 officers and 5,009 enlisted men. The battalions were broken up and the personnel used as fillers for the regular establishment.

On 1 December 1940, "Tommy" Holcomb was named to a second term as Major General Commandant. Defense battalions were being dispatched to Samoa, Midway, Johnston, and Palmyra islands. The 1st Marine Brigade had departed from Quantico in the fall for Guantanamo, and on 1 February 1941, while at sea en route to Culebra for Fleet Landing Exercise 7, it was redesignated the 1st Marine Division, with Major General Holland M. ("Howlin' Mad") Smith commanding. When the Division came back from maneuvers in May 1941 it had three infantry regiments, the 1st, 5th, and 7th, and it had outgrown Quantico as a base, so some of the Division went to Parris Island, while a new amphibious base was being readied at New River, North Carolina. Onslow Beach was used for landing exercises in the summer, and in September 1941 the Division began moving into Tent Camp One of what would eventually become Camp Lejeune.

On the West Coast, the burgeoning 2d Marine Brigade had spread out to a temporary camp, first called Camp Holcomb, then Camp Elliott, on the sandy flats of Kearny Mesa outside San Diego. On 1 February 1941, the 2d Marine Brigade, like the 1st, was expanded to a Division and the reactivated 9th and 2d Marines, in that order, joined ranks with the 6th Marines. More training area was needed and on 10 March 1942 the vast Rancho Santa Margarita, 132,000 acres, twenty miles of Pacific beach, and one-time scene of Gillespie's adventures, would be purchased.

In 1939 the General Board of the Navy had stated Marine Aviation's mission as follows:

> *Marine Aviation is to be equipped, organized, and trained primarily for the support of the Fleet Marine Force in landing operations and in support of troop activities in the field; and secondarily as replacements for carrier-based aircraft.*

It was a good statement of mission. The aircraft groups followed the brigades in their expansion. On 7 July 1941 the 1st Marine Aircraft Wing was organized at Quantico and three days later the 2d Marine Aircraft Wing came into being at San Diego. While this was going on, a brigade of Marines was landing in Iceland. In May 1941, there were 25,000 British troops in Iceland and Churchill, needing them elsewhere, invited Roosevelt to take over the occupation as a kind of extension of the Monroe Doctrine. About this time the 6th Marines had sailed from San Diego with orders to join the 1st Marine Division in the Caribbean. The intention was to send a U. S. corps consisting of the 1st Marine Division and the 1st U. S. Infantry Division to secure the Azores. Then, on 5 June 1941, President Roosevelt directed the Chief of Naval Operations to sail a Marine brigade in fifteen days' time to Iceland. The occupation of the Azores was shelved, and the 6th Marines, after passaging the Canal, were diverted northward to be the nucleus of the 1st Provisional Marine Brigade, under command of Brigadier General John Marston. The 4,095 Marines sailed from Charleston on 22 June, tarried at Argentia while last-minute negotiations nudged the unenthusiastic Iceland government into accepting their protection, and then on 7 July reached Reykjavik.

The Marines moved into British camps or built new ones using British Nissen huts, most of them in the southwest corner of the island near Reykjavik. The brigade adopted the British "Polar Bear" shoulder patch and the 6th Marines picked up the custom of singing in the Mess, but even a rum ration could not make English rations palatable, so the Marines ate U. S. Navy rations—when they could get them—along with locally purchased mutton and fish.

Churchill, meeting with Roosevelt in mid-Atlantic (the meeting which produced the Atlantic Charter), paused at the island and reviewed the Brigade. He remembered later that "there was a long march past in threes, during which the tune 'United States Marines' bit so deeply into my memory that I could not get it out of my head."

The first element of a U. S. Army brigade arrived on 6 August 1941 and the last battalion of Marines sailed away 8 March 1942. By that time the war with Japan was already three months old.

12

1941–1944
"...from shipboard to small islands..."

Pearl Harbor

At 0759 on Sunday morning, 7 December 1941, the sergeant of the guard at the Marine Barracks, Naval Ammunition Depot, Oahu, made a careful entry in his log, "Twenty-eight Japanese planes flew over Depot toward Schofield Barracks." Within minutes the USS *Arizona* had taken the first bombs of the Pearl Harbor attack. Major Alan Shapley, senior Marine officer, was thrown from the foremast a hundred feet into the water but managed to swim to Ford Island. At the Navy Yard, Marines from the barracks and 3d Defense Battalion went to their battle stations. At Camp Catlin the 4th Defense Battalion tried to get its 3-inch AA guns into action. At Ewa Air Station, Marine Aircraft Group 21 (MAG-21) was caught on the ground and had all of its fighters and dive bombers knocked out.

Farther west, Midway, Johnston, and Palmyra islands, each with its Marine defense battalion detachment, were all bombarded by Japanese naval gunfire. The shelling of Guam began on 8 December; two days later 6000 Japanese came ashore and overwhelmed the 153-man Marine garrison and 80-man Insular Guard.

Most of the 1st Defense Battalion was at Wake Island, under Major James P. S. Devereux. Marine Fighting Squadron 211 (VMF-211) had arrived on the island four days earlier with twelve brand-new F4F-3 Grumman Wildcats. Seven were destroyed on the ground in the first attack on 8 December. The remaining five were used up one by one until 22 December, when the last two took off on a final mission. The next day, before dawn, the Japanese rammed two old destroyer-transports onto the reef and put ashore 1000 men from the Special Naval Landing Force. By 0730 Major Devereaux had concluded there was no purpose in further resistance. Under a white flag he walked south down the road and surrendered.

The 4th Marine Regiment, under white-haired Colonel Samuel L. Howard, had arrived in the Philippines from Shanghai on 1 December. They were put under General Douglas MacArthur's command and ordered to Corregidor to take over the beach defenses. The final Japanese assault came the night of 5 May. At noon the following day General Jonathan M. ("Skinny") Wainwright, USA, sent out a Marine captain and a field music under a white flag to arrange a parley. Colonel Howard sadly told his adjutant to burn the 4th Marines' colors.

By then other Marine forces were already moving westward. The 2d Brigade, stripped out of the 2d Marine Division, sailed from San Diego on 6 January 1942 for American Samoa. A 3d Brigade similarly was pulled from the East Coast 1st Marine Division in March and sent to Western Samoa. The 4th Defense Battalion moved forward into the malaria-ridden New Hebrides the end of March, and on 30 April the Efate airstrip (crushed coral rolled out with water to almost concrete consistency) was ready to receive MAG-24 aircraft.

The 6th Defense Battalion and Marine Aircraft Group 22 were on Midway. MAG-22 had two squadrons, Major Floyd B. Parks's VMF-221 with twenty-one

near-useless Brewster Buffalo F2As and Major Lofton
R. Henderson's VMSB-241 with seventeen old Vought
Vindicator SB2U-3s. On 26 May the USS *Kitty Hawk*
brought in seven new Grumman Wildcat F4F-3s and
nineteen Douglas Dauntless SBD-2s.

For MAG-22 the Battle of Midway began at dawn on
4 June. VMF-221 engaged a striking force of 108
aircraft headed for Midway. Thirteen F2As and two
F4Fs were lost. Parks was among those killed. VMSB-
241, attacking without escort, made a glide-bombing
attack with the SBDs against the carriers *Akagi* and
Soryu (or perhaps it was the *Kaga*). Eight of the
attacking SBDs, including Henderson's, were shot
down by the protecting Zeroes. At the end of the day
only two Marine fighters and eleven dive bombers were
still operational, but by then the U. S. fleet was fully in
position. By 6 June, four Japanese carriers had been
sunk and the Battle of Midway was won.

In Washington, the Joint Chiefs of Staff had decided
that the Pacific, with its large watery spaces, was the
obvious place for the two Marine divisions then being
readied for deployment. On 9 April 1942 General
Joseph T. McNarney, acting Army Chief of Staff, had
sent a memorandum to the Chief of Naval Operations,
Admiral Ernest King, stating the proposition that Army
amphibious operations would be "merely the spearhead of a prolonged, heavy, land operation," whereas
"in the Pacific, offensive operations for the next year or
more promise to comprise a series of landing operations from shipboard to small islands with relatively
minor forces. This is the type of amphibious warfare
for which the Marines have apparently been specially
organized. . . . It might be wise to recognize these
differences. . . ."

In mid-May the 1st Marine Division, under the
command of Major General Alexander A. ("Sunny
Jim") Vandegrift, had left the East Coast for New
Zealand. The Japanese were well into New Guinea and
threatening Darwin. Rabaul, in Northern New Britain,

had been developed into a major air and naval base. In the Solomons they had taken Tulagi, seat of the British colonial government, and had begun to build an airfield on neighboring Guadalcanal.

Guadalcanal

On 26 June, two weeks after his arrival at Wellington, Vandegrift was abruptly summoned to Auckland to meet with Vice Admiral Robert L. Ghormley, Commander South Pacific Area, and told there was to be a landing against the Japanese in the Guadalcanal-Tulagi area with a target date of 1 August. The Division's third regiment, the 7th Marines, was to stay in Samoa and its place taken by the 2d Marines (still in San Diego). Also he would get the 1st Marine Raider Battalion (from New Caledonia) and the 3d Marine Defense Battalion (still at Pearl Harbor). The brilliant but sometimes difficult Rear Admiral Richmond Kelly Turner would be Attack Force Commander; Rear Admiral V. A. C. Crutchley, Australian Navy, would have the Screening Force; and Rear Admiral Frank J. Fletcher, with three carriers, would have the Support Force.

The Division intelligence officer, Colonel Frank B. Goettge, went off to Australia to find out what there was to know about Guadalcanal and Tulagi and learned his best sources would be ex-missionaries, planters, and other persons of more dubious island trades. The Australians also had a well-established coastwatcher system, set up in 1939 to watch the Germans and now in place to watch the Japanese. While Colonel Goettge was reading the *Pacific Island Handbook* and fishing through British Colonial Office files, the Division operations officer, Lieutenant Colonel Gerald Thomas (of Belleau Wood) and the logistics chief, Lieutenant Colonel Randolph McC. Pate, had gone back with Vandegrift to Wellington to get on with the planning and to start out-loading.

An unexpected exasperation was coping with the

longshoremen's union and finally troop labor had to do it, working the docks in pelting rain, to the tune of "Bless 'Em All," ankle-deep in soggy corn flakes. On 17 July a B-17 took off for a visual and photo reconnaissance. The photos taken were pieced together into a kind of photo mosaic (with great gaps where the clouds were). Altogether, the intelligence-collection effort indicated that the Japanese were concentrating at Lunga Point. It was guessed that there was an infantry regiment and an antiaircraft battalion on Guadalcanal, say five thousand Japanese, and fifteen hundred more on nearby Tulagi.

Admiral Turner agreed to delay the landing until 7 August. The Amphibious Force sailed on 22 July, arrived in the Fijis for the rehearsal on the twenty-eighth, and sortied for the objective area on the thirty-first.

Tulagi was a banana-shaped island about three miles long tucked under the belly of Florida Island which, in turn, lay twenty miles north of the bigger Guadalcanal. Gavutu and Tanambogo were two fly specks a mile east of Tulagi, connected to each other by a causeway.

The 1st Raider Battalion, under Lieutenant Colonel Merritt ("Red Mike") Edson, came to Tulagi on 7 August on board four APDs—World War I four-piper destroyers converted into high-speed transports—and landed on 0800 across Blue Beach on the southwest end of the island. They were to be followed by the 2d Battalion, 5th Marines. There was a patter of small-arms fire when they landed, but it was almost noon before a serious fight developed. By evening Edson had pushed the defenders back into a deep ravine lined with coral caves. During the night the Japanese came boiling back out in four *banzai* attacks. In the morning the Marines learned, after counting the dead, that there had been about five hundred defenders, most of them members of the 3d Kure Special Landing Force.

Gavutu and Tanambogo were assigned to the 1st Parachute Battalion, with their landing scheduled for four hours after the touchdown at Tulagi. (It was a surface landing; in the course of the war the parachute Marines would never make a combat jump.) The parachutes were a light battalion, about a third the size of an infantry battalion. There was a hard fight and the 3d Battalion, 2d Marines, had to be landed next morning to finish the job.

The main landing on Guadalcanal itself began at 0910, five miles east of Lunga Point. There was no opposition. (There were only 2230 Japanese, not 5000, on the island and most of these were naval construction workers—"termites," the Marines would call them —busy at work on the airfield.) Colonel LeRoy P. Hunt's 5th Marines went ashore first, followed an hour later by the 1st Marines under Colonel Clifton ("Lucky") Cates, who had been wounded six times and also gassed in World War I. Two air raids in the afternoon lent urgency to the unloading. Gear came ashore faster than the shore party could handle it and by nightfall the beach was chaotic. Night found both the 1st and 5th Marines holding a line along the Tenaru (or what they thought was the Tenaru—it was really the Ilu—their maps were wrong).

In the morning the advance began with a kind of pincer movement, the 5th Marines going straight for the airfield and the 1st Marines hooking around to the south and coming in from the jungle. The airfield was taken without difficulty but at 1230, forty Japanese bombers came over, going for the transports. There was a council of war that night aboard Amphibious Force flagship, the *McCawley*. Fletcher had lost twenty-one of his ninety-nine fighters, was running short of fuel, and was pulling his carriers out to the south. Crutchley was concerned about his cruisers in the confined seas. Kelly Turner stated his transports could not stay unprotected in the objective area. Vandegrift said he had to check on the situation at Tulagi before he could possibly concur. It was then about midnight and Vandegrift was scarcely aboard the minesweeper that was to take him to Tulagi when a Japanese task force came into Sealark Channel at flank speed, all guns blazing. It was the Battle of Savo Island and before morning Crutchley's force was nearly all gone; sunk in what forevermore would be called Iron-bottom Sound.

In the morning what was left of the fleet sailed away and the Marines were left on the beach, short of supplies and badly disposed, with 11,145 men on the big island and 6805 on Tulagi and Gavutu-Tanambogo. Vandegrift fanned out a defensive perimeter running from the Tenaru (or Ilu) south and west around the airfield and then up to Lunga Point, and put his engineers to work completing the nearly finished runway.

Japanese Reinforcements

In Tokyo, the Imperial General Staff on 8 August informed Lieutenant General Haruyoshi Hyakutake, commander of the Seventeenth Army, that his mission was to retake Guadalcanal. To do this he would be given fifty thousand men, including the 2d Sendai Division, the 38th Division, the Kawaguchi Brigade, the Ichiki Detachment, the 8th Tank Regiment, and an artillery group. The troop list was impressive but the assigned units were scattered from Guam to Manchuria. No matter: Imperial doctrine said to move fast and attack quickly. Hyakutake flew down to his headquarters on Rabaul and began day-and-night bombing. The Ichiki Detachment (actually the 2d Battalion, 28th Infantry, reinforced) had fought well in the Philippines and at Singapore and on 12 August it arrived at Truk from Guam. Hyakutake thought a surprise landing near the mouth of the Ilu, almost at the point where the Americans had landed, and a quick march onto the airfield might do the trick. Colonel Kiyono Ichiki agreed. He started forward from Truk on 17 August.

On 13 August, Captain Martin Clemens, one of the

Australian coastwatchers, had come in through the
lines and announced that there were Japanese scattered throughout the hinterlands, disorganized, many
weaponless, and without much fight in them. Clemens
was using some of the old members of the Solomon
Islands Police Force as scouts, and they were good at it.
One brought in a report of a Japanese radio station,
and a company of the 1st Marines was sent out on 19
August to get it. The patrol made contact, won the
fight, and when they searched the bodies of the dead
Japanese were surprised to learn that they were not
Naval Landing Force but Imperial Army. The Marines
had made first contact with the Ichiki Detachment.

On 12 August, Vandegrift had sent a message:
"Airfield Guadalcanal ready for fighters and dive
bombers." On 20 August the *Long Island* launched its
aircraft from a position two hundred miles southeast of
Guadalcanal. Captain John L. Smith's VMF-223 had
brand-new Grumman Wildcat F4F-4s. Major Richard
C. Mangrum's VMSB-232 had the SBD-3, latest version
of the Douglas Dauntless. First planes began to land at
about 1700 on Henderson Field, named for Major
Lofton Henderson, who had been killed at Midway.

That same night Colonel Ichiki sent his men across
the Tenaru, hitting the 2d Battalion, 1st Marines.
Marine machine guns and mortars, with the help of the
artillery, chopped them down. The 1st Battalion, 1st
Marines, moved upstream at daybreak, crossed, and
came down on the Japanese flank. Ichiki was caught
between the two battalions and the sea. He burned his
colors and shot himself through the head.

At noon on the twenty-first, steely-eyed John Smith
brought down his first Zero. On the twenty-fourth,
VMF-223 intercepted a raid and got sixteen of the
twenty-seven attackers, including three shot down by
Midway-veteran Captain Marion Carl. The Marines
shot down thirteen of sixteen bombers on the twenty-
sixth, Smith and Carl each getting two. Mangrum's
dive bombers caught four destroyer-transports coming

down the Slot on the twenty-eighth and only one got
away undamaged. On the twenty-ninth, VMF-223 got
eight more enemy planes, and on the thirtieth they
got fourteen, four by Smith and three by Carl. They
called themselves the Cactus Air Force after the code
name for Guadalcanal. The Wildcats were neither as
fast nor as nimble as the Zeroes, but they were
tougher. Marine fighter tactics were to come down
from 25,000 or 30,000 feet in one screeching pass onto
the backs of the Japanese—their fighters and bombers
both flamed easily—and then dive for home. Colonel
William J. Wallace arrived on 30 August at Henderson
as MAG-23 commander and with the Group's remaining two squadrons, VMF-224 and VMSB-231.

Makin Raid

Three weeks earlier, on 8 August—the same day that
Edson's Raiders were mopping up on Tulagi and
Hyakutake was getting his orders to retake Guadalcanal
—two companies of the 2d Raider Battalion, under
Evans Carlson, loaded out of Hawaii in two big mine-
laying submarines, the *Nautilus* and *Argonaut*. Carl-
son's executive officer was the President's son, Major
James Roosevelt. Target for Carlson's Raiders was
Makin atoll in the British-mandated Gilbert Islands.
The two subs got there before midnight 16 August.
Intelligence had two hundred fifty Japanese on the atoll
and a shore battery covering the entrance to the lagoon
(but again intelligence was wrong; there were only
seventy Japanese on the island and no shore battery).
The Raiders put their rubber boats in the water.
Everyone got ashore safely, although not exactly where
they had intended. The Japanese strung themselves
across the coastal road in a fierce show of strength and
about dawn a fire fight developed. With daylight a
3500-ton merchant ship and a small patrol craft could
be seen in the lagoon. The *Nautilus*, firing blind, sank
both vessels. Two Japanese Type 95 scout planes came

over, dropped a few bombs, and left. Twelve more planes came over at 1320 and bombed things in earnest. Two seaplanes sat down in the lagoon to off-load reinforcements and the Marines sank them with antitank fire. The Japanese then boldly counterattacked, three times in all that afternoon, and managed to convey to Carlson the notion that he was greatly outnumbered. He decided to get off the beach after dark but had all kinds of trouble with the rubber boats and their cranky outboard motors. At midnight Carlson said every man was free to make his own choice: try to get through the surf to the subs or stay on the beach. By dawn he was ready to surrender, and he sent out a captain and corporal to parley. The captain and corporal, after some adventures of their own, came to the conclusion that there were no live Japs left on the island. Heartened by this intelligence, Carlson reorganized his two scrambled companies, swept the island, shot two Japanese survivors, blew up the radio station, and burned what supplies he could find. The subs then came into the mouth of the sheltered lagoon to pick up the Raiders. (In the confusion nine Marines were left behind. The Japanese found them when they reoccupied the island and later cut off their heads.) The *Nautilus* got back to Pearl Harbor on 25 August and *Argonaut* came in a day later.

Edson's Ridge

Meanwhile Edson's Raiders (two sister battalions were never less alike) had moved from Tulagi to Guadalcanal. One of their precious destroyer-transports, the *Calhoun*, was hit unloading rations at Lunga on 30 August and had gone down. On the night of 2 September two more APDs were sunk. On 7 September the Raiders went aboard two of the three remaining destroyer-transports, the *Manley* and *McKean*, for a raid west of Tasimboko. They attacked at daylight, captured a full battery of 75-mm guns, and more importantly gathered a poncho full of documents that confirmed that Major General Kiyotake Kawaguchi's heavily reinforced brigade had arrived and was poised for an attack against Henderson Field.

The Raiders and what was left of the 1st Parachute Battalion were consolidated into a single battalion under Edson and on 12 September they occupied a low grassy ridge a mile south of Henderson Field. That night Kawaguchi, supported by naval gunfire, made three assaults against Edson's line. Next night, there were two more attacks against the center, then Kawaguchi switched his attention to the parachutes on the left flank. Edson's battalion, down to four hundred effectives, bent back but did not break; the 2d Battalion, 5th Marines, came up to help and in the morning eight hundred dead Japanese were counted on the ridge.

On 3 September Brigadier General Roy Geiger (he who had commanded Squadron 7 in France) had arrived to be ComAirCactus, with headquarters in the Japanese-built wooden shack called "the Pagoda." By the first of October nearly all the original pilots of VMF-223 and VMSB-232, except for the iron men Mangrum, Smith, and Carl, were gone. Major Leonard K. ("Duke") Davis's VMF-121 arrived on 9 October and what was left of the two squadrons could be pulled out. One of "Duke" Davis's captains, Joseph J. Foss, would get his first kill on 13 October. (The war would end with Smith and Carl the sixth- and seventh-ranking Marine aces, with nineteen and eighteen and one half Japanese aircraft shot down respectively. Foss would be No. 2, with twenty-six planes to his credit.)

On the ground side, the 1st Marine Division, after over a month without reinforcement or substantial resupply (and often down to two meals a day, including captured Japanese stores), were joined by 7th Marines, fresh from Samoa. The commanding officers of the 1st and 2d Battalions, 7th Marines, were those two eminent bush fighters, "Chesty" Puller and Herman Han-

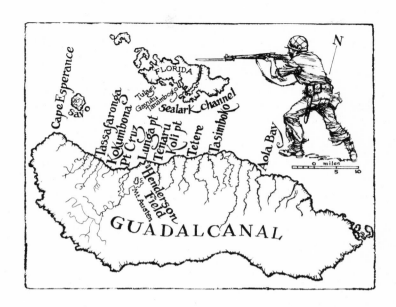

neken. Puller was sent with his battalion on 23 September to swing through the Mount Austen area (the kind of reconnaissance in force he particularly enjoyed) with orders to link up with the 1st Raider Battalion at Kokumbona. Lieutenant Colonel Samuel B. Griffith (a Chinese-language student who had translated the words of an obscure Chinese revolutionary named Mao Tse-tung) had moved up from executive officer to command of the Raiders. Puller on his second day out developed a fight on the slopes of Mount Austen and the 2d Battalion, 5th Marines, was sent to reinforce him. Edson, now a colonel and commanding officer of the 5th Marines, was dispatched to take command of the three battalions. There was some confused fighting along the Matanikau. It did not go well and the three battalions had to be pulled back.

On 7 October, Edson was given five battalions with which to try again beyond the Matanikau. They met Colonel Tadmasu Nakaguma's 4th Infantry Regiment, intent on raiding the airfield, and the fight coalesced around the mouth of the river. Nakaguma broke off on the 9th after losing about seven hundred men.

General Hyakutake had arrived at Guadalcanal that same day to take personal command. The 2d (Sendai) Division was present and reinforced up to about twenty thousand men. Henderson Field was heavily pummeled, beginning 13 October, from the air and from the sea (including bombardments by the battleships *Haruna* and *Kongo*) and by the morning of the fourteenth the Pagoda had been leveled and only forty-two of the ninety airplanes on the field would fly. Hyakutake, coming from the direction of Kokumbona, set his ground attack in motion on 16 October, probing first along the Matanikau, then swinging deeper and coming against the center of the American line. The 164th U. S. Infantry had arrived on 13 October, and, with this reinforcement, Vandegrift had divided his perimeter into five defense sectors, roughly along regimental lines. The center where the Sendai struck on the twenty-third was assigned to the 7th Marines but only Puller's 1st Battalion was manning the twenty-five hundred yards of jungle front. Puller asked for help and the 3d Battalion, 164th Infantry, was fed in to reinforce. It was in this fight that Sergeant John ("Manila John") Basilone performed prodigies with two sections of heavy machine guns and became the first enlisted Marine of World War II to win the Medal of Honor. The Japanese came again the next night. This time it was Hanneken's 2d Battalion that bore the brunt of the attack. On the morning of 26 October, the Sendai, with some 3500 dead, began withdrawing into the interior.

There was a changing climate in the South Pacific. On 18 October Admiral William F. ("Bull") Halsey succeeded Admiral Ghormley as area commander. On 28 October, I Marine Amphibious Corps was formed, with headquarters at Noumea, to coordinate all Fleet Marine Force units in the South Pacific. Reinforcements converged on Guadalcanal. On 4 November, the

8th Marines arrived from Samoa. On the same day, Carlson's Raiders and the 1st Battalion, 147th U. S. Infantry, landed at Aola Bay, forty miles east of Lunga.

Matanikau

Beginning 1 November, Vandegrift made another attack across the Matanikau, the 5th and 2d Marines reinforced under Edson moving out toward Kokumbona five and a half miles to the west. After three days the advance was stopped short of Kokumbona by Vandegrift because of events taking place east of the Lunga perimeter. On 1 November Hanneken had been sent with his battalion to see what was happening at Koli Point, well east of Vandegrift's perimeter but short of Aola Bay. Hanneken reached his objective coincident with the landing of the 230th Imperial Infantry. Hyakutake as well as Vandegrift was receiving reinforcements. Substantial parts of the 38th (Hiroshima) Division were being brought down the Slot by the Tokyo Express. Vandegrift decided to call off Edson's attack and concentrate on an envelopment of the Koli Point force. He sent out the rest of the 7th Marines and the 164th Infantry. The trap was somewhat porous. Some of the Japanese were caught in a pocket at Gavaga Creek, others oozed out. Carlson had been ordered to move his battalion out of Aola Bay to cut off any Japanese who might escape the Koli Point envelopment. He made his first solid contact on 12 November. Staying in the jungle until 4 December, he marched his battalion one hundred fifty miles, fought a dozen actions, killed five hundred enemy, and shunted the remainder into the inhospitable interior—at a cost of sixteen Raiders killed, eighteen wounded.

With Koli Point resolved, Vandegrift had turned his attention once again to Kokumbona. On 10 November, the 2d Marines, reinforced with elements of the 8th Marines and the 164th Infantry, moved out to the west but after one day's advance were halted because of intelligence of another strong attack in the making. The main body of the 38th Division, ten thousand men embarked in eleven transports, escorted by a dozen destroyers, started down the Slot on 12 November. Patrol planes reported a huge Japanese task force two hundred miles to the northwest. That day, 12 November, the Americal Division's second regiment, the 182d Infantry, was landed at Guadalcanal and their escort, Rear Admiral Daniel J. Callaghan with five cruisers and eight destroyers, went out to meet the Japanese task force. The gun duel began during the early morning hours of the thirteenth at three thousand yards. Admiral Callaghan in the *San Francisco* and Admiral Scott in the *Atlanta* were killed, but the Japanese task force got the worse of it and was forced to retire. Planes from Henderson Field caught the crippled battleship *Hiei* and battered her further, so that she had to be scuttled. Next day, 14 November, Marine and Navy air also got to the transport group and sank seven of the eleven transports. The remaining four transports continued doggedly on toward Guadalcanal. There was another big-gun naval action in Sealark Channel. The U. S. battleship *South Dakota* was badly damaged; the Japanese battleship *Kirishima* was sunk. The four remaining Japanese transports drove themselves aground between Cape Esperance and Tassafaronga and the four thousand survivors went off to join Hyakutake.

On 18 November, Vandegrift moved out once again to the west, this time with the 8th Marines, the 164th Infantry, and two battalions of the newly arrived 182d Infantry. Once again there was a meeting engagement. Hyakutake, reinforced at such terrible cost, was coming against the airfield in yet another attack. The head of his column collided with two Americal battalions the night of 19–20 November and a two-day battle followed. On the twenty-third, the 8th Marines passed through the 164th Infantry to continue the attack, but the advance was still not conclusive.

On 29 November, Japanese efforts to resupply their forces by sea touched off yet another naval battle. On 29 November a torpedo attack by eight Japanese destroyers sank the *Northampton* and put three other U. S. cruisers out of action, but even this brilliant attack could not reverse the swing of the pendulum. As December began, the Japanese came to the reluctant conclusion that they had lost the contest for Guadalcanal. By this time, Vandegrift was insisting that the 1st Marine Division be relieved and moved to a healthier climate. The surgeons estimated that a third of the Division, ranks riddled with malaria and malnutrition, was medically unfit for combat.

On 8 December, the Americal Division's third regiment, the 132d Infantry, arrived. Next day command of the island passed from Vandegrift to Major General Alexander M. Patch, USA. That same day, the 5th Marines sailed for Australia, followed shortly by the 1st Marines and 7th Marines. First elements of the U. S. 25th Division arrived on 17 December. On 2 January, Patch's force was designated the XIV Corps. Two days later, the 6th Marines landed, making the 2d Marine Division essentially complete (although commanded by the ADC, Brigadier General Alphonse De Carre, so as not to have a Marine major general ashore who was senior to Patch.) For a brief time, then, XIV Corps had three divisions—the Americal, the 25th, and the 2d Marine—some fifty thousand strong with which to fight the Japanese remnant.

Hyakutake was thought to still have about twenty-five thousand men. Patch's plan was to have the Americal Division hold the perimeter while the 25th Division and the 2d Marine Division attacked to the west. But Patch had the services of the 2d Marine Division only briefly. The 2d Marine Regiment embarked for New Zealand on 15 January, followed shortly by the 8th Marines. Patch then combined the newly arrived 6th Marines with the 147th and 182d Infantry Regiments into a provisional CAM (Composite

Army-Marine) Division and the final drive began 22 January. U. S. Army elements closed on Cape Esperance on 9 February but the Japanese were gone. Hyakutake had begun his evacuation on 1 February and had completed it on the eighth, taking off some thirteen thousand men.

The six-month campaign had cost Hyakutake perhaps 25,000 dead. Another 1000 Japanese soldiers (admittedly mostly laborers) had been taken prisoner. Six hundred Japanese planes had been destroyed. The naval battles had cost each side twenty-four fighting ships: 126,240 tons for the Allies, and 134,838 tons for the Japanese. Ashore, U. S. Marine losses were 1044 dead, 2894 wounded, 55 missing, and 8580 recorded cases of malaria. The U. S. Army lost 446 dead, 1910 wounded. Marine air had lost 55 killed, 127 wounded, 85 missing.

New Georgia

On 26 December, Brigadier General Francis P. ("Pat") Mulcahy, CG of the 2d Marine Aircraft Wing, arrived at Henderson Field to relieve Louis E. Woods as ComAir-Cactus. As a captain in France in World War I, Mulcahy had been one of the few Marines to get a confirmed German aircraft kill. On 15 February 1943 the conglomeration of Army, Navy, Marine, and New Zealand air units in the Solomons was combined under Commander, Aircraft, Solomons (ComAirSols).

In December the Japanese had been discovered hard at work on an incredibly well-camouflaged airfield at Munda on the northern end of New Georgia. Across the Kula Gulf, another field was being completed on Kolombangara. The Japanese already had four fields operational on Buka and Bougainville and five on New Britain in the vicinity of Rabaul. Fortunately, on 12 February, VMF-124 arrived at Henderson Field with twelve new gull-winged Vought Corsair F4Us. They were faster and had twice the range of any fighter the

Japanese had. Within six months all eight Marine fighter squadrons in the South Pacific would have the Corsair.

From Henderson Field northwest to Rabaul was 565 air miles. From Port Moresby in New Guinea northeast to Rabaul was 445 miles. MacArthur would advance along the latter axis, Halsey along the former. Halsey's first move up the Solomons was the 55-mile jump to the Russell Islands, halfway to New Georgia from Guadalcanal. Two new Raider battalions, the 3d under Lieutenant Colonel Harry E. ("Harry the Horse") Liversedge and the 4th under "Jimmy" Roosevelt, had come forward to Espiritu Santo. On 21 February, Liversedge's battalion made an unopposed landing on rain-soaked Pavuvu in the Russells. An airstrip was begun on neighboring Banika and beginning 14 March, MAG-21 set itself up in business with three squadrons of Wildcats.

On 15 March, at Espiritu, all four Raider battalions

were brought together into the 1st Raider Regiment
under Liversedge, and in the next weeks Raider reconnaissance patrols were sent out to scout the middle
Solomons.

Major General Noboru Sasaki arrived to take command of the Kolombangara-New Georgia sector on 31
May. He had the 229th Infantry, reinforced, on New
Georgia and a battalion of the 13th Infantry on Kolombangara. Rear Admiral Minoru Ota, who was already
there, had the Kure 6th Special Naval Landing Force on
New Georgia and the Yokosuka 7th SLNF on Kolombangara.

The U. S. plan for New Georgia was inordinately
complex, six or seven landings in all, of which the
Marines would take part in four. The Japanese were
reported closing in on a New Zealander coastwatcher
at Segi Plantation at the southeastern end of the island.
Accordingly, Lieutenant Colonel Michael S. Currin
landed there on 21 June with two companies of his 4th
Raider Battalion (Roosevelt had gone home), rendezvoused with the coastwatcher, and then made a four-
day jungle march to Viru Harbor, which he took on 1
July. Meanwhile, his other two companies had landed
with a larger Army outfit on nearby Vangunu Island.

The main landings were on 30 June. The 9th Marine
Defense Battalion landed on Rendova across Blanche
Channel from Munda behind the 43d Division's 103d
U. S. Infantry. D-Day was violent in the air if not on the
ground. American planes shot down 101 Japanese
aircraft (58 by Marine pilots) out of 130 engaged. On 3
July, the 43 Division began shuttling across Blanche
Channel to Zanana Beach, six miles east of Munda,
while the 9th Defense Battalion and the Army artillery
banged away at Munda airfield.

On the other side of the island, New Georgia was
linked to Kolombangara by barge terminals at Enogai
and Bairoko. From there, an overland trail led to
Munda. Liversedge with his regimental headquarters,
1st Raider Battalion, and two battalions from the 37th

Division landed at nearby Rice Anchorage in the predawn of Independence Day, 4 July, then made a wet march through mangrove swamps to Enogai Inlet, developing a fight on the seventh which lasted until the tenth. He paused until the eighteenth, when he was joined by Currin's battalion. On the twentieth, Liversedge moved out with his two Marine and two Army battalions against Bairoko (through which reinforcements, including the 13th Regiment, were funneling to Munda) and got into a hornet's nest of well-emplaced machine guns and 90-mm mortars for which he had nothing heavier than 60-mm mortars. After taking 243 casualties he fell back on Enogai to wait for heavier-calibered help. (When Army patrols went into Bairoko on 23 August they found it deserted.)

Meanwhile, most of the 37th and 25th Divisions had to be committed to help the 43d Division (while the 9th Defense Battalion's 155-mm "Long Toms" continued to pound the strip) before Munda was eventually secured on 5 August. Marine fighter squadrons 214 and 221 moved onto the field on 14 August. The Japanese still had a good airfield and perhaps ten thousand men on Kolombangara. It was decided to bypass it and move on to Vella Lavella. The 4th Marine Defense Battalion followed the Army's 35th RCT ashore there on 15 August. This gave the Allies control of the whole New Georgia group.

Bougainville

The next step up the ladder of the Solomons would be a big one, to Bougainville, largest of the islands, much like Guadalcanal, only wilder. There were supposed to be about thirty-five thousand Japanese on Bougainville, most of them clustered around the airfields. It was decided the Marines would set up their own airfield behind a force beachhead line. Midway down the west side of the island, in Empress Augusta Bay, there were two miles of what looked like good beach in the lee of the fishhook formed by Cape Torokina. An airstrip there would be only two hundred ten miles from Rabaul.

D-Day was set for 1 November 1943. Landing force would be the I Marine Amphibious Corps, until now an administrative headquarters at Noumea, New Caledonia. Commanding general was Vandegrift, promoted to lieutenant general. He would have the 3d Marine Division for the assault and the Army's 37th Infantry Division in reserve. The 3d Marine Division, commanded by Major General Allen H. ("Hal") Turnage, had come out to New Zealand in April 1943 and had gone into camps near Auckland. From there, after strenuous training, it had moved up to Guadalcanal.

To support the Bougainville operation AirSols had 52 squadrons (14 of them Marine) totaling 728 aircraft. Major General Ralph J. Mitchell had arrived in the South Pacific in April to take command of the 1st Marine Aircraft Wing from Geiger and on 20 November he became ComAirSols.

A diversion was needed to put the Japanese off as to the real target. A discarded operation order for a division landing on Choiseul was dusted off and the 2d Parachute Battalion, under Lieutenant Colonel "Brute" Krulak, reinforced to about 725 men, landed there the night of 27–28 October from the hard-worked destroyer transports, met with a coastwatcher and some natives, and pretended to be the 3d Marine Division. The Japanese started to reinforce from Bougainville, which was what was wanted, and Radio Tokyo announced that 20,000 Americans were ashore at Choiseul. On the night of 3–4 November, with the real landing at Empress Augusta Bay already accomplished, Krulak's battalion was lifted off by landing craft. Another part of the diversion was the landing of the New Zealand 8th Brigade Group on 27 October in the Treasury Islands sixty-five miles southeast of Empress Augusta Bay. Fighting would go on there until 12 November.

H-Hour at Cape Torokina was 0645 on 1 November. The beach was bisected by the Koromokina River. The 9th Marines were to land on the left of the Koromokina and the 3d Marines reinforced with the 2d Raider Battalion were to land on the right. The 3d Raider Battalion was to take Puruata Island. The plan was to put all eight battalions ashore at once, so the transports could go back for the 21st Marines and the 37th Division. There was more resistance than expected. The 1st Battalion, 3d Marines, landing inside the hook of Cape Torokina on the extreme right flank, was caught in a vicious crossfire including a 75-mm gun that knocked out six landing craft before it was eliminated by a brave sergeant. On the left flank surf conditions were bad. Something like eighty-six landing craft broached to and were smashed, so that the beach was abandoned and the 9th Marines came in behind the 3d Marines. Nevertheless, by nightfall the Marines had 14,000 troops and 6200 tons of supplies ashore despite the interruption of a 120-plane raid from Rabaul.

The Japanese defenses were under the overall command of the old antagonist, General Hyakutake, headquartered at Rabaul. In addition to the mauled formations that had escaped from Munda he had the full-strength 6th Division and the splendid Kure 7th Special Naval Landing Force. The 23d Infantry Regiment was sent marching to Torokina under command of a Colonel Kawano. Hyakutake's plan was to send down elements of the 17th Division from Rabaul to land beyond the American left flank, while Kawano came down the trails against the perimeter. Only four destroyers got through from Rabaul. On the night of 6–7 November about 475 Japanese landed off to the left of the beachhead; they dug in behind the Koromokina River and it took two days and three battalions to kill them all.

The Raiders had moved out to the northeast on Piva Trail and on 5 November had set up a blocking position where it intersected with Numa Numa Trail. A Japanese battalion bounced off the block and withdrew to Piva village. On the morning of 10 November, the Marine Corps Birthday, two battalions of the 9th Marines passed through the Raiders and went on into Piva village behind a carpet of one-hundred-pound bombs laid a hundred and twenty yards in front of them by two Marine torpedo squadrons putting to practical test the "yard-a-pound" rule of thumb.

By now the 21st Marines were ashore and the 37th Infantry Division was in process of landing. General Vandegrift had left for Washington, where he was to become the next Commandant on the first of the year, and his place as Corps commander was taken by stocky, cold-eyed Roy Geiger. The 37th Division took over the left half of the perimeter. There were twenty-two air raids in November, offering plenty of targets for the 3d Defense Battalion's 90-mm guns. The 3d Marines were now out in front. From 19 to 24 November they fought six actions, called the Battle of Piva Forks. On the twenty-ninth the 1st Parachute Battalion went off on a raid down the coast, to a place called Koiari. They ran into a thousand or more Japanese and it turned out badly. They had to be taken out under covering fire from three destroyers and 155-mm guns firing at extreme range from Torokina.

What was left of the 23d Imperial Infantry had consolidated on some high ground the Marines called Hellzapoppin Ridge. The 21st Marines finished them off in a series of fights that went from 12 to 23 December. Except for the 3d Defense Battalion (which would stay until June 1944) it was now time for the Marines to leave Bougainville. The American Division had arrived to relieve the 3d Marine Division, and on 15 December the Army's XXIV Corps had taken over from IMAC. Bougainville had cost the Marines 423 dead, 1418 wounded. It also marked the end of ground action in the South Pacific for the Marines. Halsey's line of advance in the South Pacific had now merged with that of MacArthur's drive up through the Southwest Pacific.

To pound Rabaul, Mitchell, as ComAirSols, planned to use his medium and heavy Army bombers and also fighter sweeps, a technique that had worked well at cleaning out Kahili. His star performer at fighter sweeps was Major Gregory R. ("Pappy") Boyington. Flying P-40s with the Flying Tigers in China Boyington had shot down six Japanese planes. Now thirty-one years old, he had gotten no victories in his first Solomons tour as CO of VMF-112 during the summer of 1943. In September he was given the chance to reorganize VMF-214. They took the name "Black Sheep" because the squadron had been filled out with pool pilots and other odds and ends. By the first of the new year Boyington's own score stood at twenty-five. On 3 January he took his squadron over Rabaul at twenty thousand feet. About fifty Japanese fighters came up to meet them. Boyington got three more planes before his Corsair's main gas tank caught fire. Several hours later a Japanese submarine picked him up from his rubber raft and took him into Rabaul. Boyington survived a harsh captivity and emerged at the end of the war as the Marine Corps' ranking ace with twenty-eight air-to-air victories.

The Japanese took their remaining aircraft out of Rabaul in February and the Marine SBD dive-bombers and TBF torpedo-bombers were able to go in earnest against the shipping servicing the Japanese base. After the big ships were sunk or driven off, the light bombers went after the all-important barges and did so well that by March the Japanese at Rabaul were no longer even receiving their mail.

Cape Gloucester

MacArthur had decided that Cape Gloucester on New Britain would be the next target for the 1st Marine

Division, which had been rebuilding slowly in Australia since arriving there from Guadalcanal. They had been re-equipped (the beloved bolt-action Springfield '03 giving way to the semiautomatic Garand M-1) and in August a Sixth Army inspection team had given them a combat efficiency rating of "excellent." William H. Rupertus now had the Division. The new ADC was Brigadier General Lemuel C. Shepherd, Jr. In late December the Division moved to staging areas on the east coast of New Guinea. Across the Straits was crescent-shaped New Britain, three hundred thirty miles long, mountainous, wild, heavily jungled. At the northwestern corner of the island was Cape Glouces-ter, where there was an airfield. At the other end of the crescent was Rabaul itself. There were an estimated 70,000 Japanese on New Britain, most of them in the north. Marine amphibious scouts and some Australians had gone into the objective area several times and there were the usual ubiquitous coastwatchers. Divi-sion Intelligence came up with a minimum-maximum of 7416 to 9816 Japanese, which was pretty close. Command of western New Britain was under Major General Iwao Matsuda. He had the 65th Brigade with the 53d and 141st Regiments.

D-Day, several times postponed, was finally set for 26 December 1943. The 1st Marine Division embarked the day before Christmas. No big transports were available but none were really needed for the short inter-island haul. The assault echelons went in APDs, the much-used destroyer-transports, from which they would go ashore in landing craft. The support groups were in LCIs which hopefully would be able to beach. The reserve and the heavy equipment and vehicles were in LSTs. Christmas was spent at sea and at 0300 on the morning of the twenty-sixth the troops were broken out for "steak-and-eggs" (a taste developed in Australia), which would become the traditional D-Day breakfast.

There was a fringing reef but there were breaks in it

and the plan was to pass through the reef in two places. The 7th Marines were to land across Yellow Beach, about seven miles down the east coast from the Cape. The 1st Marines (less its 2d Battalion) would then land behind the 7th, and, on order, pass through, and attack toward the airfield. The 5th Marines would be in reserve. Meanwhile, the 2d Battalion, 1st Marines, would land on the other side of the Cape over Green Beach at Tauali, to block either reinforcement or withdrawal by the Japanese along the west coast trails.

H-Hour was 0745. Initially there was no enemy, nothing behind the narrow beach but a dense wall of jungle, but within an hour 3d Battalion, 7th Marines, had developed a line of bunkers beyond Yellow One. The 3d Battalion, 1st Marines, passed through and by mid-morning had developed a good-sized fight. That afternoon there was an air raid by eighty-eight planes from Rabaul. Most of them were knocked down by Army P-38s but a U. S. destroyer was sunk, and three others damaged. Across the Cape, the 2d Battalion, 1st Marines, had landed at Tauali with no more resistance than a brush with a Japanese patrol but could not make radio contact with the Division ten miles away, because of the hill mass, dominated by 6600-foot Mount Talawe, which separated them.

The monsoon rains began in earnest that night. There was also an attack against the center of the Marine perimeter by the 2d Battalion, 53d Imperial Infantry. In the morning the 1st and 3d Battalions of the 1st Marines moved up the axis of the coast road against no opposition to within a mile and a half of the airfield. In front of them the 1st Battalion, 53d Infantry, had a line of defenses which the Marines would call Hell's Point. The Japanese were pushed back from there on the twenty-eighth. That same day the 5th Marines were landed and next day both regiments went forward, the 5th Marines moving up on the left of the 1st Marines, and by nightfall most of the airfield had been taken.

Even so, Matsuda still had most of his Brigade intact, including the 141st Regiment, and he was thought to be in the high, heavily jungled ground south and west of the beachhead. On the 29th, Rupertus told Shepherd to take the 7th Marines plus the 3d Battalion, 5th Marines, and destroy Matsuda. Three battalions were to advance abreast through the rain-sodden hills until contact was made, then the reserve battalion would hook around in an envelopment. A captured order told the Marines that "Aogiri Ridge" was to be held at all costs. This ridge was reached on 8 January. Lieutenant Colonel Lewis Walt now had the 3d Battalion, 5th Marines. He put his shoulder to a 37-mm gun and, using canister, blasted his way to the top. Matsuda tried a counterattack on the night of the ninth, failed, and fell back. There was one more hill, a big one, six hundred sixty feet high. The 3d Battalion, 7th Marines, under Lieutenant Colonel Henry W. ("Bill") Buse, Naval Academy '34, went forward against Hill 660 on the thirteenth. The first assault failed, Buse dug in for the night, and next morning worked around the west face of the hill and came down on the Japanese. By dusk he had the ridge. The Japanese counterattacked with two companies at daybreak on the sixteenth. Matsuda then broke off contact but it was not known if he was moving east or south.

"Chesty" Puller, now executive officer of the 7th Marines, took a 384-man "patrol" across the island to Gilnit on the south coast and back again, but he found nothing except a few stragglers. Matsuda was not in the interior but moving along the north coast, leaving behind a trail of dead and dying Japanese. The 5th Marines went after them, paused at Iboki, sixty miles from Cape Gloucester, then under a new regimental commander, the slender and quiet Colonel Oliver Prince Smith, made a fifty-seven-mile shore-to-shore amphibious move on 6 March to take Talasea airfield at the tip of Willaumez Peninsula. On 28 April 1944, the 1st Marine Division was relieved by the 40th Infantry

Division. New Britain had cost the Marines 310 killed, 1083 wounded. The Division, re-embarked, hoped they were going back to Australia. Instead they were headed for a muddier camp at Pavuvu in the Russell Islands, and perhaps even more rain than in New Britain.

13

1943–1945
"...all organized resistance has ceased."

Tarawa

At the Quebec Conference, in August 1943, the line of advance for the Central Pacific offensive was marked out as from the Gilberts, to the Marshalls, to the Marianas, and thence to the Carolines. First objectives, then, would be the Gilbert Islands, stretching loosely across the Equator like so many carelessly-flung coral necklaces.

The V Amphibious Corps—two divisions, one Army, one Marine—under Major General Holland M. Smith would be the landing force. The 27th Infantry Division, led by Major General Ralph C. Smith, USA, would land at Makin. The 2d Marine Division, which had been resting in New Zealand since coming out of Guadalcanal, would land at Tarawa under command of a third Smith, this one the soft-spoken, gentlemanly Julian C. Smith.

Tarawa atoll is an extended thumb and forefinger. Betio island is the thumbnail, two miles long, half a mile wide, and at no point more than ten feet above sea level. Three runways forming a flat letter A filled most of the island. The rest was fortifications: coconut logs, coral, a lot of reinforced concrete, and over two hundred guns of all calibers up to four fine 8-inch rifles taken at Singapore. There were 5236 souls on the island, 2619 combatants in the Sasebo 7th Special Naval Landing Force and 3d Special Base Force, the rest airfield specialists and labor troops; all were under command of Rear Admiral Keichi Shibasaki, who was of the opinion that the Americans could not take the island in a million years.

The Marines chose to land on the north shore which faced on the lagoon. There was a fringing reef on that side, five hundred to a thousand yards of coral. Landing craft couldn't cross it; amphibian tractors might. The 2d Division had something over a hundred of them, thin-skinned Alligators, enough to lift the first three waves. A pier, solidly built of coconut logs and coral, bisected the north beach, jutting out five hundred yards. Any guns left intact on the pier would enfilade the waves coming in to the beach. The three-day prelanding bombardment called for 1500 tons of bombs and 2000 tons of naval shells.

H-Hour was to be 0830, 20 November 1943, but when that hour came the shore batteries were not yet quiet and so H-Hour was postponed until 0900. The assault waves began taking 37-mm and 76-mm fire three to four thousand yards off the beach. A scout-sniper platoon reached the pier and began burning out gun emplacements with flamethrowers. About fifteen minutes later, first elements of the 2d Battalion, 8th Marines, touched down on Red Beach Three just east of the pier. The 2d Battalion, 2d Marines, coming in west of the pier on Red Beach Two got badly shot up; its battalion commander was killed in the water. Farther west, at some distance, 3d Battalion, 2d Marines, landed on the extreme right flank of Red Beach One. The battalion had gotten separated from its command group and the senior company commander, Major Michael P. Ryan took charge.

The 1st Battalion, 2d Marines, waded in across the

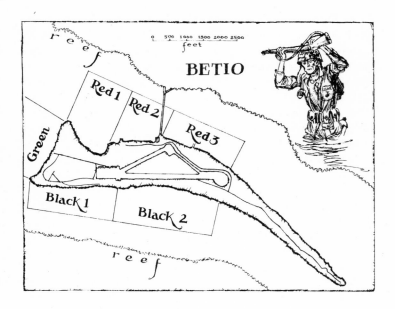

fire-swept reef behind 2d Battalion, 2d Marines. The 3d
Battalion, 8th Marines, which was to follow the 2d
Battalion, 8th Marines, onto Red Three was caught
unloading from landing craft at the edge of the reef and
was badly shelled. Colonel David Shoup, commanding
the 2d Marine Regiment, landed about 1030 and set up
his command post in a blasted Japanese blockhouse.
As night fell, Shoup, with parts of four battalions, held
a shallow box-shaped perimeter around the base of the
pier. Separated from him and over on the right flank,
two Sherman tanks had landed and with these Ryan
had started toward Green Beach on the western tip of
the island. During the night, made bright with star
shells and burning gasoline, some guns from the 10th
Marines got ashore. The 1st Battalion, 8th Marines,
spent the night out in the water in landing craft, started
in at daybreak, and took heavy losses. Needing more
troops, Julian Smith got the release of the 6th Marines,
which was in Corps reserve.

On D-Plus-One, Shoup, already wounded, attacked south across the waist of the island, his four battalions in two columns. By nightfall he had reached the south shore. Ryan, still separated from the rest of the landing force, had secured Green Beach by noon. The 1st Battalion, 6th Marines, under Major William Jones, got ashore late in the afternoon. Sometime during the day Shibasaki had expired. His last message to Tokyo ended, "May Japan exist for ten thousand years."

Next morning, Jones attacked at right angles to Shoup's position and by dark the Marines had the western two-thirds of the island. That night the Japanese tried three desperate and futile *banzai* attacks. The following morning the fresh 3d Battalion, 6th Marines, passed through the Marine line and pushed to the eastern tip of the island. At 1321, 23 November, Julian Smith declared the island secured. The seventy-six hours of fighting had cost 984 Marine dead and 2072 wounded. The only enemy left alive were 17 wounded prisoners and 129 Korean laborers.

The 27th Infantry Division landed on Butaritari island in the Makin atoll on schedule on 20 November. Ralph Smith used a 6472-man regimental landing team built around the 165th Infantry Regiment. There were 848 Japanese on Butaritari, about a third of them first-class fighting troops, and these were taken care of in four days.

After Tarawa, Holland Smith recommended the "assignment of at least one Marine Aircraft Wing specifically for direct air support in landing operations." What were needed were escort carriers to provide the platforms from which to operate, but the Navy was chary about giving these decks to the Marines. So, for the time, Marine aviation in the Central Pacific would be limited to rear-area missions. The 4th Marine Base Defense Aircraft Wing had been activated in August 1942 and on Christmas Day 1943, Brigadier General Lewie G. Merritt brought the forward echelon forward to Tarawa.

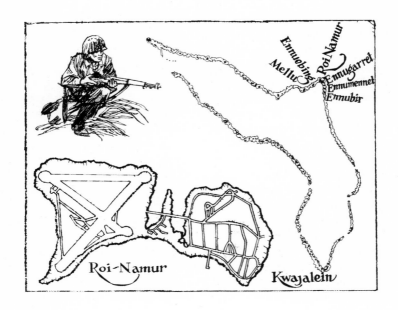

The Marshalls

Next objective in the Central Pacific would be Kwajalein (the world's largest atoll) in the Marshall Islands, a
part of Japanese trust territories since World War I.
The V Amphibious Corps would again be the landing
force, this time with the Army's 7th Division and the
new 4th Marine Division under Major General Harry
("the Dutchman") Schmidt. The Army was to take
Kwajalein island itself at the southeast corner of the
atoll. The Marines were to land on the twin islands of
Roi and Namur at the northeast corner. D-Day was set
for 31 January 1944.

Roi-Namur was supposed to have three thousand
defenders but was nowhere near so well fortified as
Betio had been. Heaviest guns were a pair of twin
5.5-inch dual-purpose naval rifles. As at Tarawa, the
landing would be made on the lagoon side of the
islands. Amphibian tractors were now coming off

the assembly lines in quantity and 4th Marine Division had three times the number the 2d Division had had at Betio. There was to be two days of heavy, deliberate bombardment.

D-Day operations called for the 25th Marines to make five separate landings on the mellifluously named islets of Mellu, Ennuebing, Ennugarret, Ennumennet, and Ennubir, which flanked the "big" islands of Roi and Namur (neither of which measured much more than a mile along its longest axis). The 25th Marines would be followed by the 4th Division's artillery regiment, the 14th Marines, which would set up to cover the main landings the following day. These landings went well except for troubles with the amphibian tractors. There were plenty of them but their crews were half-trained, relations with their mother LSTs were acrimonious, their radios were unreliable, their sea-keeping ability marginal; when their engines stopped so did their pumps, and they had a distressing habit of sinking.

D-Plus-One's plans called for the 23d Marines to land on Roi and the 24th Marines to land on Namur. (The two islands were linked by a causeway.) Roi was skinned clean of vegetation and most of it was taken up by an X-shaped airfield. Namur to the east had most of the supply installations and was still pretty well covered with pandanus and such. H-Hour was delayed until 1100. The 23d Marines, which had a fresh amphibian tractor battalion to lift it, was on the mark, but the 24th Marines were to use yesterday's tractors and there seemed to be only sixty-two of them left. The 23d Marines landed on Roi against virtually no opposition, raced across the island in a pell-mell formless attack, slaughtering dazed and bewildered Japanese (half of the defenders were already dead from the naval bombardment), securing the island by nightfall.

The 24th Marines found it tougher going. At dark, with two-thirds of Namur in their possession, they halted for the night. The Japanese tried a half-hearted *banzai* attack. Next morning, the 24th Marines went forward supported by tanks and half-tracks, and at 1428 on 2 February Namur was declared secure. The 4th Marine Division plus naval gunfire had killed 3563 Japanese at a cost of 313 dead, 502 wounded. Meanwhile, the 7th Infantry Division had landed on Kwajalein island itself on 1 February and in four days killed 4823 enemy, losing 173 soldiers dead, 793 wounded.

Eniwetok

The next objective would be Eniwetok atoll at the northwest edge of the Marshalls. Ready at hand was the unused V Phib Corps reserve, a brigade-size force, called Tactical Group 1, under hot-tempered Marine Brigadier General Thomas E. ("Terrible Tommy") Watson, consisting of two regiments: the 22d Marines and the 106th U. S. Infantry. There were three islands in the atoll to be taken. Engebi, a triangular piece of coral, had the airfield and was at the northern curve of the necklace. Twenty miles south of Engebi, across the lagoon, was Eniwetok island itself, and northeast of Eniwetok island was Parry island. Once again, the landing was to be made from inside the lagoon.

On 17 February 1944, behind a curtain of naval gunfire, the amphibian tractors ground ashore on three islets adjacent to Engebi to secure supporting artillery positions. The next morning the 22d Marines made the main landing, its three battalions in the classic "two up and one back" formation. Touch-down was at 0842, 18 February. There was a fairly wild night (the defenders had a new trick—a "spider web" of tunnels made up of buried oil drums laid end to end) but in the morning it was all over and the U. S. flag went up while someone sounded colors on a captured Japanese bugle.

Next morning, the 106th Infantry landed at Eniwetok at 0915, found it tougher going, and were joined at 1330 by the 22d Marines' 3d Battalion. After two days of hard fighting, Eniwetok island was declared secured on

ENIWETOK ATOLL

the twenty-first, and next day the 22d Marines went on
to take Parry island. Sixty-six prisoners had been taken
and about 3400 Japanese killed. The Marines had lost
254 killed and 555 wounded. U. S. Army casualties
were 94 killed and 311 wounded.

There were four more big Japanese bases in the
Marshalls—Mille, Jaluit, Wotje, and Maleolap—but if
they were cut off from reinforcement and kept neutralized by air attacks, they would be impotent and could

be left to wither away. To this end MAG-31 started flight operations from Roi on 15 March and MAG-13 began flying from Majuro on the twenty-first. The 4th Marine Base Defense Aircraft Wing echeloned its headquarters forward to Kwajalein on 9 March. Later MAG-22 from Midway would join the Wing. Ten fighter and four bomber squadrons would continue the long-term monotonous, but necessary, task of neutralizing the bypassed Marshall atolls. (How well they would do the job was revealed after the war: of the 13,701 Japanese on the four atolls, 7440 would die, 2564 from the bombing, the rest from disease and starvation. Ninety per cent of the damage was attributed to the Marine squadrons.)

The Marianas

The Air Force needed airfields in the Mariana Islands, fifteen hundred miles from Japan, if the new B-29s were to reach the Empire. The Navy wanted advanced bases there for future moves against the Philippines and eventually against the Japanese home islands, and also hoped that such an attack would bring out the Japanese main battle fleet, absent since Guadalcanal, to a final, decisive action. There were three main islands to go after: Saipan, Tinian, and Guam.

Some eight hundred ships and 162,000 men rendezvoused in the Marshalls for the long step to the Marianas. All this made up Spruance's Fifth Fleet. The Joint Expeditionary Force was under Kelly Turner. Holland Smith, now a lieutenant general, had two jobs: Expeditionary Troops, and Northern Troops and Landing Force. NTLF had the 2d Marine Division, commanded by newly promoted Tommy Watson, and the 4th Marine Division, still under Harry Schmidt. Saipan was first, fourteen miles long by six wide, rugged, mountainous, ringed with a coral reef, and with a Japanese and Chamorro civilian population. D-Day for Saipan was 15 June 1944. The assault on Guam, for which there was a Southern Troops and Landing Force, was to be three days later, on the eighteenth. Tinian was then to follow. Ralph Smith's 27th Infantry Division was in floating reserve and the 77th Division was to be held in Hawaii as strategic reserve.

Saipan was the headquarters of the Japanese Central Pacific Fleet under Admiral Chiuchi Nagumo, who had been Commander Striking Force at Pearl Harbor and Midway. The headquarters of the new 31st Army was also there, under elderly Lieutenant General Yoshitsugo Saito. The 31st Army was subordinate to the Central Pacific Fleet but the command lines were convolute and the admiral and the general did not get along. Nagumo thought the landing would be on the east coast, in Magicienne ("Magazine") Bay, and soon. Saito thought it would be on the west coast near Charan Kanoa but not until November. By careful count there were 29,662 defenders on Saipan. Army troops included the 43d (Nagoya) Division, the 47th Independent Mixed Brigade, the 9th Tank Regiment, two engineer regiments, and an antiaircraft regiment. Most of the soldiers had come recently from the Kwantung Army in China. Naval defenses, chiefly the 1st Yokosuka Special Naval Landing Force, were concentrated around Tanapag Harbor on the northwest coast. Key terrain feature was Mount Tapotchau, 1552 feet high, in the center of the island. The one important airfield was Aslito field at the southern end of the island.

Saito had been right; the Marines were going to land across the beaches north and south of the sugar-mill town of Charan Kanoa. The 2d Division was on the right, farther south, with the 23d and 25th Marines in the lead. Seven hundred amtracks were to carry the assault waves, coming in behind new armored amphibians mounting 75-mm guns. H-Hour was 0840. There was much mortar and artillery fire as the tractors came across the reef. The Marines took two thousand casualties the first day. Five of the original battalion commanders were hit. One battalion—the 2d Battalion, 6th Marines—had four different commanders before dark.

The situation ashore was not good but the Navy got one reaction they wanted: the Japanese Combined Fleet came out from its hiding places to meet the Fifth Fleet. Spruance met with Holland Smith and Kelly Turner the morning of 16 June on board the *Rocky Mount*. He was sending Marc Mitscher's Task Force 58 out to meet the Japanese fleet. The Guam landing would be postponed. The 27th Division would be landed on Saipan and the 77th Division would be brought forward from Hawaii.

Ashore, by noon on the sixteenth, two battalions of the 2d Division had gotten through Charan Kanoa. Meanwhile, the 4th Division was attacking straight ahead, clearing the beach so that the 165th Infantry could come ashore. At about 0330 the next morning the 9th Tank Regiment hit the 2d Division, and the tanks got almost to the 6th Marines command post before being stopped. With daylight on the seventeenth the Marine attack started forward slowly. Marshy Lake Susupe lying behind Charan Kanoa separated the two divisions and proved troublesome. Momentum picked up on the eighteenth. The 4th Division, with its regiments abreast, pushed across the island to Magicienne Bay. On the 4th Division's right flank, the 165th Infantry had curled south and taken Aslito airfield, and on 165th's right, the 105th Infantry had moved to the cliffs on the southern tip of the island, so that by the nineteenth a Japanese battalion had been compressed into a pocket at Nafutan Point.

It was on 19 June that Task Force 58 shot down 346 Japanese aircraft off Guam in the "Marianas Turkey Shoot." Next day Spruance pressed home the attack and, although it cost 100 American planes, took out 3 Japanese aircraft carriers in the Battle of the Philippine Sea.

On the twentieth, while the 2d Division held fast as a pivot, the 4th Division swung around so that there was

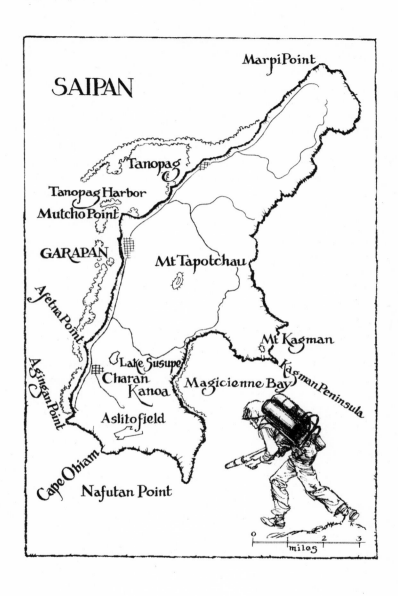

SAIPAN

Marpi Point

Tanopag

Tanopag Harbor

Mutcho Point

GARAPAN

Afetna Point

Mt Tapotchau

Mt Kagman

Aginean Point

Lake Susupe

Charan Kanoa

Magicienne Bay

Kagman Peninsula

Aslito field

Cape Obiam

Nafutan Point

0   2   3
miles

a line facing north. Holland Smith now ordered the 27th Division to leave one battalion in the south to clean out Nafutan Point and to move in between the 2d and 4th Divisions. On the twenty-third, the three divisions jumped off behind a preparation laid down by eighteen battalions of artillery. On the left, in the 2d Division's zone, the 2d Marines on 24 June entered Garapan, once a town of fifteen thousand, now empty and nearly flattened, and the 8th Marines started up the slopes of Mount Tapotchau. On the right, the 4th Division took Hill 600 (and renamed it "Hot Potato Hill") which covered Kagman Peninsula, which in turn formed the northern lip of Magicienne Bay.

In the center, the 27th Division had bogged down. After conferring with Spruance and Kelly Turner, Holland Smith relieved Ralph Smith of his command. A Marine general Smith relieving an Army general named Smith was a ready-made newspaper sensation and the effects of it on inter-Service relations would be felt for years. Next day Lieutenant Colonel Rathvon McC. ("Tommy") Tompkins, who had the 1st Battalion, 29th Marines (a separate battalion attached temporarily to the 2d Division), made a brilliant flanking attack to the top of Mount Tapotchau, getting above the Japanese defenders.

On the night of 26 June the Japanese in the Nafutan Point pocket (they were the 317th Battalion, 47th Brigade) came boiling out, punched through the 2d Battalion, 105th Infantry, and reached the flight line on Aslito (renamed Isely) airfield. Some five hundred were eventually killed by the 25th Marines who were in reserve and the artillerymen of the 14th Marines.

In the north, as the island narrowed, the 4th and 27th Divisions continued in the assault and the 2d Division passed into reserve. On 6 July, Saito pressed his *samurai* sword to his breast, drew blood, and was ceremoniously shot by his adjutant. At about the same time Admiral Nagumo put a bullet through his own brain. By now Major General George W. Griner, USA, had arrived from Hawaii to take over the 27th Division. Holland Smith told him to expect a *banzai* attack. It came early on the morning of 7 July. Two to three thousand Japanese found a three-hundred-yard gap separating the 1st and 3d Battalions of the 105th Infantry, poured through, and were finally stopped by the 3d Battalion, 10th Marines, firing at pointblank range with 105s. Next day General Smith sent in the rested 2d Division to relieve the 27th Division and by 9 July Marpi Point was reached at the northern tip of the island. It was a two-hundred-twenty-foot cliff honeycombed with caves. Urged on by the remaining Japanese soldiers, many of the civilians committed mass suicide by leaping from the cliff. The alternate method preferred by most of the soldiers was to blow themselves up with hand grenades.

American casualties for Saipan numbered 16,525 of whom 12,934 were Marines. Of the nearly 30,000 Japanese defenders, all but about 1000 perished. On 18 July, Premier Hideki Tojo, mortified by the defeat in the Battle of the Philippine Sea and the loss of Saipan, submitted his resignation to the Emperor.

Guam

Peanut-shaped Guam, largest and southernmost of the Marianas, twenty-eight miles long, four to eight miles wide, was not unlike Saipan, but bigger, more jungle, and no cane fields. The southern half of the island, where not cultivated, was high jungle country. The northern half was flatter, less lush, but covered with dense brush and undergrowth. The natives of Guam were called Chamorros, a name they disliked, a brown people, their aboriginal blood liberally mixed with Spanish, Filipino, and Japanese. On the western side of the island were two coral fingers, Cabras Island and Orote peninsula, sticking out into the sea and forming Apra harbor. North of Cabras, along the coast road, was the town of Asan and then the capital, Agana, about twelve thousand souls in normal times. South of Orote the road ran to Agat and then petered out to a little more than a track that went on around the island. Behind Apra harbor was Mount Tenjo, going up to a thousand feet.

Lieutenant General Takeshi Takashina, a vigorous veteran of Manchuria, was the senior Japanese officer present. His command included the 38th Infantry Regiment, reinforced, the 48th Independent Mixed Brigade, and the 10th Independent Mixed Regiment, about 13,000 Army troops altogether. There were also 5500 members of the Imperial Navy, under Captain Yutaka Sugimoto, the most significant unit being the 54th Naval Guard Force (whom the U. S. Marines would call "Imperial Marines" and who would fight exceedingly well). Tumon Bay, north of Agana, was the most obvious landing site and Takashina had fortified it heavily. There was the usual large inventory of artillery of mixed calibers and origins, the most formidable being nineteen 8-inch guns, not all of which were in position, the Japanese not having gotten down seriously to the business of fortifying Guam until after the Marshalls had fallen.

Major General Roy Geiger would be Commander, Southern Troops and Landing Force. His headquarters was the III Amphibious Corps, a redesignation of what had been I Marine Amphibious Corps. He had the 3d Marine Division under Major General Allen Turnage, the 1st Provisional Marine Brigade under Brigadier General Lemuel Shepherd, the usual Corps troops including plentiful artillery, the 9th and 14th Defense Battalions (with which to garrison the island after the assault), and, in reserve, the 77th U. S. Army Division.

Landing day, called W-Day for this operation, originally to have been 18 June, now was set for 21 July. There was the usual problem of a fringing reef but this was becoming almost routine—the amphibian tractors would take the assault waves into the beach, then come back to transfer line at the reef's edge and pick up the

GUAM

0 2000 4000 6000 8000 10000
yards

Ritidian Point

Pacific Ocean

Tumon Bay

Mt Barrigada

Adelup Point

Asan Point

Agana

Cabras

Asan

Apra Harbor

Fonte hill

Pago Bay

Orote
Point

Sumay
airfield

Mt Tenjo

Agat

Gaan Point

Mt Alifan

Bangi Point

Facpi Point

succeeding waves from the landing craft. There would be two landings, about five miles apart. Turnage's 3d Marine Division would make the northern landing, avoiding Tumon Bay, and going in on a wide crescent-shaped beach between Adelup and Asan points. Shepherd's Brigade would land just south of Agat. H-Hour was 0830. Air and naval gunfire had flattened Agana, Asan, Agat, and nearly everything above ground on Orote peninsula. Most of the big-caliber coastal guns had been knocked out or neutralized; not so with the lighter guns. The 3d Marine Division landed with three regiments abreast behind a barrage of rockets fired from LCI gunboats, the first waves being armored amphibians mounting 37-mm and 75-mm guns. As they came across the reef the Japanese started dropping artillery and mortar fire on them, and then brought them under cross fire from machine guns hidden in the cliff faces. The 3d Marines, on the left, met stiffening resistance as they moved forward into a vise formed by the Chonito Cliff and the Fonte heights. The 21st Marines, in the center, went through the town of Asan and continued west against the higher ground farther inland. The 9th Marines, on the right flank and on easier ground, swung south, secured Asan point, and reached the causeway to Cabras Island by evening.

Shepherd's Brigade had harder fighting. Put together on Guadalcanal, the Brigade had two regiments, the 22d Marines, veterans of Eniwetok, and the new 4th Marines, made up of the Raider battalions, reorganized into infantry and given the designation of the regiment lost at Bataan. The Brigade landed with the 4th Marines on the right, 22d Marines on the left, both with two battalions abreast. Separating the two regimental beaches was Gaan point. The Japanese had hollowed it out and in the nose were two short-barreled 75-mm guns that piled up two dozen amphibian tractors landing the 22d Marines. Gaan point stayed "hot" most of the day. Alifan ridge was a mile behind the beach, the 4th Marines got halfway there before nightfall. The 22d Marines went through Agat and curled toward the base of Orote peninsula. The 305th U. S. Infantry, on temporary loan from the 77th Division as Brigade reserve, came into the beach about dark.

Sometime after midnight the Japanese came out of their caves and boiled toward the Brigade beachhead. Takashina used up two battalions of the 38th Regiment in the attack. When morning came, the 4th Marines resumed the advance and by nightfall had reached the crest of Mount Alifan. The 305th Infantry moved into the center of the Brigade beachhead and the 22d Marines started north astride the Agat-Agana Road. By 23 July they had cut across the base of Orote peninsula to Apra harbor.

The 3d Division was also heavily engaged. In the first three days, the 3d Marines had been held stalled in front of Fonte hill; the 21st Marines had doggedly made their way inland against successive ridgeline positions; and the 9th Marines had taken Cabras Island. The 9th Marines could now spare a battalion to come to the help of the 3d Marines. Lieutenant Colonel Robert Cushman arrived with the 2d Battalion, 9th Marines, the night of 24 July. The next morning, his battalion passed through the 3d Marines leading edge, crossed the Mount Tenjo Road, and went up the slope of Fonte hill, driving a wedge into the Japanese defenses. That same day, the twenty-fifth, patrols from the 9th and 22d Marines made contact on the rim of Apra harbor and the two beachheads were tenuously linked. Most of the 77th Division was ashore by now and the 4th Marines had come up on the left of the 22d Marines on Orote peninsula.

That night, 25–26 July, Takashina made his big effort. On Orote peninsula, the Naval defenders came charging out of a mangrove swamp in a saki-inflamed, suicidal extravaganza. In the north what was left of the 10th Independent Mixed Regiment came against Cushman's battalion on Fonte hill. Company F, under a tall Mississippian, Captain Louis H. Wilson, was at the apex of the Marine salient, and during the night seven separate attacks were beaten off. Elsewhere on the Division perimeter there were two penetrations and some of the attackers got back to the field hospital, where there was a weird scene of wounded Marines fighting in bandages and underwear. By morning, the fire was out of the attack on both fronts and Takashina had used up the equivalent of ten battalions. On Fonte, Lou Wilson, three times wounded, collected a patrol and tidied up his company position before allowing himself to be evacuated.

Takashina himself was killed on the twenty-eighth. That same day, the 22d Marines reached the fire-blackened skeleton of the old Marine barracks and next day took Orote airfield. During the last days of the month the 77th Division moved up on the right of the 3d Marine Division and on 31 July the two divisions started forward in a shoulder-to-shoulder sweep. MAG-21 began flight operations at Orote airfield on 4 August and eventually grew to twelve squadrons. On 7 August the rested Brigade came in on the Division's left flank, and three days later the last Japanese defenders were pushed over the northern cliffs.

American casualties were 1919 killed, 7122 wounded, 70 missing; a total of 9111. Japanese losses were put at 17,300 killed, 485 prisoners, although for months, even years to come (as late as 1972), hardy survivors would be killed or captured, running up the count.

Tinian

Tinian is just south of Saipan, separated by about two and a half miles of water. Smaller than Saipan (about twelve miles long, north to south), Tinian is also less rugged, mostly a fairly regular low plateau, densely planted in those days in sugar cane. The cane fields in

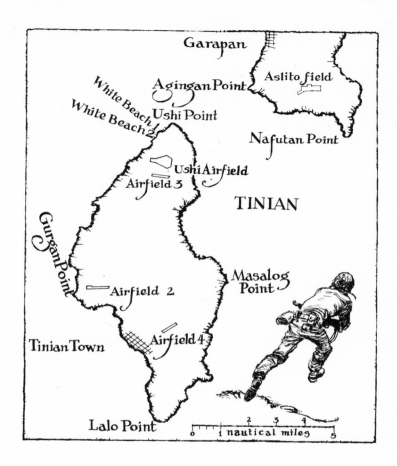

the center of the island promised room for six 8500-foot runways for the B-29s that were to bomb the Japanese home islands.

The Japanese commander was Colonel Keishi Ogata, a veteran of the Kwantung Army. He commanded the 50th Infantry Regiment, 29th Division, plus a battalion of the 135th Infantry and the usual reinforcements. Also under Ogata's orders was the 56th Naval Guard Force. In all there were 4700 Army and 4110 Navy.

Near the northern tip of the island there were two

beaches, both very small, one about sixty yards wide and the other with a usable length of about seventy-five yards. Reconnaissance showed mines between the high- and low-water marks, but obviously the Japanese did not expect a landing over such narrow beaches.

The plan was for the 4th Marine Division (now commanded by Clifton Cates—Harry Schmidt had moved up to command of V Amphibious Corps) to make a shore-to-shore landing while Tommy Watson's 2d Division demonstrated off Tinian Town in the south. By 15 July, all the artillery on Saipan had been grouped in the south of the island from where it could cover Tinian. Naval gunfire support was also plentiful. Air support would come from Army and Marine squadrons already in place on Saipan, as well from carrier-based Naval aviation.

J-Day was 24 July. At 0745, the 24th Marines came across White One, the northern, more narrow beach, in column of battalions, while the 25th Marines landed with two battalions abreast on White Two. Opposition was "light" on White One, "moderate" on White Two. About mid-day the 23d Marines moved into line on the right flank.

Colonel Ogata, still committed to a doctrine that said to defend at the waterline, started his counterattack in motion that afternoon. At 0200 in the morning the 1st Battalion, 135th Infantry, hit the center of the Marine line. The 25th Marines were very solidly in position on good ground and the attackers made no impression. At 0300, the 50th Infantry attacked, found the boundary between the 25th Marines and the 23d Marines, and a couple of hundred of them got through as far as the light artillery positions. About this same time the 56th Naval Guard Force was destroying itself against the 24th Marines on the left flank.

The next day, 25 July, the 2d Marine Division came ashore, took Ushi airfield, swung around and came up on the 4th Division's left flank. The 24th Regiment went into reserve and the two divisions started a shoulder-to-shoulder systematic sweep southward. On 31 July the 4th Division moved through Tinian Town. Early next morning, there was a *banzai* attack of sorts and at daylight the body of a colonel was found hanging on the wire. It might have been Ogata. As the Japanese were compressed into the southern part of the island, there was a repetition of the death hysteria that had gripped Saipan. On 1 August our patrols reached the southern coast and Harry Schmidt was able to announce that "all organized resistance had ceased." By 12 August, 13,262 civilians had been rounded up and put safely into stockades. By count, 6050 Japanese defenders were dead, 255 others were prisoners. The Marines had lost 290 killed, 1515 wounded, and 24 missing.

Peleliu

The Palaus are about midway between the Marianas and the southern Philippines, say five hundred miles from Mindanao, easy medium-bomber range. Biggest island is Babelthuap but the Americans were interested more in Peleliu at the southern end of the group. Six miles long, two miles wide, shaped something like a lobster's claw, Peleliu had a big airfield filling most of its flat lower end. Off the northern end was the smaller island, Ngesebus, connected to Peleliu by a causeway. The backbone of Peleliu, north of the airfield, was a coral-limestone ridge, going up to about two-hundred feet, and forming the upper half of the lobster's claw. The natives called the ridge Umurbrogol.

The Palaus were to be another III Phib Corps operation. Expeditionary troops would be the 1st Marine Division, coming up from muddy Pavuvu, and the untried 81st U. S. Division from Hawaii. The Marines would take Peleliu, while the Army demonstrated off Babelthuap and then moved on to take Angaur, seven miles southwest of Peleliu. Major General William Rupertus still had the 1st Marine Division which was reinforced for the operation to a strength of 28,484.

A very canny lieutenant general named Sadea Inoue commanded the Palau Sector Group. On Peleliu he had the 2d Infantry Regiment from his own 14th Division (one of Japan's oldest and best), two more infantry battalions, and reinforcements which included tanks and a mixture of guns, among them a new 200-mm rocket launcher. That made about 6000 Japanese soldiers. There were also 4100 Imperial Navy, including the usual Naval Guard Force.

D-Day was set for 15 September 1944. On 12 September the bombardment began. Afterward it was called the "least adequate" of the Pacific War, partly because of the length of time, partly because of poor targeting, but, in fairness, mostly due to the Japanese soldier's skill with pick and spade. Rupertus's scheme was to land all three infantry regiments abreast on the wide beach on the west side of the island right off the airfield. The 7th Marines (now commanded by Herman Hanneken) would land on the southernmost beach and clear out the lower end of the island. The 5th Marines, under Colonel Harold D. ("Bucky") Harris, would land in the center and drive straight across the airfield. The 1st Marines, under "Chesty" Puller, would land on the left and swing to the north along the axis of Umurbrogol ridge. Four days, someone suggested, would be all it would take.

H-Hour was 0830. Conduct of the defense devolved upon Colonel Kunio Nakagawa, commander of the 2d Infantry Regiment. The first wave of Marines were met at the beach by nothing heavier than small-arms fire and then, in accordance with Inoue's plan, the guns and mortars opened up and it was a repeat of Saipan and Guam. Twenty-six LVTs were knocked out. At about 1630, Nakagawa hit between the 1st and 5th Marines in a tank-infantry thrust. His attack was stopped cold, but by dark less than half the Marines' D-Day objectives

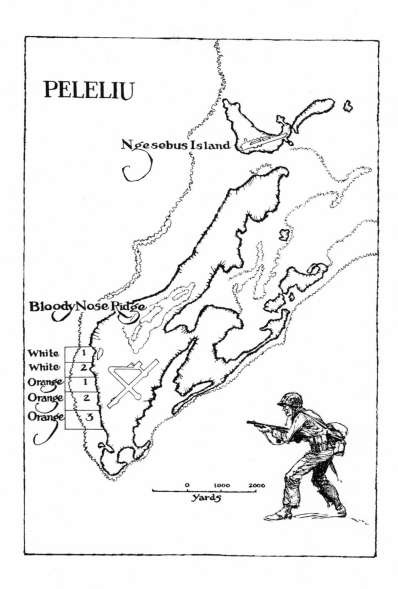

PELELIU

Ngesebus Island

Bloody Nose Ridge

White 1
White 2
Orange 1
Orange 2
Orange 3

0   1000   2000
Yards

had been taken. During the night there were probes but no major counterattacks, no senseless, drunken *banzais*. Next day, in the south, Hanneken's Marines moved well against what appeared to be one battalion. "Bucky" Harris's 5th Marines drove straight across the airfield, hurt most by artillery and mortars dropping on them from the ridge. Puller's 1st Marines butted their heads against what was already being called the "Bloody Nose." There was a general advance on the seventeenth, the 7th Marines finished cleaning out the southern tip, the 5th moved north of the airfield (130 ruined Japanese aircraft were counted), and the 1st Marines, at terrible cost, clawed a few yards farther up the slopes of Bloody Nose. On the twentieth, Geiger met with Rupertus and over Rupertus's objections told him to get ready to re-embark Puller's regiment, Geiger was bringing in the 321st RCT. The battered 1st Marines, with 1749 casualties (56 per cent) was relieved by the 7th Marines and started back for Pavuvu. The 321st (which, with the 322d RCT had taken Angaur in three days of fighting) landed on the twenty-third, moved up the coast road on the left of Bloody Nose ridge, and, using the road as a line of departure, attacked up the ridge on a broad front. It was decided to add a third prong to the attack by passing "Bucky" Harris's 5th Marines behind the 321st, having Harris clear the northern end of the island, and then attack south along the ridge. By nightfall on 26 September, the 5th Marines had swept the northern end but were bothered by heavy mortar fire coming from Ngesebus Island. On the twenty-eighth, the 3d Battalion, 5th Marines, made a shore-to-shore landing onto Ngesebus behind sixteen Sherman tanks and thunderously supported by naval gunfire, artillery, and close air support from VMF-114. (The Marine Corsair squadron had arrived two days earlier.)

This left just the center section of the Umurbrogol. By 1 October another Corsair squadron, VMF-122, had arrived and Marine Aircraft Group 11 was in place.

Delivering their ordnance a thousand yards from take-off, the Corsairs had two novelties to offer—rockets and napalm. On the twelfth the island was declared "secure," and a few days later the 81st Division relieved the 1st Marine Division. In a battle in many ways worse than Tarawa, Rupertus had taken 6265 casualties, 1241 of them dead. The Marines had buried 10,695 Japanese and taken 301 prisoners. Ironically, MacArthur was already on his way back to the Philippines and Peleliu wasn't really needed.

Night Fighters and Marine Carriers

Also present at Peleliu was VMF(N)-541, a Marine night-fighter squadron equipped with Grumman Hellcats. The first night-fighting squadron, VMF(N)-531, had been activated at Cherry Point in November 1942. The only aircraft then available were surplus PV-1s—twin-engined Lockheed Vega Venturas which were really patrol aircraft. Later squadrons were given radar-equipped F4U Corsairs and F6F Hellcats, but a single-place fighter wasn't the complete answer either. A second man was needed to work the radar. Even so, the one Japanese aircraft shot down in the Palaus by a Marine was on the night of 31 October by VMF(N)-541.

Two more Marine fighter squadrons and a torpedo-bomber squadron arrived on Peleliu in October and, after the island was finally secured, took up the sometimes dangerous "milk run" neutralization of the remaining Palaus and bypassed Yap. The 2d Marine Aircraft Wing, coming up from the New Hebrides, was designated Garrison Air Force, Western Carolines, with two operating groups, MAGs 11 and 25.

In April 1944, a 9th Marine Aircraft Wing had been activated at Cherry Point and in May the 3d MAW had come out to Ewa. As of the end of June, Marine aviation had a strength of 5 wings, 28 groups, 126 aircraft squadrons, and 112,626 personnel, of whom 10,457 were pilots. In August, General Vandegrift went

out to Pearl Harbor to confer with Admiral Chester
Nimitz on the question, once again raised, of putting
Marines back on board aircraft carriers. It was decided
that Marines would be put on a certain number of
escort carriers, or CVEs, of which the Navy now had
35.

In the Central Pacific the 4th MBDAW, with Louis
Woods, now a major general, as its commander,
dropped the "Base Defense" from its designator and
became simply the 4th Marine Aircraft Wing." Also, in
October 1944, Marine Carrier Groups, Aircraft, Fleet
Marine Force Pacific, was activated in Santa Barbara,
California, to get on with the implementation of the
Nimitz-Vandegrift decision. There were to be eight
carrier air groups, each with an eighteen-plane fighter
squadron and a twelve-plane torpedo-bomber squad-
ron. The fighters would be F4Us (greatly improved
since rejected by the Navy as carrier fighters in 1942)
and the torpedo bombers TBMs, the latter being the
General Motors model of the Grumman Avenger. The
Marine Corps had also gotten into the medium-bomber
business, apparently for no reason other than that the
Army Air Force was overstocked with North American
Mitchell B-25s (which the Navy called PBJs). Eventually, five squadrons of Marine PBJs would serve in the
South and Southwest Pacific and two in the Central
Pacific.

The Philippines

The reoccupation of the Philippines began on 20 October 1944 with landings on the east coast of Leyte by X
and XXIV Corps. On loan to XXIV Corps were 1528
Marines, mostly from V Phib Corps artillery, and a sign
sprang up on the beach, "By grace of God and a few
Marines, MacArthur's back in the Philippines." Also
present was Major General Ralph Mitchell, who was
looking for work for his underemployed 1st Marine

Aircraft Wing which was still in the northern Solomons.

The Leyte landings caused the Japanese Combined Fleet to sortie and the Battle for Leyte Gulf resulted, a decisive affair fought in three parts and one in which the new Japanese *kamikaze* tactic of slamming aircraft into ships caused much consternation. General Mitchell, ashore at muddy Tacloban airfield on 25 October, worked a pair of signal flags to help bring in forty Navy planes that had lost their carrier decks. But when the battle was over, the Imperial Navy, in the postwar words of one Japanese reporter, "as a Navy, had ceased to exist."

MacArthur wanted the Marine night-fighter squadron at Peleliu moved up to Leyte and on 3 December, VMF(N)-541 came in at Tacloban with its F6F Hellcats. MAG-12's four squadrons of FG-1s, the Goodyear version of the Corsair, began arriving a few hours later, and, by the end of the first week of December, five Marine squadrons totaling eighty-seven aircraft were trying to operate from the mud of Tacloban. On 7 December, Marine air helped cover a landing by the 77th Division on the west side of Leyte south of Ormoc. The Japanese made a desperate effort to reinforce and there were transports and destroyers to sink as well as bombers and fighters to battle.

The Army landed on Mindoro on 15 December against no opposition, Marines contributing to the air cover and also flying interdiction strikes against Japanese fields on Luzon. Late in the month MAG-12 moved from muddy, crowded Tacloban seven miles south to Tanauan, an airstrip made of Marston matting laid over beach sand. MAG-14, meanwhile, was in the process of moving north from Green Island to a coral strip at Guian on Samar. When the Sixth Army's landings at Lingayen on Luzon began 9 January 1945, both MAG-12 and -14 were in support.

Colonel Clayton C. Jerome, CO of MAG-32, and

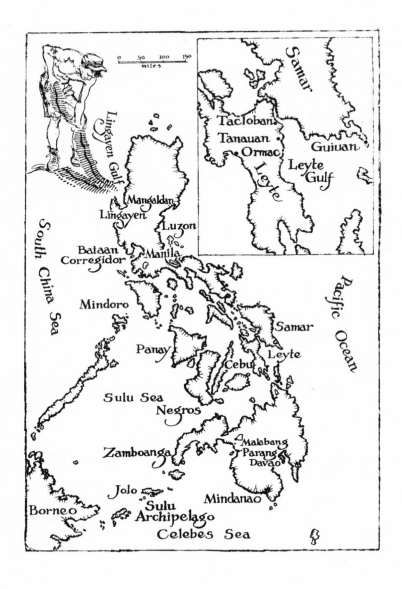

0 50 100 150
miles

Lingayen Gulf

Mangaldan
Lingayen
Luzon
Manila
Bataan
Corregidor

South China Sea

Mindoro

Panay

Cebu

Sulu Sea
Negros

Zamboanga

Jolo
Sulu
Archipelago

Borneo

Celebes Sea

Samar
Leyte

Pacific Ocean

Malabang
Parang
Davao

Mindanao

Samar
Tacloban
Tanauan
Ormac
Guiuan
Leyte
Gulf
Leyte

Lieutenant Colonel Keith McCutcheon, operations officer of MAG-24, went ashore at Lingayen on 11 January with a jeep and a driver and found a seasonally dry rice paddy at Mangaldan. Bulldozers went to work, first Marine SBDs began to arrive on 25 January, and by the month's end, seven squadrons of Marine dive bombers, 174 aircraft in all, were present and ready for operations. Preparations for the move of MAGs 24 and 32 to the Philippines had begun in October at Bougainville, dedicated to the principle, in McCutcheon's words, that "close air support aviation is only an additional weapon to be employed at the discretion of the ground commander."

Colonel Jerome, as senior Marine officer present, commanded MAGSDAGUPAN ("Marine Aircraft Groups, Dagupan"). First strikes were flown on 27 January. MAGSDAGUPAN was to give priority of support to the 1st Cavalry Division in its drive for Manila. The dash got under way on 1 February and the cavalrymen reached the city in sixty-six hours (although complete reduction of the Japanese defenses would require almost a month's more hard fighting). Twelve miles northwest of Manila General Yamashita had eighty thousand troops invested in the twenty-five-mile-long Shimbu Line. MAGSDAGUPAN would pound this line for the next several weeks and give some measure of support to all ten U. S. divisions operating on Luzon plus five "regiments" of guerrillas who were roaming the mountains and jungles.

Next came Zamboanga, a tail-like appendage extending southwest from the big island of Mindanao. The U. S. 41st Infantry Division put two regiments ashore there on 10 March. Jerome and McCutcheon followed the GIs to San Roque field, a mile inland. The first Corsair landed on 14 March, and the next day Marines were flying missions. The new aggregation— MAGs 12, 24, and 32—was called MAGZAM (Marine Aircraft Groups, Zamboanga) and it would eventually total 293 aircraft. MAG-14 would stay on Samar but would furnish close support to operations on neighboring Panay and Cebu, as well as longer-legged missions to Mindanao.

There was a series of Army D-Days to be supported: the 40th Division's landing on Panay on 18 March, the Americal Division's landing on Cebu on 26 March, the 40th Division's landing on Negros on 29 March, the 41st Division's operations in the Tawatawi group stretching to the southwest (particularly the Jolo island landing on 9 April), and toughest nut of all, the main landings on Mindanao. X Corps was to land at Parang on the south coast on 17 April. MAG-24, still in Luzon, was to support from Malabang field which was held by guerrillas. Flight operations stopped at Mangaldan on 14 April (which was just as well—spring rains were dissolving the rice-paddy airstrip) and the Group staged down to Malabang on Mindanao. The 24th Division, covered by Marine air, took Davao, Mindanao's principal city, on 3 May.

Iwo Jima

Think of a bad-smelling pork chop, burned black, five miles long and two and a half miles wide, about eight square miles in all, and that was Iwo Jima. It lay in the Volcano-Bonin archipelago, almost at the midpoint of a line drawn from the B-29 bases on Tinian and the home islands—seven hundred miles from the Marianas, six hundred sixty miles from Tokyo. The Japanese had completed two airfields on the island and were working on a third. Although the bony knob at the shank end of the pork chop, five-hundred-fifty-six-foot-high Mount Suribachi, was itself extinct, the core of the island was still hot. The volcanic rock tunneled easily and the loose black sand combined well with cement to make a first-class concrete.

Short, squat fifty-four-year-old Lieutenant General Tadamichi Kuribayashi commanded at Iwo. In what was nominally the 109th Infantry Division, he had the

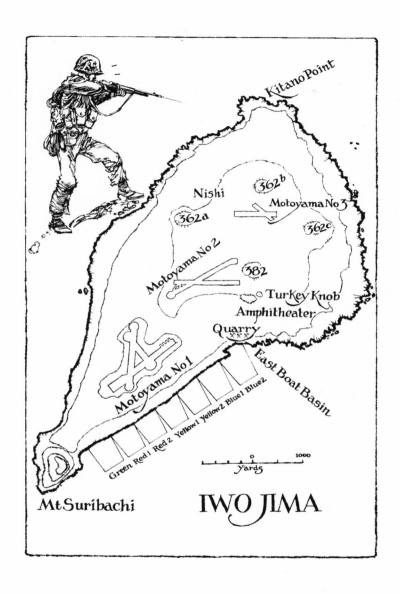

Kitano Point

Nishi

362b

Motoyama No 3

362a

362c

Motoyama No 2

382

Turkey Knob

Amphitheater

Quarry

Motoyama No 1

East Boat Basin

Green Red 1 Red 2 Yellow 1 Yellow 2 Blue 1 Blue 2

0   1000

Yards

Mt Suribachi

IWO JIMA

2d Independent Mixed Brigade, the 145th Infantry Regiment, a battalion of the 17th Regiment, a brigade artillery group, and the 26th Tank Regiment. In the artillery group there were five antitank battalions, also batteries ranging from 70-mm to 8-inch coast defense guns, all kinds of mortars, including a new 320-mm spigot mortar, and rockets improvised from 8-inch naval shells. There was also a naval force, mostly antiaircraft and construction. Suribachi with seven successive galleries of defenses was a fortress in itself. North of Suribachi a broad belt of fortifications passed across the island between Airfields 1 and 2 and another belt filled the space north of Airfield 2. Kuribayashi had published a set of "Courageous Battle Vows" and these were pasted to the inner walls of the pillboxes. One of the vows was "Each man will make it his duty to kill ten of the enemy before dying." In all, there were about twenty-three thousand Japanese defenders.

For the assault against Iwo Jima, Lieutenant General Holland Smith would again be Commanding General, Expeditionary Troops. Landing Force was the V Amphibious Corps under Major General Harry Schmidt and there would be three Marine divisions. The 4th Division, commanded by Clifton Cates, would come forward from Hawaii as would the 5th Marine Division, new and untried but well salted, commanded by Major General Keller E. Rockey (sometimes called "the Great Stone Face"). In floating reserve would be the 3d Division coming from Guam and led by Graves B. ("the Big E") Erskine.

D-Day was first set for 20 January 1945 but when the Fleet got involved in the Philippines this was postponed, first until 3 February, and then a second time until 19 February. The photo interpreters had pegged a total of 642 blockhouses, pillboxes, and gun positions. There was a drumfire of carefully targeted Army and Navy air attacks for the seventy-four days before the landing. The immediate prelanding preparation was limited to three days, not as much time as the Marines would have liked. Prevailing winds dictated the choice of the eastern beaches, left flank almost at the foot of Suribachi, right flank at East Boat Basin. As there was no fringing reef, landing craft would be able to beach. There were to be seven assault battalions and the beaches from left to right were Green, Red One, Red Two, Yellow One, Yellow Two, Blue One, and Blue Two. The first wave of armored amphibian tractors touched down at 0902 and the troop-carrying tractors began disgorging their passengers three minutes later. There was nothing to oppose them except some small-arms fire and an occasional mortar shell. Rockey's 5th Marine Division landed across the Green and Red beaches, the 28th Marines on the left, 27th Marines on the right. The 28th Marines were to turn left and take Suribachi while the 27th Marines cut across the island. Cates's 4th Division, meanwhile, with the 23d and 25th Marines landing across Yellow and Blue beaches, would move against Airfield No. 1. That was the plan and by 0945 all seven assault battalions were ashore.

Then the pounding started as Kuribayashi brought all his carefully ranged guns and mortars to bear along with the deadly scissors of crisscrossing automatic fire. Gunnery Sergeant "Manila John" Basilone, now commanding a machine-gun platoon in the 1st Battalion, 27th Marines, said, "Come on, you guys, we got to get these guns off the beach," started over the rise, and was killed. From late morning until early afternoon virtually no landing craft could make the shore. Wheeled vehicles could not move through the sand. Tracked vehicles did little better. Tanks ran into deadly 47-mm fire. What artillery was ashore had to set up in the open, almost abreast of the infantry. Not until late afternoon did the reserves begin to land. At 1800, when the advance ended for the day, the Marine beachhead swung in an undulating line from the base of Suribachi around the southern edge of the airfield to the East Boat Basin just beyond the right flank of the landing beaches. That night, there were probes by infiltrators and bypassed defenders popped up here and there but no big wild *banzai*. In the morning the Marines continued the attack. Cates's 4th Division was to wheel northward. Rockey's 5th Division was to go in two directions: the 27th Marines were to hook around to the north on the west side of Airfield No. 1 in coordination with the 4th Division while the 28th Marines went against Suribachi.

Liversedge had the 28th Marines and he started up Suribachi at 0830 on 20 February, his 2d and 3d Battalions in the assault, the 1st in reserve. A day's fighting gained the regiment two hundred yards. Next morning they were at it again, all three battalions in line. The Japanese erupted from the mountain in a counterattack. It failed. The attack against Suribachi beat its way up hill again on the twenty-second. Next morning the mountaintop seemed silent. A squad-sized patrol went forward, feeling its way. It was followed by a larger, platoon-sized patrol. There was a short hard fight and the crest was taken. It was about 1015, 23 February. The lieutenant had a small American flag. He and his Marines put it on the end of a piece of Japanese pipe and stood it up on the hilltop. A couple of hours later a four-man patrol brought up a larger flag from LST 779. It was fastened to another pipe; the four Marines had trouble getting it into position so another Marine and a hospital corpsman gave them a hand. Associated Press photographer Joe Rosenthal took their picture.

Suribachi had been taken, but the attack to the north had come almost to a halt. The belt of fortifications between the Airfields No. 1 and No. 2 had no flanks and it was worse than Suribachi. On D-Plus-One, the 27th Marines on the left had made good gains. In the center, the 23d Marines stayed abreast, but on the right, against the toughest resistance, the 25th Marines had barely made two hundred yards. Next day, 21 February, the 26th Marines passed through the 27th Marines in the 5th Division's zone, while the 21st Marines came

ashore and relieved the 23d Marines. Harry Schmidt
decided the main effort against Airfield No. 2 would be
in the zone of the fresh 21st Marines. They attacked on
the twenty-fourth, behind a thunderous preparation by
naval gunfire, artillery, and carrier-based air, and supported by all the tanks that could be mustered from
both the 4th and 5th Divisions. Fifteen tanks got loose
on Airfield No. 2, and in an hour and a half the 21st
Marines ("fighting on a pool table . . .") had advanced
half a mile.

Erskine was now ashore with the rest of the 3d
Marine Division (except for the 3d Marines which
stayed afloat as a last reserve) and Schmidt put him
into the center of the line. The 9th Marines (the
"Striking Ninth") passed through the 21st Marines and
after three days of hard fighting held two hills north of
Airfield No. 2. Next afternoon, 28 February, the 21st
came back into the attack, took the ruined rubble of
Motoyama village, and started up into the hills overlooking unfinished Airfield No. 3. On 3d Division's
right, Cates's 4th Division was fighting hard for Hill
382 and on their left, Rockey's 5th Division was
stopped by Hill 362A. Schmidt now shifted the weight
of his attack to his flank divisions. The 28th Marines
were brought north from Suribachi, attacked Hill 362A
on 1 March, and by nightfall had the crest. The 4th
Division called Hill 382 the "Meatgrinder." It was 2
March before the 2d Battalion, 24th Marines, succeeded in sticking to the top of the hill.

There were two more hills numbered "362," but
quite separate from Hill 362A. Hill 362B, in the 5th
Division zone, was taken on 3 March by the 26th
Marines. Hill 362C, in the 3d Division's zone, was
defended by the dismounted 26th Tank Regiment. They
fought hard and were compressed into Cushman's
Pocket (named for "Bob" Cushman's heavily engaged
2d Battalion, 9th Marines). On 7 March, Erskine's 3d
Division made a silent predawn attack with no artillery
preparation, took the tankers by surprise, and made a

good advance. Two days later the 3d Division plunged forward again, broke their way through to Iwo's northeastern shore. The 9th Marines faced east toward the 4th Division, the 21st Marines faced west toward the 5th Division, and the final compression began. The remaining defenders made a last wild counterattack against the 4th Division the night of 8 March, getting at the juncture of the 23d and 24th Marines. After that it was simply a case of mopping up. Last die-hards were eliminated on Turkey Knob and in the Amphitheater on 10 March, and 4th Division patrols pushed on to the northeast coast.

Rockey's 5th Division still had a powerful Japanese remnant under Kuribayashi's personal command in front of them at Kitano Point, the northwestern tip of the pork chop. With help from Erskine's 3d Division, Kitano Point was taken on 26 March and the island was declared secured. That night a shapeless last-ditch counterattack hit the 5th Pioneer Battalion near Airfield No. 2. There were many Japanese officers among the attackers (forty *samurai* swords were picked up later) and it was rumored that one of the 223 dead was Kuribayashi. On 16 March he had sent a last message to Imperial General Headquarters: "I . . . humbly apologize to His Majesty that I have failed to live up to expectations. . . . Bullets are gone and water exhausted. . . . Permit me to say farewell. . . ."

Of the 71,245 Marines who had gone ashore, 5931 had been killed, 17,372 wounded. Admiral Nimitz could well have been speaking for both attacker and defender when he said of this bitterly fought battle, "Uncommon valor was a common virtue."

Okinawa

One of the consequences of heavy Navy losses to the *kamikazes* was to put Marine fighter squadrons on board the big attack carriers. VMFs 124 and 213 in the *Essex* took part in Admiral William F. Halsey's great

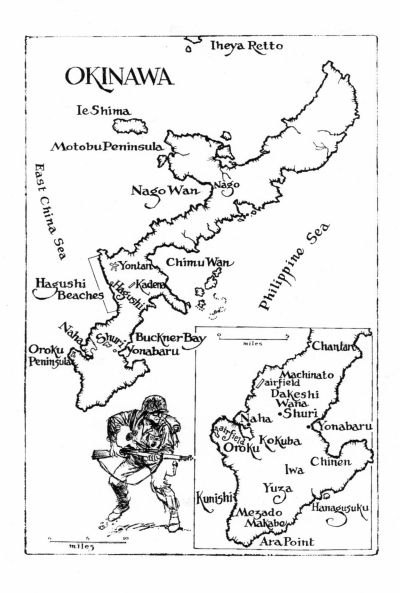

OKINAWA

Iheya Retto

Ie Shima

Motobu Peninsula

East China Sea

Nago Wan · Nago

Yontan · Chimu Wan

Hagushi Beaches · Hagushi · Kadena

Naha · Shuri · Buckner Bay
Yonabaru

Oroku Peninsula

Philippine Sea

miles

Chantan

Machinato airfield
Dakeshi
Wana · Shuri
Naha
airfield · Kokuba · Yonabaru
Oroku
Chinen
Iwa
Kunishi · Yuza
Mezado · Hanagusuku
Makabe
Ara Point

miles
0   5   10

raid against the Indo-China ports and airfields in January 1945, and when Admiral Raymond A. Spruance sent his fast carrier task force against the Japanese home islands, during Iwo Jima, there were eight Marine squadrons on board the *Bennington, Bunker Hill, Essex,* and *Wasp.* In mid-March, the Marine squadrons in the *Essex* and *Wasp* were replaced with all-Navy air groups, but the *Franklin* had come out with two fresh Marine squadrons. She had just joined Vice Admiral Marc A. Mitscher's task force when on 19 March, a little after daybreak and fifty-five miles off Japan's coast, a Japanese plane put two bombs into her flight deck. She was gutted and VMFs 214 and 452 were knocked out of the war after only two days' carrier combat. This left four squadrons operational in the *Bunker Hill* and *Bennington.* Both carriers would have a part to play in the seizure of Okinawa.

Okinawa would be the point of final intersection of Nimitz's drive across the Central Pacific and MacArthur's march up from the Southwest Pacific. The island was about sixty miles long and from two to eighteen miles wide, looking something like a long skinny insect with a number of peninsular legs sticking out each side. The northern part was wild and mountainous; the south, below the narrow Ishikawa waist, was more open, heavily cultivated, but still hilly with several ridges crossing the island from east to west.

Spruance would be in overall charge of the operation. Kelly Turner, with 1213 ships, would once again have the Joint Expeditionary Force. Lieutenant General Simon Bolivar Buckner, Jr., USA, who had the Tenth Army, would command the Expeditionary Troops ashore. Under him he would have as Northern Landing Force the III Amphibious Corps, still commanded by Roy Geiger, with the 1st and 6th Marine Divisions. Southern Landing Force would be the XXIV U. S. Army Corps under Major General John R. Hodge, USA, with the 7th, 77th, and 96th Divisions. The 2d Marine Division would go along as a demonstration force and the 27th Division would be in floating reserve.

All the land-based air support was grouped under Tactical Air Force, Tenth Army, with Marine Major General Francis Mulcahy as tactical air commander. Carrier-based air support came more directly under Turner and included eighteen escort carriers (of which four had Marine squadrons on board) and also the planes from the big carriers of TF 58 when they were sent in to help.

By official count there were 182,112 men in the Tenth Army of whom 81,165 were Marines. L-Day was to be Sunday, 1 April 1945, which was both Easter and April Fool's Day. Naval gunfire and air preparation began seven days before the landing. On 26 March a Marine reconnaissance battalion and two regiments of the 77th Division took five islands of the Kerama Retto group thirty miles west of Okinawa against light resistance. On L-Day the 2d Marine Division was to feint a landing in the extreme south while the two corps landed abreast over the Hagushi beaches on the western side of the island close to Yontan and Kadena airfields. After cutting the island in half, III Corps would swing north and XXIV Corps, making the main effort, would go south toward Shuri Castle and Naha.

The 2d Marine Division under Major General LeRoy P. Hunt lost a transport and an LST to a *kamikaze* attack shortly after dawn while getting into position for the demonstration. The landing craft embarked their troops, made their run in toward the beach, and then turned away. Meanwhile, the real landing was under way with touchdown scheduled for 0830. From left to right, the 6th and 1st Marine Divisions were landing on the northern or Blue Beaches and the 7th and 96th Infantry Divisions were coming across the southern or Purple Beaches, each division with two regiments abreast. By noon Shepherd's 6th Division had taken Yontan airfield. (After Guam, the 1st Provisional Marine Brigade had added the 29th Marines and became

the 6th Marine Division.) By 4 April Major General
Pedro del Valle's 1st Marine Division had cut across
the island and secured Katchin peninsula. XXIV Corps
on his right flank had taken Kadena airfield on 2 April
and by 4 April had swung to the right into a line of four
regiments stretching across the narrow waist of the
island. So far the fighting had been negligible. The
Japanese were known to have from 55,000 to 65,000
troops on the island. Where were they?

The highly capable Lieutenant General Mitsuru Ushijima had elected not to defend the beaches or the
airfields. In his "Battle Instruction Number 8," issued 8
March 1945, Ushijima said: ". . . we must make it our
basic principle to allow the enemy to land in full . . .
until he can be lured into a position where he cannot
receive cover and support from the naval gunfire and
aerial bombardment, we must patiently and prudently
hold our fire. Then, leaping into action, we shall open
fire and wipe out the enemy. . . ." His Thirty-second
Army included two divisions, a brigade, a tank regiment, and a great deal of artillery. He had concentrated
his strength in the south. Using the east-west ridges, he
had organized three defense lines. The first followed
Kakazu ridge. The second and strongest was in front of
Shuri Castle and covered the capital city of Naha. The
third line was well to the south and passed through
Kunishi ridge. Ushijima himself was in a command
post dug in under Shuri Castle. (It had been nearly a
hundred years since Commodore Perry had marched
his bluejackets and Marines to Shuri Castle—to the
consternation and ultimate undoing of the elderly
Regent.)

It was against Ushijima's first line that XXIV Corps
moved on 4 April, 7th Division on the left and 96th on
the right. The advance ground to a stop on the slopes of
Kakazu ridge and by the twelfth, the day of Roosevelt's
death, all forward momentum had been lost. The 27th
Division was moved into line on the right of the 96th
and a three-division attack jumped off on 19 April. A

mile-wide gap opened between the 27th and the 96th, and it took eight days of hard fighting before Kakazu ridge was cleared.

On the northern end of the island Shepherd's 6th Division had swung to the left to take Motobu peninsula, above Nago Bay, beginning the attack on 12 April with his new regiment, the 29th Marines. The key piece of terrain, twelve-hundred-foot Yae Take, proved more than the 29th Marines could handle by themselves. The veteran 4th Marines moved up to help, got to the top of the Yae Take on 16 April, and by the nineteenth the fight for Motobu was over. The 22d Marines in the meantime had reached the northern end of the island.

Buckner's problem now was how to get things moving in the south. The Marines were urging an amphibious landing to turn the enemy position. The 2d Marine Division was available and General Vandegrift, who visited Okinawa on 21 April, seconded Geiger's nomination that it be used, but Buckner decided in favor of a shoulder-to-shoulder frontal assault. On 27 April Del Valle's 1st Marine Division was assigned to XXIV Corps and on 1 May relieved the badly battered 27th Division. The 77th Division also moved into line, relieving the 96th Division, so that the Corps front, from left to right, was 7th Division, 77th Division, and 1st Marine Division.

On 4 May, Ushijima "leaped into action" all along the line, his tanks and infantry coming in close behind a drumfire artillery preparation. The Corps front was briefly punctured at the 7th and 77th Division boundary. Buckner ordered Geiger to join him on the southern front with the rest of III Phib Corps. Mopping up in the north was turned over to the 27th Division and the 6th Marine Division moved in on the extreme right flank of the line, the 1st Division sliding over to the left. It was now a two-corps front: Geiger's III Amphibious Corps on the right, Hodge's XXIV Corps on the left. In front of the 1st Marine Division was Dakeshi ridge and beyond that was Wana ridge. In front of the 6th Marine

Division was the western anchor of the Shuri line, a complex of low, rounded hills dominated by "Sugar Loaf." A general advance began on 11 May.

The 22d Marines crossed the Asa Kawa by footbridge and two days later were clawing their way up Sugar Loaf. It was then joined by the 29th Marines, and by the eighteenth the Shuri line had been breached. The 4th Marines relieved the 29th Marines, threw off a night counterattack, and continued to advance, crossing the Asato, and by 23 May, as the spring "plum rains" began to fall, the 6th Marine Division was on the outskirts of Naha.

Meanwhile, the 96th Division had taken Conical Hill, the eastern bastion of the Shuri line, and the 77th Division and 1st Marine Division were converging on Shuri Castle itself. On 12 May, the 7th Marines had gotten to the top of Dakeshi ridge and on 15 May started against Wana ridge. By the twenty-first, the 1st and 5th Marines were within assaulting distance of Shuri Castle itself.

Ushijima now decided to withdraw to his third and final defensive line. His columns on the roads south of Shuri were cut into bloody ribbons by air and naval gunfire; nevertheless, Ushijima completed his withdrawal in good order. The rear guard left at Shuri had been ordered to hold until 31 May. On the twenty-ninth, Company A, 5th Marines entered Shuri Castle and at 1015 reported it secured.

With a solid week of rain, the whole front had turned soggy. The Naval garrison, commanded by Rear Admiral Minoru Ota (who had defended Bairoko against Liversedge's Raiders), was still intact on Oroku peninsula. Shepherd, ordered to take the peninsula (a problem not unlike the one he had faced on Guam in taking Orote peninsula), elected to make a shore-to-shore landing. With the 22d Marines attacking on the landward side to seal off the base of the peninsula, the 4th Marines led off in the landing, touching down at 0600

on 4 June, followed later in the day by the 29th
Marines. All three Marine regiments joined to com-
press the Naval defenders into one last pocket near
Oroku village. (Ota signaled: "The Naval Base Force is
dying gloriously. . . .") The Ota Force was eliminated
on 14 June.

Ushijima's remnants of Kunishi ridge still showed
fight. Del Valle's 1st Marine Division started against
the ridge. The 7th Marines crossed half a mile of flat
paddy land on 11 June in a night attack and four days
later got to the crest. On the eighteenth, the 8th
Marines, brought in from Saipan, relieved the 7th.
General Buckner, watching them jump off from the
Division observation post, was struck by fragments of
a Japanese shell and ten minutes later was dead.
Geiger, by seniority, became as of that minute Commanding General, Tenth Army, the first Marine to
command a field army.

Marine Air at Okinawa

III Phib Corps' four "VMOs" (or light observation
squadrons) with their "Grasshoppers" had moved into
Yontan and Kadena airfields immediately after the
landing. Within a week Marine Aircraft Group 31 was
operating its F4U Vought Corsairs from Yontan and a
few days later MAG-33 was at Kadena, so that within
ten days of the landing, two hundred Marine aircraft
were shore-based. MAG-22 arrived in May from Midway and was put in at Ie Shima an offshore island
taken by the 77th Division. In June, MAG-14 came up
from the Philippines. In all, at final count, there were
twenty-two Marine squadrons ashore.

In addition, there was some support from ten Marine
squadrons at sea. The escort carrier *Block Island*, with
its squadrons of Corsairs, Hellcats, and Avengers flew
its first strike on 10 May, and was joined on 21 May by
the *Gilbert Islands*. Both carriers, however, were used

more to neutralize the airfields in Sakishima Gunto, midway between Okinawa and Formosa, than in direct support of the ground fighting. Two *kamikazes* got to the attack carrier *Bunker Hill* on 11 May. This left just the two squadrons in the *Bennington*: VMFs 112 and 123. In almost continuous combat from 16 February to 8 June 1945, the two squadrons had shot down 82 enemy planes, destroyed 149 more on the ground, dropped over 100 tons of bombs, and fired more than 4000 rockets. Their own losses were 18 pilots killed, 48 planes lost.

The End

On 21 June General Geiger announced that "all organized resistance has ceased" and next morning, at 1000, there was a formal flag-raising in front of Tenth Army headquarters. That same day, Lieutenant General Mitsura Ushijima dressed himself in full uniform, and told his chief of staff, Lieutenant General Cho, "I'll take along my fan since it is getting warm." The two generals made the ceremonial abdominal cuts and then their adjutant took off their heads with his sword. Three days later patrols from the 32d Infantry found their graves.

In all its dimensions Okinawa had been the biggest amphibious operation of the Pacific war. A total of 107,539 Japanese and Okinawans had been killed on the island; 7401 had been taken prisoner. The Japanese had lost 7830 airplanes, 3041 of them shot down by Navy and Marine pilots. The United States had lost 768 planes. The U. S. Navy had lost 36 ships sunk, 368 damaged, more than at Pearl Harbor, and the number of Navy dead, 4907, exceeded the total of either the Army or Marines. The Marines had lost 2899 killed, 345 died of wounds, and 11,677 wounded.

On 2 September 1945, the Japanese officially surrendered aboard the battleship *Missouri* in Tokyo Bay.

Standing little-noticed on a deck filled with U. S. and foreign dignitaries was one solitary senior Marine, Lieutenant General Roy Geiger, who had succeeded Holland Smith as Commanding General, Fleet Marine Force, Pacific.

14

1946–1950

"...very serious and urgent matter..."

Occupation of Japan

On 10 August 1945 Japan sued for peace under terms
of the Potsdam Declaration and on 14 August President
Truman announced that the war had ended. The war
had cost the Marines 86,940 dead and wounded and
there had been eighty Medals of Honor. The Corps'
main effort was in the Pacific; but there had been
diverse employment for Marines around the globe.
There had been service afloat in the capital ships of the
Fleet. A few Marines had served with the British in
Europe and the Middle East. Others had been with the
partisans in Yugoslavia and some with the guerrillas in
the Philippines and China.

If Japan had not sued for peace, both the III and V
Amphibious Corps would have been involved in the
invasion of the Japanese home islands. As it was, when
the war ended, Halsey's Third Fleet was the closest
Allied force to the Empire. Task Force 31 was formed
to land at Yokosuka naval base near Tokyo. The 4th
Marines would come forward from Guam. Two other
regiments, provisional ones, were formed the old-fash-
ioned way from ships' crews and Marine detachments:

a three-battalion Fleet Marine Landing Force, and a three-battalion Naval Landing Force. The British carrier task force contributed a battalion of sailors and Royal Marines.

The reception they would get ashore was an unknown quantity; there was considerable apprehension as to possible treachery and last-ditch fanaticism. Task Force 31 dropped anchor in Tokyo Bay off Yokosuka on 28 August. After some cautious preliminaries, the 1st and 3d Battalions, 4th Marines, touched down on the beach in the main landing at 0930 on 30 August. White flags were everywhere and the few remaining Japanese were wearing white arm bands. That afternoon Nimitz and MacArthur also came ashore—MacArthur to stay for six years as Japan's virtual ruler.

A week later the provisional units were dissolved and their component parts went back to the Fleet. MAG-31 came up from Okinawa to be the supporting aircraft group. The survivors of the "old" 4th Marines, captured at Corregidor, were found and released from their captivity, and there was a formation at which they received the colors of the "new" 4th Regiment. By the end of December redeployments had brought the regiment down to a single battalion. In January 1946 the regimental headquarters left for Tsingtao to rejoin the 6th Marine Division and the remaining battalion was converted into the 2d Separate Guard Battalion and had little to do but police the Yokosuka naval base.

The V Amphibious Corps, still commanded by Harry Schmidt, was assigned the responsibility of occupying Kyushu. Major objectives were Nagasaki, still reeling from history's second atomic bombing, and Sasebo naval base. On 22 September the 5th Marine Division's transports arrived off Sasebo and were courteously directed to safe berths by Japanese pilots. The next day, the 2d Marine Division landed at Nagasaki. MAG-22 arrived from Okinawa and was operational before the month's end.

The Japanese were as docile and cooperative in

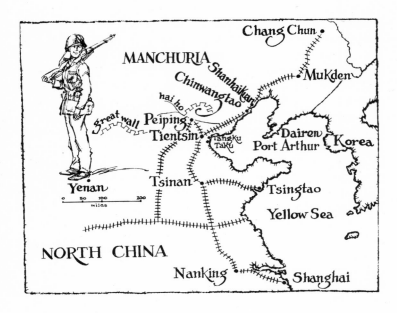

defeat as they had been fanatical and intransigent in battle. The 5th Marine Division left for home in December, followed in January by V Phib Corps headquarters. Both were deactivated in February 1946. The 2d Marine Division stayed on in Japan until June 1946.

Occupation of China

Occupation of North China proved less tranquil. Nominal mission for III Amphibious Corps, now under Keller Rockey, would be to disarm and repatriate the Japanese (there were 630,000 of them); more importantly and unwritten, the Marines were to get to North China before the Russians could come sweeping down from Manchuria and were to hold it against the Chinese Communists until the Chinese Nationalists could redeploy northward.

The 1st Marine Division, having come from Okinawa through the tail of a typhoon and an adventuresome passage through the mine-strewn Yellow Sea, arrived off Taku Bar during the early hours of 30 September 1945, landed administratively, and started their way up the Taku-Tientsin rail line, the same line traveled in 1900 and 1927 by Smedley Butler. The line was guarded by well-uniformed Chinese soldiers. The Marine rank-and-file thought them Chinese Nationalists; they were not. They were "puppet" troops under Japanese control. The 2d and 3d Battalions, 7th Marines, moved on into Tientsin without incident. The next day, 1st Battalion, 7th Marines, sailed from Taku for Chinwangtao, shipping point for the coal mines in Tangshan. It was held to be vital that 100,000 tons of coal be shipped to Shanghai each month, or else the public utilities and factories would shut down.

The headquarters of III Phib Corps and 1st Marine Division found opulent billeting in the European quarter of Tientsin; the 1st and 11th Marines were in and around the city. On 6 October General Rockey received the official surrender of fifty thousand troops in front of Tientsin's municipal building. The 5th Marines had gone on up to Peiping, the regimental headquarters establishing itself in the old Legation Guard Barracks. On 10 October, fifty thousand more Japanese were surrendered there. The Japanese prisoners were not immediately disarmed; the Americans were learning that they were the one disciplined force upon which they could depend.

Farther south, Lemuel Shepherd's 6th Marine Division had arrived at Tsingtao on 10 October. The Japanese garrison of ten thousand was surrendered at the race course on 25 October. Beyond the city limits, except for roads and rail lines held open by the Japanese, Shantung peninsula was under Communist control.

During October, the U. S. Fourteenth Air Force brought into Peiping the Ninety-second and Ninety-fourth Chinese Armies (some fifty thousand men—a Chinese Nationalist army equated to a U. S. division) and U. S. Navy amphibious shipping ferried the Thirteenth CNA to Chinwangtao. The Chinese Nationalists controlled the cities; the legendary Communist Eighth Route Army dominated the countryside. Also adrift were the puppet troops cast loose by the Japanese and independent "people's armies," indistinguishable from outright bandits. Against U. S. advice Chiang Kai-shek started moving his new strength north into Manchuria.

The 1st Marine Aircraft Wing set up its headquarters in the old French arsenal outside of Tientsin. MAGs 12 and 24 were at Peiping and MAGs 25 and 32 were at Tsingtao. On 31 October, Major General Claude E. Larkin passed command of the wing to Louis Woods.

By the first of November the Marines had formally accepted the responsibility for guarding all railroad bridges over a hundred meters in length and Marine guards were riding virtually all trains. On 14 and 15 November, Major General DeWitt Peck (who now had the 1st Marine Division) on an inspection trip from Tangshan to Chinwangtao had his train stopped twice by firing incidents, presaging more serious events to come.

Black Marines

Up until World War II, the Corps had thought of itself, not quite accurately, as all-male and all-white. Actually, the pay rolls of Captain Mullan's company show that he enlisted an "Isaac Walker, Negro" on 27 August 1776 and another recruit was shown on 1 October 1776 as "Orange . . . Negro." There were probably others. Hard-pressed recruiters in the Revolution were not apt to be finicky as to pedigree. But when the Marine Corps was re-created in 1798, the recruiting regulations, directed toward shipboard service, provided that "No Negro, Mulatto or Indian to be enlisted . . ." and there were specific instructions "not to enlist more Foreigners than as one to three natives." These precautions were thought necessary to insure the reliability and loyalty of the Marine guard. As late as 1852, a Navy commander would write Archibald Henderson: "It is useless to disguise the fact that the crews of our ships are now composed of foreigners and the most worthless class of our native population; with such materials to manage, a large guard of Marines is, in my judgment, highly desirable, if not absolutely necessary."

By mid-1941 President Roosevelt had taken steps to erase discrimination in the Armed Forces and General Holcomb, eyeing the probability that Negroes would be coming into the Corps, directed a study be made as to how they could best be used. A board headed by Keller Rockey, then a brigadier general, recommended they be used in a composite defense battalion.

Soon after the war began, the Corps was ordered to accept Negro enlistments. Colonel Samuel A. Woods, Jr. (who had entered the Marine Corps from the Citadel, Charleston, South Carolina, in 1916) was named to head the program. A training camp was built at Mumford (later changed to "Montford") Point across the New River from Camp Lejeune and the first recruits arrived in late August 1942. The new unit was designated the 51st Composite Defense Battalion.

In January 1943 a commissary or steward's branch was established. There were also to be Negro "pioneer infantry"—a euphemism for labor troops. At first, all black Marines were to be trained by the 51st Defense Battalion, but this load was lightened in March 1943 when a Recruit Depot Battalion was activated. Initially, all drill instructors and officers were white but the white NCOs were to be replaced as fast as black NCOs could be trained. Intermingling of "colored and white enlisted personnel" was to be avoided and in no case were "colored" NCOs to be senior to white men in the same outfit.

The 51st Defense Battalion left Montford Point on 20 January 1944, its departure a riotous affair which was later investigated and blown up out of all proportion.

The battalion, its strength on 31 January standing at 1478, sailed from San Diego and on 27 February arrived at Funafuti, Ellice Islands, a back-water of the war, where it relieved elements of the 7th Defense Battalion. In September 1944 it moved on to Eniwetok, where it relieved the 10th Antiaircraft Battalion, and in June 1945 a composite group from the battalion went to Kwajalein. In late November the battalion returned to the United States, arriving at Montford Point the day after Christmas. The men were put on leave and the battalion disbanded the end of January 1946.

There was also a 52d Defense Battalion, organized 15 December 1943, which departed from Montford Point on 19 August 1944, staged through San Diego and Pearl Harbor, and arrived at Roi-Namur on 22 October, relieving the 15th Antiaircraft Battalion. The 52d echeloned forward to Guam in May 1945 and in November, after the war's end, was divided into two groups. One went to Eniwetok, the other to Kwajalein—to defend against what threat is not clear. In January 1946, the men with the longest periods of obligated service remaining were put into a heavy antiaircraft group and sent to Saipan. The remainder of the battalion reassembled at Guam, sailed for San Diego in March, arrived at Montford Point in April, and were redesignated the 3d Antiaircraft Battalion in May. The Saipan Group was disbanded in February 1947, its remaining personnel being transferred into provisional depot companies.

Fifty-one Marine depot companies and twelve Marine ammunition companies were formed during the war. Assigned to Service Command, their job was to serve as shore party labor during landings and to work supply points in forward field depots and, by one of the vagaries of the war, these black Marine units saw more combat than the more selective Negro defense battalions. They did notably well, beginning at Saipan, through Tinian, Guam Peleliu, and Iwo, and on to Okinawa.

In truth, there had been no great rush of Negro

volunteers into the Marine Corps. Of a total of 19,168 black Americans who served during World War II, 16,039 were drafted. As late as April 1944, a Headquarters Marine Corps study was recommending against "colored" officers. A year later, the first three Negro officer candidates reported to Quantico. One was a sergeant major, two were first sergeants; all three were college graduates, but all three failed the course: one physically, the other two academically. The first Negro second lieutenant in the Marine Corps Reserve was commissioned on 10 November 1945. The war was over and with the rest of his class he was placed immediately on the inactive list. Not until 28 May 1948 did a Negro attain a Regular commission (but by 1971 there would be 288 black officers on active duty, including two lieutenant colonels).

For the peacetime Marine Corps, General Vandegrift approved a quota, not to exceed 10 per cent, of Negroes in the Corps but it was a puzzling problem as to where these segregated units could fit into the structure of the shrinking postwar Marine Corps. Then, in June 1949, the Secretary of the Navy decreed that "no distinction" was to be "made between individuals wearing the uniform. . . ." The segregated boot camp at Montford Point was closed in September 1949. By the eve of the Korean War, June 1950, of a strength of about 74,000 Marines in the Corps, some 1500 were Negroes; some in the steward's branch but most on general duty.

Women Marines

There had been "Reservists (Female)" in World War I. Authorized on 12 August 1918, three months before the Armistice, they had been recruited up to 305 members and called, by a bit of cloying whimsy, the "Marinettes." Despite, or perhaps because of this experience, the Marine Corps was the last of the four armed services to organize a Women's Reserve in World War II. Pressed and prodded on the issue, General Holcomb, with undisguised reluctance, wrote to the Secretary of the Navy on 12 October 1942: ". . . in furtherance of the war effort, it was believed that as many women as possible should be used in noncombatant billets, thus relieving a greater number of the limited manpower available for essential combat duty."

By Holcomb's own frequently recounted story, when he went home that night to the Commandant's House and announced his decision to bring women into the Corps, Archibald Henderson's portrait fell off the wall. President Roosevelt was more approving, and on 7 November 1942 the U. S. Marine Corps Women's Reserve was authorized. Mrs. Ruth Cheney Streeter of New Jersey was selected to head the program and was commissioned a major. Public announcement of the new Reserve was made on 13 February 1943. Total strength, to be attained by 30 June 1944, was set at 1000 officers and 18,000 enlisted women.

Officer candidates initially went to Mount Holyoke College in Massachusetts, and enlisted recruits went to Hunter College in the Bronx, New York. Uniforms were adaptations of regulation Marine "greens" and "blues." Lipstick was to match the winter cap cord and muffler, and was known to the trade as "Montezuma Red." Girdles were required articles of dress. In mid-summer 1943, training of both officers and enlisted women was shifted to Camp Lejeune and, at Mrs. Roosevelt's instigation, weapons instruction was included.

Women Marines could be assigned to any of over two hundred job classifications ranging alphabetically from "accountant" to "woodworking-machine operator," but the great majority filled clerical billets, and by June 1944 constituted 85 per cent of the enlisted personnel at Headquarters Marine Corps. When the war ended in August 1945, there were 820 women officers and 17,640 enlisted women, serving as far west as Hawaii, and General Vandegrift would remark they ". . . could feel responsible for putting the 6th Marine Division into the field."

By December 1945 two-thirds of them (including Ruth Streeter, promoted to colonel) had been released from active duty. It was planned that all would be gone by September 1946, but then a decision was made to keep a small cadre on active duty and in June 1948 integration of women into the Regular Marines was authorized.

Demobilization

Congress in 1945 set the peacetime strength of the Corps at 107,000, nearly six times its prewar size but less than a quarter of its peak wartime strength of 485,053. In the wartime structure, weighted entirely in the direction of the Pacific, there had been two corps, six divisions, and five aircraft wings. For peacetime it had been decided that there would be a Fleet Marine Force, Atlantic, as well as a Fleet Marine Force, Pacific, each with a division and wing (albeit at peacetime strengths) plus supporting combat and combat service units.

Discharges were regulated by a point system based on length of service, time overseas, wounds, and medals. The wartime formations as they came home were shrunk to cadres. The 4th Division (Saipan, Iwo Jima, Tinian) was deactivated in November 1945, followed by the 3d Division (Bougainville, Guam, Iwo Jima) in December. The 5th Division (Iwo Jima), home from Japan, went off the active list in January 1946. The 6th Division (Okinawa) would be disbanded in April 1946.

The 2d Division (Guadalcanal, Tarawa, Saipan, Tinian) on coming back from Japan in June 1946 was home-ported at Camp Lejeune with the 2d Wing close by at Cherry Point. The 1st Division (Guadalcanal, Cape Gloucester, Peleliu, Okinawa) on coming out of China would go to Camp Pendleton and its companion, the 1st Wing, to El Toro. There would also be a brigade on Guam.

In late 1946 the U. S. Mediterranean Squadron (later to be the Sixth Fleet) was re-established. Afloat with the squadron was a battalion landing team from the 2d Marine Division. Rotated at six-month intervals, it would see much use and service in the next quarter-century. The arrangement by which the Marines provided security guards to embassies and legations was formalized. (By 1972, ninety-seven diplomatic posts would have such guards, usually a seven- or eight-man detachment commanded by a staff noncommissioned officer, all trained and administered by the Marine Security Guard Battalion headquartered in Washington.) The Basic School for new second lieutenants (and for some older ones whose wartime training had been slighted) was re-established, not at Philadelphia Navy Yard, but at Quantico. The more advanced courses at Quantico were regularized into an Amphibious Warfare School with junior and senior courses. Personnel strengths had not yet bottomed out. By the end of 1946 they were plunging below the hundred thousand mark. There was a brief experiment, under the peculiar "J" tables of organization, with a division and brigade structure which would have separate battalions and no regimental echelon.

Unification and the Marine Corps

Following U. S. Army blueprints, there were strong pressures, endorsed by President Truman, for the "unification" of the U. S. Armed Forces, all Services to be merged under a single Department of War, with a single chief of staff and a national general staff. In the spring of 1946, there was a series of Congressional hearings on a bill encompassing most of the War Department's merger plan. The bill was beaten down, largely because of the stalwart countertestimony of General Vandegrift, but another similar bill appeared in 1947. The National Security Act, as it was passed in 1947, created the Department of Defense with the subordinate Departments of the Army, Navy, and Air Force. The future status of the Marine Corps was left unclear.

General Vandegrift's term as Commandant ended on 31 December 1947. The choosing of the next Commandant was up to President Truman. The two leading contenders, Clifton B. Cates and Lemuel C. Shepherd, Jr., offered remarkably similar credentials. How to choose between two such men? President Truman called them to the White House and told them that as a military man he had always believed in seniority. Said President Truman to General Shepherd: "General Cates is senior to you and he's older than you are. I'm going to make him Commandant this year, and I trust that I'll be able to have you follow him four years from now."

Clifton Bledsoe Cates, urbane, given to wearing a trench coat and seldom without a cigarette in a lengthy holder (perhaps out of kindness to his gas-injured lungs) thus became the nineteenth Commandant. Cates, who in combat had commanded every size unit, from platoon to division, now had a new battlefield: Capitol Hill, and the fight would be to keep the Marine Corps alive.

On 11 March 1948, James Forrestal, the first Secretary of Defense, assembled the chiefs of the Army, Navy, and new Air Force at Key West, Florida, for a four-day discussion of roles and missions. General Cates was not invited. After the conference, the press was informed that the Marines were not to constitute a second land army; that there would be a four-division ceiling on their wartime strength; and that a Marine would not exercise tactical command higher than corps level. A few days later, the ailing James Forrestal was replaced as Secretary of Defense by a West Virginia politician, Louis A. Johnson, who had little love for the Navy and none for the Marine Corps. Unopposed by a complaisant Secretary of the Navy, he directed sharp cuts in Fleet Marine Force strength for fiscal years

1949 and 1950 (the budget dollar is the device by which Congress regulates the size of the U. S. military establishment) so that FMF force structure came down to eight infantry battalions and twelve aircraft squadrons. (In a bit of pettiness, Johnson in 1949 also forbade the future official observance of the Marine Corps Birthday on 10 November. This prohibition was observed in the breach by round-the-world "private" parties. Even the most minuscule Marine Security Guard sponsors a party; these have come to rival, in foreign capitals, the U. S. ambassador's traditional Fourth of July reception.)

In the fall of 1949, there was another series of hearings before the House Armed Services Committee. In his testimony, Cates pointed out that the Marine Corps had no voice or vote in Joint Chiefs of Staff proceedings and that Secretary Johnson had quashed a proposal that the Commandant be allowed to sit in on JCS meetings treating items dealing with the Marine Corps. Sympathetic Congressmen drafted a bill making the Commandant of the Marine Corps a member of the JCS. The bill was not acted upon that year but the seed was sown.

End of the China Experience

In December 1945, General of the Army George C. Marshall had come out to China at President Truman's behest to attempt to mediate the differences between the Nationalists and the Communists. There was a brief cease-fire beginning 13 January 1946; then the situation worsened. For the Marines it meant dealing with blown bridges, derailments, and ambushes. Under the point system, combat veterans were going home by the thousands and for every two that went home there was only one replacement.

On 1 April 1946, the 6th Marine Division was deactivated and its remaining pieces reorganized into the 3d Brigade, its infantry core being the 4th Marines whose colors had come over from Japan. (Symbolically, if not actually, the 4th Marines, the old China regiment, had returned to China.) The Brigade did not last long. On 10 June, III Amphibious Corps was redesignated Marine Forces, China. Authorized strength was set at 24,252—less than half the strength of III Phib Corps when it landed in September 1945. The 3d Brigade was disbanded and the 4th Marines put under the 1st Marine Division. MAGs 25 and 32 left for home.

On 29 July 1946, a platoon-size motorized patrol from the 11th Marines, escorting a supply convoy, was ambushed at An Ping (where Seymour's column had turned back in 1900). Three Marines, including the lieutenant, were killed; twelve more were wounded.

On 1 August, the Tsingtao garrison was reduced to just the 3d Battalion, 4th Marines, and the rest of the regiment sailed for home. On 18 September, General Rockey turned over command of Marine Forces, China, to Major General Samuel Howard (who had commanded the 4th Marines when it was surrendered at Corregidor). In December, the 7th Marines left for the States and the reduced 11th Marines departed for Guam.

On the night of 4 April 1947, there was a stiffish raid against the ammunition supply point at Hsin Ho, near Tangku. Five Marines were killed, sixteen wounded. Soon thereafter, the headquarters of the 1st Marine Division and 1st Marine Aircraft Wing departed and on 1 May a new consolidated command, Fleet Marine Force, Western Pacific, was created. The 5th Marines sailed away in April and May and by the first of September 1947, all remaining Marines were concentrated at Tsingtao. Down to two infantry battalions, they were charged with the defense of the Seventh Fleet naval base and also with having a battalion ready for airlift to Shanghai, Nanking, or Tientsin, to go to the aid of American nationals if need be. (Under the short-lived "J" tables of organization that did away with the regimental echelon yet tried to keep the regimental numbers alive, the 2d Battalion, 1st Marines, had become the "1st Marines" and the 3d Battalion, 4th Marines, the "3d Marines.")

By the fall of 1948 Tsingtao had become an island in a Communist sea and the imminent collapse of the Chinese Nationalists was obvious to even the most sanguine. In December the battalion-size 9th Marines came forward from Guam, staged through Tsingtao, and went to Shanghai to assist in the evacuation of American nationals. The 1st Marines left Tsingtao in February 1949 and the 3d Marines went afloat in the harbor. They sailed for home in May, and by June 1949, the last Marine elements had cleared Tsingtao and China.

Vertical Envelopment

Amphibious assaults against fortified beaches had been written off by many military experts as a nuclear age improbability. General Omar Bradley, USA, Chairman of the Joint Chiefs, gave his opinion to the House Armed Services Committee that amphibious operations were a dead letter and that there would never again be another major amphibious assault.

At Quantico the thinking was otherwise. In July 1946, six months before his death, General Geiger, having viewed the Bikini bomb tests, wrote to General Vandegrift, ". . . it is trusted that Marine Corps Headquarters will consider this very serious and urgent matter and will use its most competent officers in finding a solution to develop the technique of conducting amphibious operations in the atomic age."

A board to study the matter was convened under General Shepherd, who had returned from China to become Assistant Commandant. Shepherd's report, delivered on 16 December 1946, recognized that wide dispersion had to be reconciled with control, flexibility, and concentration of striking power. It concluded that carrier-based helicopters offered the best possible solution to the critical ship-to-shore movement and it recommended the activation of an experimental helicopter squadron at Quantico. Within three days, Vandegrift had approved the report, but helicopters came more slowly.

On paper, there was a requirement for ten helicopter aircraft carriers and two hundred forty helicopters, each capable of lifting a squad. HMX-1, organized at the end of 1947, got its first five helos early in 1948. Each would lift, somewhat precariously, two passengers. In May, in a Marine Corps Schools amphibious command post exercise at Camp Lejeune, these early choppers simulated the landing of a regiment. Later in the year the Piasecki HRP-1, the "Flying Banana," and the first true transport helicopter, came into the inventory, and in November, Quantico published a slender pamphlet, bound in blue paper, "PHIB-31, Employment of Helicopters (Tentative)."

In June 1950, ten days before the North Koreans crossed into South Korea, President Truman came to Quantico to see a simulated helicopter assault. Not greatly impressed, the old National Guard battery commander grinned, patted the barrel of a 75-mm pack howitzer, and said, "I like this best."

15

1950–1953
"If I only had the 1st Marine Division...."

A Brigade for Korea

Before dawn on Sunday, 25 June 1950, Far Eastern
time, seven infantry divisions and one armored division
of the North Korean People's Army crossed the 38th
Parallel into South Korea. In Washington, in the frantic
first hours that followed, no one seemed to have time
for General Cates. On 29 June he buttonholed the Chief
of Naval Operations, Admiral Forrest Sherman, in the
halls of the Pentagon and offered a regimental combat
team and aircraft group for immediate service. Sherman was only mildly interested. The next day, Cates
got to see Navy Secretary Matthews, who said he
couldn't recall any discussion on the possibility of
using Marines in Korea. But at Cates's urging, Sherman on 1 July sent Vice Admiral C. Turner Joy,
commanding U. S. Naval Forces Far East, an eyes-only
message authorizing him to offer the Commander-in-
Chief Far East a Marine air-ground brigade. General
MacArthur, CINCFE, fired back a dispatch to the Joint
Chiefs of Staff asking for the Marines. MacArthur's
request was put on the JCS agenda for 3 July. Cates
arrived at the meeting uninvited but was allowed to sit

in. That night he was able to write on his desk calendar, "Attended JCS meeting. Orders for deployment of FMF approved." The next day, 4 July, Lemuel Shepherd, now a lieutenant general and Commanding General, Fleet Marine Force, Pacific, left Honolulu for Tokyo to confer with MacArthur, and took with him his G-3, "Brute" Krulak.

At Pendleton, on 7 July, the 1st Provisional Marine Brigade was stripped out of the skeleton 1st Marine Division and put under slender white-haired Brigadier General Edward A. Craig. Then fifty-four, Craig had been commissioned in 1917, had commanded the 9th Marines at Guam, and had been Schmidt's G-3 at Iwo. It would be an air-ground brigade. Core of the ground element would be the 5th Marines, commanded by Lieutenant Colonel Raymond L. Murray, a tall, rangy Texan who had fought exceedingly well at Guadalcanal. The air element of the Brigade would be Marine Aircraft Group 33 under Brigadier General Thomas H. Cushman. Cushman, who was also Deputy Brigade Commander, was fifty-five and like Craig had come into the Corps in 1917. He had been one of the aviation pioneers in Haiti and Nicaragua and during World War II had commanded a wing. There were three fighter-bomber squadrons, equipped with late model F4U Corsairs, in the Group. There was also a light observation squadron, VMO-6, just activated. VMO-6 was taking eight light OY airplanes (in the hope that four could be made to fly) and four two-place HO3S-1 Sikorsky helicopters hastily brought west from Quantico.

In Tokyo, MacArthur, meeting with Shepherd on 10 July, moved to his wall map of Korea and stabbed at the port of Inchon with the stem of his corncob pipe, "If I only had the 1st Marine Division under my command again, I would land them here. . . ." Shepherd told him that the rest of the 1st Marine Division could be ready by the first of September.

The Brigade, strength 6534, sailed from San Diego on 12 July. Craig and Cushman, who had gone on ahead by air with an advance party, met with MacArthur on the nineteenth. MacArthur reiterated that if the Division could be assembled by September he would land at Inchon, march to Seoul, cut North Korean lines of communication, and isolate the North Korean People's Army. Walker's Eighth Army would then break out of the Pusan perimeter and the North Korean invasion would be crushed in classic hammer-and-anvil fashion ninety days after it had begun.

The perimeter was roughly a quarter-circle drawn at a radius of a hundred miles from Pusan—although the front was by no means as definite or solid as lines on the map would indicate. By the last week of July, the whole business threatened to collapse and on the twenty-fifth MacArthur ordered the Brigade to Pusan as the last available reserve. The 24th and 1st Cavalry Divisions, badly understrength, were in process of falling back to new positions along the Naktong, while the 25th Division had been shifted to the Western flank to cover Chinju. The Brigade would have to act as kind of a fire brigade.

Pusan Perimeter

First elements of the Brigade came ashore at Pusan on 2 August. At dawn the next day, the 5th Marines moved west some forty miles by truck and rail to an assembly area at Changwon. By now the NKPA were pressing close to Masan and the Brigade was given Sachon as its objective as part of a 25th Division counterattack. The 5th Marines jumped off on 7 August, eighth anniversary of their landing at Guadalcanal. The soldiers of the 25th Division watched with outspoken envy and admiration the quality of close air support delivered by the Corsairs. Cushman's two day fighter-bomber squadrons, VMF-214 and VMF-323 with their gull-winged F4Us, were working from the aircraft carriers USS *Sicily* and *Badoeng Strait*. The night fighter squadron, VMF(N)-513, was at Itazuke in

MANCHURIA

Yalu River

Chosin Reservoir
Yudam-ni • Hagaru ri
Koto-ri •
Hamhung •
Hungnam
Majon-ni
Wonsan
Pyongyang Kojo

Hwachon 38°

Panmunjom Chunchon
Seoul Hongchon
Inchon Wonju
han river
Andong
Yellow Sea
naktong river
Pohang
Chinju Masan
Sachon
Pusan
Sea of Japan

KOREA

USSR

0 20 40 60 80 100
miles

Japan, under Fifth Air Force control, and was being used for night heckler missions.

On 13 August, with the 5th Marines about to enter Sachon, Craig was suddenly ordered to disengage and move seventy-five miles north to the "Naktong Bulge," a salient created by the 4th NKPA Division crossing the river near Obong-ni, where the 5th Marines were given "No-Name Ridge" to take. Murray assaulted in column of battalions on the 15th and on the fourth try reached the crest. That night the NKPA counterattacked. The Marines made their first acquaintance with the vaunted Russian-built T-34 tanks and tore them up with rocket launchers, recoilless rifles, and 90-mm tank fire. Next morning the 4th NKPA Division, badly battered, retired across the river, harried by Cushman's Corsairs.

The NKPA came across the Naktong again on 3 September, this time with their 9th Division, hitting the newly arrived 2d U. S. Infantry Division's 9th Regiment. The 5th Marines came charging up and in three days the 9th NKPA Division had been pushed back six miles with heavy losses. On 5 September the Brigade went into reserve to load-out for Inchon.

There had been 74,279 Marines on active duty, 27,656 of them in the Fleet Marine Force (with further cuts planned for fiscal year 1951 by Louis Johnson), when Cates made his proposal that a brigade go to Korea. On 19 July, Truman authorized the call-up of "citizen-Marines." Mobilization of the Organized Marine Corps Reserve brought in 33,528 well-qualified officers and men, many of them World War II combat veterans. Three understrength battalions were dispatched from Lejeune to Pendleton to serve as cadre for the 1st Marine Regiment. Hearing that his old regiment was being put on a war footing, "Chesty" Puller, now CO of the Marine Barracks at Pearl Harbor, pestered the Commandant with telephone calls and cables asking for its command. Oliver Prince Smith, who had been Assistant Division Commander at Peleliu, had been named as CG, 1st Marine Division. He acceded to Puller's request. The two men, Smith and Puller, were very different; Smith, tall, ascetic, professorial; Puller, bandy-legged, gnarled, always outspoken, often profane; but the two worked well together. The Division headquarters and the 1st Marines (put together in ten days from the Lejeune battalions, filled out with Reserves and drafts from posts and stations) sailed from San Diego in mid-August, Meanwhile, Homer L. Litzenberg, CO, 6th Marines at Lejeune, having sent his battalions off to Pendleton, was told to form the 7th Regiment from what was left.

Orders reached El Toro on 16 August telling Major General Field Harris (Naval Academy, class of 1917) to take the headquarters of his 1st Marine Aircraft Wing and MAG-12 with Corsair squadrons VMF-212, VMF-312, and VMF (N) 542 to the Far East. All cleared the West Coast by 1 September.

Inchon

MacArthur, in his *Reminiscences*, says:

> *The target date, because of the great tides at Inchon, had to be the middle of September. This meant that the staging for the landing at Inchon would have to be accomplished more rapidly than that of any other large amphibious operation in modern warfare. . . . My plan was opposed by powerful military influences in Washington. The essence of the operation depended upon a great amphibious movement, but the chairman of the Joint Chiefs of Staff, General Omar Bradley, was of the considered opinion that such amphibious operations were obsolete–that there would never be another successful movement of this sort.*

The Attack Force would have come up to Inchon from the Yellow Sea through narrow and tortuous

Flying Fish Channel. When the tides went out they ripped through the channel at seven or eight knots, leaving vast mud flats across which even amtracks could not expect to crawl. The hydrographers said the best date would be 15 September. Morning high tide (an incredible 31.2 feet) would be at 0659, evening high tide at 1919. The landing would have to accommodate to these times.

Much of the Navy's Amphibious Force was a rusty travesty of the great World War II amphibious armadas. Many of the LSTs to be used in the landing had to be reclaimed from Japanese charters. Some came complete with Japanese crew. Other crews had to be made up from Navy Reserves flown to Japan.

Now came an aggravation from another quarter. On 21 August, Congressman Gordon L. McDonough of California had written President Truman urging that the Commandant of the Marine Corps be given a voice in the Joint Chiefs of Staff. Truman answered with a tart personal note, ". . . For your information the Marine Corps is the Navy's police force and as long as I am President that is what it will remain. They have a propaganda machine that is almost equal to Stalin's. . . . The Chief of Naval Operations is the Chief of Staff of the Navy of which the Marines are a part. . . ."

The story got into the newspapers on 5 September. Great cries of outrage went up from the public. Next day Truman sent a contrite apology to Cates regretting his choice of language and then manfully appeared at a Marine Corps League banquet by chance being held in Washington, but he did not recant his fundamental beliefs as to where the Marine Corps should fit in the national military establishment.

The 1st Marines, staging out of Kobe for Inchon, read about the incident in the *Stars and Stripes* and chalked on their trucks and tanks, "Horrible Harry's Police Force." The 1st Marine Division would literally form on the battlefield. The 5th Marines were loading out of Pusan. The 7th Marines were still on the high seas (one of its battalions had been in the Mediterranean and was coming by way of Suez). On 3 September the 1st Korean Marine Corps Regiment was assigned to the 1st Marine Division.

Lifting the Landing Force would be Amphibious Group 1, under Rear Admiral James H. Doyle. Superimposed on top the Landing Force was X Corps, under Major General Edward M. Almond, USA, MacArthur's former chief of staff. The 7th U.S. Infantry Division would be in reserve. Pyramided over X Corps was Joint Task Force 7.

There were estimated to be about 2200 second-rate North Korean troops in Inchon. Inland, in the vicinity of Seoul, there were thought to be about 21,500 enemy of better quality. A battalion of the 5th Marines would land at daybreak on Green Beach on Wolmi-do, an island separated from Inchon itself by a six-hundred-yard causeway. Then there would be a long wait of twelve hours until evening tide was in and the main landings could be made. The rest of the 5th Marines would then land across Red Beach to the north and the 1st Marines across Blue Beach to the south—although calling them "beaches" was a misnomer; the harbor was edged with sea walls which would have to be scaled with ladders.

Air and naval gunfire preparation of the target area began 10 September. L-Hour for Wolmi-do was 0630 on 15 September. BLT 3/5 scrambled ashore, twenty-five minutes later ran up the flag over Radio Hill. "That's it," said MacArthur, watching from the bridge of the command ship *Mount McKinley* along with Shepherd, Almond, Doyle, and Smith. "Let's get a cup of coffee."

During the day the target area became increasingly smudged with smoke from the burning city mixed with rain and fog. H-Hour for the main landings was 1730. No landmarks could be seen in the grayish-green pall, the assault waves crisscrossed during the run in to the sea wall, and all the sorting out wasn't complete before it was pitch black. The X Corps' plan was to move inland following the landing, capture Kimpo airfield, cross the Han, recapture Seoul, and then act as the anvil against which the NKPA would be crushed by an Eighth Army drive up from the south. The axis for the twenty-mile advance to Seoul was the intertwined road and railroad. In the morning the Division moved out, 1st Regiment astride and right of the road, 5th Regiment on the left. On the morning of 17 September, MacArthur and other notables came ashore to visit the front. On the highway they saw the still-smoking hulks of a column of T-34s which had tried a counterattack at dawn. MacArthur gave Craig, Murray, and Puller Silver Stars, and Smith was told that the 7th Infantry Division would land next day and move in on the right of the 1st Marines.

That same day, 17 September, Murray's 5th Marines took Kimpo airfield. Swimmers were put across the Han and Lieutenant Colonel Robert D. Taplett's 3d Battalion went over in amtracks at dawn on the 20th, followed a few hours later by the 2d Battalion. This put the 5th Marines in position on the high ground north of Seoul.

The 1st Marines, coming up along the Inchon-Seoul Road had found it tougher going, there had been a hard fight at Sosa, and it was the nineteenth before they reached the hills overlooking Yongdong-po, the city that lies across the Han from Seoul. All three battalions of the 1st Marines went in the final attack beginning on 21 September against Yongdong-po. This finished the enemy west of the Han.

On the twenty-fourth, Puller's 1st Marines crossed the river. The next day the 1st and 5th Marines went into Seoul itself, the 1st Marines attacking up Ma Po Boulevard toward Ducksoo Palace, the traditional seat of government. Supporting arms had to be used sparingly because of the civilian populace and the fighting was largely grenade and rifle, barricade-to-barricade, and house-to-house. That night the NKPA tried a final tank-infantry counterattack with everything they had left in the city. It failed, and by the twenty-seventh Seoul was secure. Two days later Syngman Rhee, escorted by MacArthur, made a triumphal re-entry into the capital. On 30 September Litzenberg's 7th Marines, who had joined the 1st Division in Seoul, moved out along the Seoul-Pyongyang highway, reaching Uijongbu, ten miles to the north under the approving eye of visiting General Cates. The 1st Cavalry Division, new armor gleaming, now passed through the 1st Marine Division, which then made a motor march back to Inchon to re-embark.

Wonsan

The next objective was Wonsan on the east coast north of the 38th Parallel. The harbor had been sown extensively with Russian-made mines and by the time these had been cleared, there was no need for an amphibious assault; the port had been taken from the land side by resurgent Republic of Korea forces. The 1st Marine Division landed administratively across the beach on 26 October and found the checkerboard-nosed Corsairs of VMF-312 already operating from Wonsan airfield.

These operations on the eastern coast were being conducted by X Corps independently of the Eighth Army. The 1st Marine Division was given a zone of action three hundred miles from north to south, fifty miles deep. The 5th and 7th Marines were to go north to Hamhung to prepare for a further advance to the Yalu. The 1st Marines were to stay behind in the vicinity of Wonsan and scoop up the supposedly shattered remnants of an NKPA division. In Tokyo they were saying the war would be over by Christmas. O. P. Smith was not so hopeful. He thought his Division badly overextended.

Immediately after landing at Wonsan on 26 October, the 1st Battalion, 1st Marines, had been sent south by rail to the picture book little seaport of Kojo, almost undisturbed by the war, thirty-nine miles down the coast. The night of 27 October the 1st Battalion was hit by a still-intact NKPA regiment and took heavy casualties in a fight that went on until mid-morning on the twenty-eighth. Having weathered that storm, the 1st Battalion stayed at Kojo until 1 November when it was relieved by the 5th Battalion, Korean Marines.

A sister unit, the 3d Battalion, 1st Marines, had been sent twenty-six road miles west of Wonsan on 28 October to secure the mountain town of Majon-ni, important because it was where the cross-peninsula roads from Seoul, Pyongyang, and Wonsan came together. Once in position the battalion found itself surrounded by the 15th NKPA Division, many members of which were more than ready to surrender (the 3d Battalion took more prisoners than its own total strength while at Majon-ni), but there was still considerable fight left in the rest. Convoys could get through to Majon-ni only with major effort and the 3d Battalion was kept supplied by free-fall airdrop with casualties going out by helicopter. On 10 November (the Marine Corps Birthday, celebrated with a makeshift cake) the 3d Battalion was joined by the 3d Battalion, Korean Marine Corps, and on the afternoon of the thirteenth, the 1st Battalion, 15th U. S. Infantry, fresh from Fort Benning, arrived. The 3d Battalion, 1st Marines, turned the Majon-ni perimeter over to the Army and left next morning by truck for Wonsan.

Chosin Reservoir

There was hard intelligence that the Chinese Communist Forces were across the Yalu but CINCFE in Tokyo at first denied and then minimized their presence, insisting that it was too late for the Chinese to intervene effectively in the war. The 1st Marine Division was to advance northwest of Hungnam along a mountain road to Chosin Reservoir, site of an important hydroelectric plant, and thence to the Yalu.

Hungnam and Hamhung, the names are confusingly similar. Hungnam is the seaport. Hamhung is the road and railroad nexus, some eight miles to the northwest. The 7th Marines under Litzenberg moved out of Hamhung on 2 November and by midnight were in heavy contact with the 124th CCF Division near Sudong-ni. The fight now went uphill through tortuous Funchilin Pass to a high plateau. The 124th broke contact on 7 November and on 10 November the 7th Marines entered Koto-ri. Three days later they were in Hagaru-ri at the southern tip of Chosin Reservoir. Marine engineers began to scrape out air strips at Koto-ri and Hagaru-ri. General Almond, X Corps commander, planned to bring his flag forward to Hagaru-ri and some Army engineers and signal troops were detailed to begin the construction. The brief autumn was almost over and the weather was turning bitterly cold. The nearest Eighth Army unit was eighty miles to the west.

On 24 November, the day after Thanksgiving (special holiday menu including roast turkey, cranberry sauce, fruit cake, and mincemeat pie), the 7th Marines moved out along the road west of Chosin Reservoir, through Toktong Pass, to Yudam-ni. Fox Company was dropped off at Toktong Pass to keep it open. Two days later the 7th Marines were joined at Yudam-ni by Murray's 5th Marines. Puller's 1st Marines had been relieved at Wonsan by the newly arrived 3d U.S. Infantry Division and his battalions were strung out along the road to keep the lines of communication back to Hungnam open: 1st Battalion at Chinhung-ni at the foot of Funchilin Pass, 2d Battalion and the regimental command post at Koto-ri, and 3d Battalion at Hagaru-ri.

On 24 November, Smith had received a warning order that his Division would make a wide sweeping envelopment to the west to form the northern arm of a giant pincer of which the Eighth Army would be the southern arm. H-Hour was to be 0800 on the 27th. This gave the 1st Marine Division the bleak prospect of crossing the near-roadless and mountainous backbone of Korea in weather that was already subzero.

Then, on 25 November, the II ROK Corps, forming the Eighth Army's right wing, was struck seventy miles southwest of Yudam-ni by a Red Chinese counterattack. The ROK Corps gave way, the right flank and rear of the 2d U.S. Infantry Division was exposed, and by the twenty-sixth the Eighth Army advance had come to a disastrous halt.

On the twenty-seventh, with the X Corps operation order unmodified, the 5th Marines dutifully attacked to the west from Yudam-ni, went a mile, and were stopped. That night it snowed and the temperature went down to 20°F. below zero. General Sung Shih-lun came out of the mountains with eight CCF Divisions in a carefully planned counterstroke with the express mission of destroying the 1st Marine Division. Three CCF Divisions hit at the 5th and 7th Marines at Yudam-ni. Other elements cut the MSR to Hagaru-ri and struck at Fox Company holding Toktong Pass. Another division attacked Hagaru-ri, defended by two-thirds of 3d Battalion, 1st Marines, two batteries of 105s, and odds and ends of service and combat support troops. The road south to Koto-ri was also cut and Koto-ri attacked by still another division.

Hagaru-ri

The situation was most precarious at Hagaru-ri. The high ground, called East Hill, that dominated the town and also the exit south to Koto-ri had been lost to the Chinese. The unfinished twenty-nine-hundred-foot airstrip had been penetrated and although the line there was restored the strip continued to be fireswept. (Transports, mostly Marine R4Ds, a military version of the Douglas C-47, would begin using the strip on 1 December, bringing in supplies and taking out the wounded. Five hundred replacements were eventually flown in, many of them direct from hospitals in Japan, barely recovered from earlier wounds.)

On 28 November, O. P. Smith flew in to Hagaru-ri and opened his command post there. He ordered the 5th Marines to hold where they were and the 7th Marines to reverse direction, attack southward, and clear the MSR from Yudam-ni to Hagaru-ri. On the twenty-ninth, the remnants of three Army battalions, badly cut up east of the reservoir, were attached to the 1st Marine Division. Few of the survivors, limping across the ice into Hagaru-ri, were in fit condition to fight.

Hagaru-ri had to be held until the Division could be reconstituted. On the twenty-ninth, Puller at Koto-ri, at Smith's instruction, put together a relief column to come up to Hagaru-ri. Lieutenant Colonel Douglas B. Drysdale, RM, had reported to the 1st Marine Division on 20 November at Hungnam with the 41 Independent Commando, Royal Marines. In addition to the Commando (14 officers and 221 enlisted men) there was Company G, reinforced, 1st Marines, on its way to rejoin its parent battalion at Hagaru-ri; Company B, 31st U. S. Infantry; two Marine tank companies with 29 tanks; altogether over 900 men and a headquarters train of some 141 vehicles. Twice Task Force Drysdale was ambushed and halted. The armor could cut through and the infantry could handle itself; the truck convoy got the worst of it. Drysdale was told to push on. By midnight on the twenty-ninth he was in Hagaru-ri with 41 Commando, Company G, and one of the tank companies. On the road behind them the truck column had been cut up into four different segments. Their situation was hopeless and by morning (except for a few hardy individuals who made their way either back to Koto-ri or forward to Hagaru-ri) all were killed or captured.

From Yudam-ni to Hungnam

On 30 November, "Ned" Almond flew in to Hagaru-ri
to see Smith, said the situation had changed radically
for the worse all across the front, there would be no
attack to the west, X Corps would fall back to Hungnam. Weapons, equipment, and vehicles were to be
abandoned as necessary. Smith demurred, and he told
Almond the Marines would fight their way out.

Next day Lieutenant Colonel Raymond G. Davis with
the 1st Battalion, 7th Marines, started across country
from Yudam-ni to relieve Fox Company still grimly
holding on to Toktong Pass. He reached there on 2
December, found only eighty-two of the original Marines unwounded. Meanwhile, Taplett's 3d Battalion,
5th Marines, led the main body out of Yudam-ni along
the road, carefully shepherded overhead by Marine air.
The column reached Hagaru-ri on 3 December having
done fourteen miles of fighting and marching in sev-
enty-nine hours.

The breakout southward from Hagaru-ri began on 6
December, led by Litzenberg's 7th Marines, followed
by Murray's 5th Marines with 41 Commando and 3d
Battalion, 1st Marines, attached. The Marines were
bringing everything out and there was a solid mass of
vehicles on the road. On the flanks, the rifle companies
leapfrogged from one piece of critical terrain to the
next. Overhead was close air support, Marine air
reserving for themselves a corridor a mile wide over
the column with Navy and Air Force working farther
out. Last elements from Hagaru-ri had completed the
eleven-mile march and entered the perimeter at Koto-ri
by midnight on the seventh.

Next morning the Division resumed its march to the
sea. Funchilin Pass was now held by the Chinese and
had to be cleared. The 1st Battalion, 1st Marines, made
a successful uphill attack from Chinhung-ni on 8
December. By the morning of 12 December the Division had closed at Hungnam. The weather along the

coast seemed almost balmy to the Marines. The Reservoir had cost them 4400 battle casualties (730 killed or died of wounds) and uncounted cases of frostbite and pneumonia. All the fight was out of the Chinese. They had lost perhaps 25,000 dead and did not press the perimeter as X Corps prepared to evacuate Hungnam.

There was a curious rumor in circulation that the Marines were going to Indochina to help the French. "Chesty" Puller, aboard the MSTS transport *General Collins*, reviewed for some of his junior officers the events of the Russo–Japanese 1907 war in Korea and was gloomy in his prognostications. The Marines unloaded at Pusan, jolted down the road, and spent Christmas in the Bean Patch at Masan.

Killer and Ripper

As the new year began, some semblance of order emerged from the chaos. Lieutenant General Matthew B. Ridgway had come out to take command, replacing Walton Walker who had been killed in a vehicle accident. The Eighth Army had succeeded in establishing a line south of Seoul. The 1st Marine Division was given a sector in the rear stretching from Pohang on the east coast northwest to Andong and spent an easy month, from 12 January to 15 February, in antiguerrilla operations, experimenting with such things as inserting reconnaissance patrols by helicopter.

Ridgway had planned a buttoned-up shoulder-to-shoulder United Nations counteroffensive (unlike Walker's freewheeling, hell-for-leather operations) called Operation Killer. The 1st Marine Division was moved to the center of the line, under IX Corps, far from blue water. They jumped off from Wonju on 21 February and with the 1st and 5th Marines in the assault took their objective, Hoengsong, eight miles to the north, three days later. That same day, the IX Corps commander died of a heart attack and O. P. Smith, by seniority and with Ridgway's endorsement, became

Corps commander. Puller, now a brigadier general, moved up to temporary command of the Division. But the press inevitably confused the quiet and courtly O. P. Smith with the sulphurous H. M. Smith. Saipan was remembered, and O. P. Smith remained in command of IX Corps only as long as it took the Army to get a more senior major general to Korea.

Operation Killer was succeeded by Operation Ripper on 7 March. In the Marines' zone of action, the attack was led off by the 1st Marines (now commanded by Colonel Francis M. McAlister) and the 7th Marines (also with a new commander, Colonel Herman ("Herman the German") Nickerson, Jr.). The Marines liked Ridgway's way of fighting. By April the Eighth Army's line was generally north of the 38th Parallel. Political considerations outweighed military momentum and there now came a pause.

Hwachon Reservoir

The 1st Marine Division was at Hwachon Reservoir when the Chinese spring counteroffensive materialized on 21 April. In one night's fighting the 6th ROK Division on the Marines' right flank was swept away and a gap opened in the line ten miles wide by ten miles deep. McAlister's 1st Marines, in reserve, was flung into action on the twenty-second, battalion by battalion, to seal off the penetration. The 7th Regiment was withdrawn and echeloned to the left. The Division was joined by the British Commonwealth 27 Brigade and by 26 April the situation was once again stabilized. On that day O. P. Smith turned over command of the Division to "Jerry" Thomas, now a major general. By 30 April, the 1st Marine Division was once again part of Almond's X Corps, and in a defensive position at Hongchon.

The second phase of the Chinese spring offensive came in mid-May. This time they hit heavily on the

Marines' right, rolling back the 2d U. S. Infantry Division. The 1st Marines, now under Colonel Wilburt S. ("Big Foot") Brown, went to the aid of the 2d Division which in turn was able to echelon to the right to retake ground lost by another collapsed ROK division. The Chinese attack ran out of steam and it was the turn of the United Nations (another fighting general, James Van Fleet, had replaced Ridgway, who had moved up to take MacArthur's place as CINCFE) to take the offensive.

The 1st Marine Division found itself back in the Hwachon Reservoir sector, moving up to Yanggu through rugged mountain country. There were North Koreans in front of them and they fought more tenaciously than the Chinese. By the first week in June all three Marine regiments were abreast on line and by 20 June the Division had taken its portion of the Corps' objective, a ridgeline overlooking a deep circular valley which was promptly nicknamed the "Punchbowl." Truce negotiations now began and the UN forces settled down into a defensive line.

The Punchbowl

Summer 1951 was quiescent. Then in September the Division was ordered to take the rest of the Punchbowl. The attack began 5 September. There were eighteen days of hard, inconclusive fighting. Thomas said flatly that the air support meted out by the Fifth Air Force was "unsatisfactory." Over Marine Corps protests, the 1st Marine Aircraft Wing had been put under operational control of the Fifth Air Force with mission assignments coming from the Joint Operations Center. This was in accordance with Air Force doctrine of a single air commander and centralized control of tactical air operations, but it did great damage to the Marine Corps' air-ground team concept, and while the general level of air support across the whole front for all divisions may have improved, that received by the 1st Marine Division was down in both quantity and quality.

Strategically, the Fifth Air Force began Operation Strangle on 5 June, an interdiction attack against the enemy's rear designed to dry up his ability to fight. Major General Christian Schilt, hero of Quilali, had succeeded Field Harris as commanding general of the Wing. During July some concessions were wrung out of the Fifth Air Force as to the assignment of Marine aircraft to Marine-requested missions.

In September 1951, HMR-161, the first transport helicopter squadron arrived in Korea. Equipped with the Sikorsky HRS-1, the squadron put theory to practice and demonstrated that it could supply an infantry battalion in combat, lift a rocket battery, and move the Division reconnaissance company to a mountaintop.

Winter 1951 found the 1st Marine Division holding eleven miles of front on the north side of the Punchbowl. On 10 January 1952, Thomas returned to Washington to become the Assistant Commandant and Major General John T. Selden took over the Division. Planners dreamed of amphibious "end runs" but they never came about. On 23 March the Division was pulled out of the Punchbowl sector and moved a hundred and eighty miles west to the left flank of the UN line, thirty-five miles of front which overlooked Panmunjom and included the defense of the Pyongyang-Seoul corridor. The British Commonwealth Division tied in on their right flank. The lines had solidified and it was trench warfare now, very much like World War I. There were no general offensives or big attacks, just nasty localized actions growing out of patrols and raids, or the loss or capture of an outpost. In mid-August 1952, there was hard fighting at "Bunker Hill" outpost. In October, there was a fight for the "Hook." In early 1953 there was a contest for "Berlin" and "East Berlin" and in March particularly hard fighting for possession of "Reno," "Carson," and

"Vegas." (Vegas was lost and recaptured by 5th Marines, now commanded by "Lew" Walt.)

During 1952 and 1953, the F9F Panther jet gradually replaced the prop-driven Corsair as the Marine Corps first-line fighter-bomber and the Douglas R4D transports were augmented by Fairchild R4Q "Flying Boxcars."

In June 1953, Major General Randolph Pate assumed command of the Division. Firing ceased at 2200 on 27 July as the truce argued out at Panmunjom went into effect. During the Korean War 4262 Marines had been killed, 21,781 wounded, twice the totals of World War I. Of the 7190 Americans taken prisoner, however, only 227 were Marines. The 1st Marine Aircraft Wing had flown 127,496 combat sorties and lost 436 aircraft. Korea had largely been fought with World War II weapons drawn from the vast stores held by the Marines at Barstow in California's desert. There were few new innovations in equipment. The basic rifle was still the M-1. Leggings, which like the bayonet had grown shorter, gave way altogether to combat boots. For cold weather a thermal insulated "Mickey Mouse" boot replaced the treacherous shoe-pac used during the first winter. An armored vest, or "flak jacket," developed at Camp Lejeune proved particularly effective against grenades and mortars and became general issue. A cold-weather training camp was opened at Pickel Meadow in California's High Sierras and all replacements passed through it. A huge artillery range was acquired at Twenty-nine Palms in California. An East Coast counterpart of the supply center at Barstow was developed at Albany, Georgia.

16

1954–1965
"...a separate service, distinct and apart..."

Post-Korea

The armistice in Korea did not signal victory but rather
a shift from a war of movement to a gray kind of war of
position which never really ended. The 3d Marine
Division had been reactivated in January 1952 and in
August 1953 it had come out to Japan to be in strategic
reserve for the Far East. The 1st Marine Division
stayed on in Korea until 1955 and then came home to
Camp Pendleton. The 1st Marine Aircraft Wing went to
bases in Japan. The 3d Marine Division, crowded out of
Japan, sent the 4th Marine regiment to Hawaii, where
it became the ground element of the 1st Marine
Brigade, and the remainder of the Division began
moving to Okinawa.

President Truman fulfilled his promise and on 1
January 1952, Lemuel Cornick Shepherd, Jr., had become Commandant. One of Shepherd's first actions
was to reorganize Headquarters Marine Corps along
general staff lines with a G-1 (Personnel), G-2 (Intelligence), G-3 (Operations and Training), and G-4 (Logistics).

The political battle for the survival of the Marine

Corps was still being waged. In January 1951 Senator Paul H. Douglas of Illinois and Congressman Mike Mansfield of Montana (both former Marines) had introduced in their respective bodies of the Congress the Douglas-Mansfield Bill which would have made it a matter of law that there would be four Marine divisions and four Marine air wings in the active structure. There had been committee hearings, sometimes acrimonious, in the Senate and the House in April and May of 1951. The proponents of the bill emphasized the "force-in-readiness" or expeditionary status of the Corps. The House Armed Services Committee in its report reaffirmed that the Marine Corps "is and has always been since its inception a separate service, distinct and apart from the United States Army, United States Navy, and United States Air Force." The bill went through various permutations and as signed by President Truman (not altogether enthusiastically, it can be assumed) it became Public Law 416, 82d Congress, and it provided for three active Marine divisions and three air wings, and coequal status for the Commandant with the Joint Chiefs of Staff when matters of direct concern to the Marine Corps were under consideration.

In the Far East there were various demands requiring the attention of the 3d Marine Division and the 1st Marine Aircraft Wing. In February 1955, when the Chinese Communists seized Ichiang island and the adjacent Tachen Islands became untenable for the Chinese Nationalists, Marines with the Seventh Fleet assisted in the evacuation of twenty-four thousand Nationalist soldiers and civilians to Taiwan. In the same year they also helped in the larger evacuation of three-hundred thousand refugees from North Vietnam to South Vietnam.

Shepherd retired on 31 December 1955 and was recalled to active duty to be Chairman of the Inter-American Defense Board. His successor as Commandant, appointed by President Eisenhower, was General Randolph McCall Pate. Born in Port Royal, South

Carolina, in 1898, Pate had served briefly as a soldier in World War I, then had gone to Virginia Military Institute (as had Shepherd) where he graduated in 1921. In the 1920s he had served in Santo Domingo and China. He was the logistic planner for Guadalcanal and had spent World War II as a staff officer. In Korea, he had commanded the 1st Marine Division in the last days of the war. Like Shepherd, he was a traditionalist. There was much emphasis on the fit of uniforms, the length of trousers, and proper civilian dress. (Secretary of Defense Charles E. Wilson testily decreed that officers serving in the Washington area should wear civilian clothes. General Pate said that Marine officers must wear hats.) Pate also brought back the swagger stick and made it near-compulsory for officers and staff noncommissioned officers.

A drill instructor at Parris Island on 8 April 1956 took his platoon on an unauthorized night-march and six of them drowned in marshy Ribbon Creek. There was a court-martial and national attention focused on recruit-training methods. David Shoup of Tarawa, now a major general, was ordered to make a searching investigation of what went on in "boot" camp. Recruit training would remain hard but not harsh; the "head-in-the-bucket" era was over.

In the same year the unstable situation in the Middle East came unhinged with the Suez Crisis. On 31 October 1956, the 3d Battalion, 2d Marines, afloat with the Sixth Fleet, landed at Alexandria and covered the evacuation of fifteen hundred civilians from thirty-three different countries. Marines also evacuated some U.N. truce team members caught between the Israelis and Egyptians, and in an action somewhat removed from the main event the Marine garrison at Port Lyautey was reinforced because of the fighting between the French and Moroccans.

There were also occasions for the controlled use of amphibious power in the Caribbean. In January 1958, after the overthrow of Dictator Pérez Jiménez in Venezuela and with mobs running rampant in Caracas, the cruiser *Des Moines* with a company of Marines embarked took station off-shore in time-honored fashion. In May, after Vice President Richard Nixon's good-will visit to Caracas turned sour, a battalion of Marines was put on board the cruiser *Boston.* In neither case did they land.

Lebanon Intervention (1958)

The largest Marine operation in these years, however, was in Lebanon. On 14 July 1958 the equilibrium of the Arab world was once again tipped violently, this time by the *coup d'état* in Iraq and the murder of pro-Western King Feisal. In half-Christian, half-Moslem Lebanon, President Camille Chamoun, confronted with open rebellion supported by Syrian troops poised on Lebanon's borders, asked for U. S. and British intervention. That same day, 14 July, President Eisenhower met with the JCS, listened to their recommendations, and made his decision: "All right, we'll send them in."

There was a contingency plan, nicknamed Bluebat, which called for two Marine battalion landing teams, one to land north, the other south of Beirut, while a British airborne brigade came in from Cyprus. As of 14 July, three battalion landing teams were present in the eastern Mediterranean, partly by coincidence, partly by design. BLT 1/8 was just north of Malta, its return to the United States delayed because of the unsettled conditions. BLT 3/6, newly arrived as relief for BLT 1/8 was steaming from Crete toward Athens. BLT 2/2 was off the southern coast of Cyprus and closest to Beirut. Also present was the headquarters of a brigade equivalent, the 2d Provisional Marine Force. This headquarters had been formed in January under Brigadier General Sidney S. Wade for a combined exercise to be held at Sardinia with the British Royal Marines and the

Italian Navy. After rioting broke out in Lebanon, General Wade and his staff had come forward into the Mediterranean.

BLT 2/2 was ordered to land over Red Beach at 1500 on 15 July. Red Beach was four miles south of Beirut, half a mile from the International Airport, and a mile north of the village of Khalde.

U. S. Ambassador Robert McClintock informed General Fuad Chehab, commander of the Lebanese Army, of the impending landing at 1330. Chehab, visibly upset, asked that the Americans remain on board their ship. Ambassador McClintock had no radio link with the Fleet so he dispatched his naval attaché to Red Beach to stay the landing. The attaché arrived at Khalde at 1520; by that time the landing had been in progress for twenty minutes, battle-clad Marines picking their way through sun-bathers and soft-drink vendors, toward the beach road and the airfield. Lieutenant Colonel Harry A. Hadd, commanding the 2d Battalion, 2d Marines, opined to the attaché that he knew of no way to reverse a landing ordered by the President of the United States. By evening, with four rifle companies ashore, Hadd's battalion had taken over the airport from the bemused Lebanese airport guards and had established a defensive perimeter.

Next morning, before dawn, Admiral James L. ("Lord Jim") Holloway arrived from London as Commander-in-Chief, Specified Command, Middle East. At 0730, BLT 3/6 began landing across Red Beach and 2d Battalion, 2d Marines, formed up into column to move into Beirut. After several false starts (Chamoun thought the Marines should come into the city; Chehab thought they should not), the column got under way about 1230 and by 1900 the battalion had control of the dock area and had put guards on the critical bridges and the U. S. Embassy. The "Basta," the rebel stronghold in the center of the city, was left alone. There were some minor confrontations with both the Lebanese

Army and the rebels, a few shots were exchanged but no casualties.

The next day the cooperation of the Lebanese Army improved markedly and on the 18th, BLT 1/8 landed over Yellow Beach four miles north of the city while air-transported elements of 2d Battalion, 8th Marines, began arriving at the International Airport from Camp Lejeune. The earmarked British brigade from Cyprus had gone into Jordan at the request of Feisal's cousin, King Hussein. Its place was taken in Bluebat by the U. S. 24th Airborne Brigade which began to arrive from Germany on 19 July. Major General Paul D. Adams, USA, was named CINC American Land Forces, Lebanon, and arrived on 26 July. Afterward, General Wade paid Adams the oblique compliment of being ". . . as fair to the Marine Corps as any Army general I've ever dealt with."

Lebanese national elections were held on 31 July and General Chehab was elected President. He took office on 23 September, having formed a coalition government with the rebels. Chamoun, who had asked the Americans to intervene, was out and Chehab, who had walked the fence, was in. In the interim, three Marine battalions had departed for home and by 18 October all the Marines were gone.

Beginning in 1958, a battalion landing team was kept afloat with the Seventh Fleet as a Special Landing Force and late in the same year MAG-11 went to Taiwan for an extended stay. The Communist-provoked civil war in Laos began in earnest in 1960. As a countermove, a Marine helicopter squadron went into Thailand in 1961 followed in May 1962 by a sizable exercise involving the 3d Marine Expeditionary Unit (made up of a battalion landing team, a helicopter squadron, and an attack squadron). Marine involvement in Southeast Asia had begun.

Shoup as Commandant

David Monroe Shoup succeeded Pate as Commandant. In naming him, President Eisenhower had gone past five lieutenant generals and four major generals. Shoup, the first Midwesterner to become Commandant, delighted in playing the earthy Indiana farm boy. In his baptismal speech in January 1960 he said, "It is good to feel the grips of the plow in my hands. . . ." and he promised that ". . . the furrow will be straight and true. . . ." He also announced, with respect to the swagger stick, "It shall remain an optional item of interference. If you feel the need of it, carry it." Shoup continued the modernization of Headquarters Marine Corps begun by Shepherd. A shrewd fundamentalist, he was skeptical of the counterinsurgency doctrines then in vogue. In private he was critical of the U. S. policy toward Castro's Cuba. Vietnam he considered a rat hole and he sought to keep the Marine commitment to the advisory effort down to a minimum.

In October 1962, after President Kennedy's ultimatum to the Soviets that the offensive missiles must be removed from Cuba, the garrison at Guantanamo was reinforced to regimental strength. The rest of the 2d Marine Division went to sea in amphibious shipping and was joined in the Caribbean by the 5th Marine Expeditionary Brigade, drawn from the 1st Marine Division, which had come through the Panama Canal from California. To support them, much of the 2d Marine Aircraft Wing deployed forward to airfields in Florida and Puerto Rico.

Budget constraints kept the strength of the Corps down to about a hundred and seventy-five thousand, so that the Fleet Marine Forces were chronically understrength; nevertheless, the operating forces reached perhaps their highest peacetime level of effectiveness. During these years technical capabilities had caught up with doctrinal aspirations. There was now a family of dependable helicopters in fairly sufficient quantity. The

Fleet also was gaining in the number of platforms from which they could be launched. The Fleet Marine Force had been restructured in 1956 and 1957, so that division elements were now largely helicopter transportable with heavier units, such as tank battalions, being moved out of the division and into Force Troops. The USS *Thetis Bay*, an old escort carrier, had been recommissioned for testing as an LPH (Landing Platform Helicopter Carrier). These experiments led to the reconfiguration of a number of former attack carriers (including the *Boxer* and *Princeton*) as LPHs. These, in turn, were followed by new-construction LPHs, beginning with the *Iwo Jima*, commissioned in 1961.

The problem of establishing high-performance tactical aircraft ashore quickly and early in an amphibious operation was approached by something called the SATS or "Short Airfield for Tactical Support." SATS, approved for development in 1958, applied aircraft-carrier components to an expeditionary airfield whose "flight deck" consisted of a new type aluminum matting.

Less esoterically, in 1962 the M-14 rifle, chambered for the 7.62-mm "NATO" cartridge, replaced the M-1, and the M-60 machine gun replaced the vintage Brownings.

Greene Becomes Commandant

Wallace Martin Greene, Jr., of Vermont succeeded General Shoup as Commandant on 1 January 1964. A graduate of the Naval Academy (class of 1930), his career before World War II had followed the familiar pattern of Basic School, sea duty, China duty, schools, and Guantanamo. At the beginning of the war he was an observer in Britain. In the Pacific he served as an operations officer in the Marshalls and at Saipan and Tinian. After the war, came more operations-planning experience at successively higher echelons. After Ribbon Creek he was sent to Parris Island to take com-

mand of the Recruit Depot. When Shoup became
Commandant in 1960, he made Greene his Chief of
Staff.

More of an internationalist than his predecessor,
Greene set up, as one of his first actions, Operation
Steel Pike. Held in concert with the Spanish Marine
Corps in the fall of 1964, it was the largest combined
amphibious exercise since World War II.

Dominican Intervention (1965)

In the spring of 1965, there was a testing of a different
sort of the Atlantic Fleet's amphibious capability. Since
the days of the 1916–1924 occupation, the Dominican
Republic had been the subject of special, almost senti-
mental, Marine Corps interest. Before and after Trujillo's assassination in May 1961, ships' visits and a
showing of the flag had helped keep a highly inflamma-
ble situation from bursting into a conflagration. In
November 1961, when a civil war threatened, an adroit
amphibious demonstration dampened it down. Similar
actions were effective in 1963, but in April 1965 the
situation got out of hand.

Late on Saturday, 24 April, word reached the 6th
Marine Expeditionary Unit (then on board amphibious
shipping, anchored south of Puerto Rico's Vieques
Island) that a Communist-inspired coup was under way
in Santo Domingo. Orders were to take station off the
southern coast of the troubled republic, hull-down, but
prepared to move in to evacuate up to twelve hundred
U. S. citizens. By 0200, 25 April, the task group was off
Haina, the sugar port and minuscule naval base just
west of Santo Domingo city. The 6th MEU included
Battalion Landing Team 3/6 and Medium Helicopter
Squadron 264. Fixed-wing support would have to come
from Roosevelt Roads in Puerto Rico. By this time the
rebels had gained substantial control of downtown
Santo Domingo, the loyalist troops had been pushed
out of the National Palace, and Donald Reid Cabral had

quit as President. The number of U. S. citizens and foreign nationals to be evacuated had grown to three thousand.

The evacuation site was the Hotel Embajador on the western edge of the city with a polo field, once used by the Trujillos, offering an elegant helicopter-landing zone. Evacuation began at 1300 on 27 April. Downtown, the U. S. Embassy, defended by an eight-man Marine security guard and thirty-six National Policemen, was receiving sporadic sniper fire. Next morning, 28 April, the National Police announced they no longer could guarantee the security of either the evacuation site or the Embassy. Accordingly, a platoon of Marines was put in at each place. The loyalists, having lost most of the city, had concentrated at San Isidro air base some eight miles away. At mid-afternoon, the military junta at San Isidro asked that a battalion of Marines be landed to help restore order. At about 1900, authority came back from Washington to land 500 Marines to protect the lives of Americans and foreign nationals. Within two hours, 526 Marines had come into the Embajador landing zone.

Early the next afternoon, 29 April, the U. S. Embassy came under heavy small-arms fire. From Washington came word that the Organization of American States was considering an International Safety Zone. By nightfall all of BLT 3/6 was ashore. During the early morning hours of 30 April, the 3d Brigade, 82d Airborne Division began arriving at San Isidro. The day's operation plan called for 3d Battalion, 6th Marines, to move east from the polo field to a north-south line just beyond the U. S. Embassy so as to establish the International Safety Zone agreed to by the OAS. The 2d Brigade, 82d Airborne, were to come in from San Isidro as far as the vital Duarte Bridge across the Río Ozama. The loyalists, relieved at the bridge, were to go forward and patrol the center of the city. All parts of the plan worked, except the last. Instead of advancing the loyalists fell back to San Isidro, where a three-cornered negotiation for a cease-fire was taking place. Next morning the Marines and Airborne pushed forward their patrols and linked up shortly after noon. Then they got orders from the U. S. negotiators to withdraw to their original positions.

Lieutenant General Bruce Palmer, USA, arrived that morning with the 2d Brigade, 82d Airborne, and took over command of all U. S. ground forces. Other arrivals that day at San Isidro were Brigadier General John H. Bouker, USMC, as commanding general, 4th Marine Expeditionary Brigade, and air-lifted BLT 1/6. A five-man peace commission from the OAS also arrived. The Marines and Army were now permitted to link up once again, which they did shortly after midnight on 3 May. Later on the third BLT 1/8 came into San Isidro by air, while BLT 1/2 arrived on board the LPH *Okinawa* to serve as floating reserve.

On 6 May, after bitter debate, the OAS voted to create an Inter-American Peace Force. On 7 May, tough and wily Brigadier General Antonio Imbert Bar-reras, one of the two surviving assassins of Trujillo, took over as head of the San Isidro group. He energized the faltering loyalist effort and began the cleanup of the remaining pocket of rebel resistance in the old part of the city.

With three BLTs ashore and one afloat, Marine strength had peaked at eight thousand. On 25 May, the first contingent of Brazilians arrived. Eventually, Par-aguay, Honduras, Nicaragua, and Costa Rica would all send small units and more than a thousand troops would come from Brazil. On 26 May the Marines began to withdraw. Last elements had gone by 6 June and the Dominican intervention, as far as the Marines were concerned, was over. Marine casualties had been nine killed and thirty wounded. U. .S Army casualties were about the same. There were those who would say that the threat of a Communist takeover was never so great as assumed by President Lyndon B. Johnson and that the amount of U. S. force sent ashore went far beyond that required. There were others who would say that the Dominican situation had been exploited as a laboratory opportunity for testing the respective strategic mobility systems of amphibious and airborne forces. Elsewhere in the world, by this time, an even more ambiguous and infinitely more costly involvement had already begun.

17

1965–1972
"Battles would be fought and re-fought"

Da Nang and III MAF

On 8 March 1965 under Brigadier General Frederick J. Karch, the 9th Marine Expeditionary Brigade, after standing off the coast for two months, landed across a fine sandy beach in the Bay of Da Nang, the first American ground-combat forces to come into Viet Nam. Battalion Landing Team 3/9 had hit Red Beach Two at 0902, looking very fierce in camouflaged helmets and armored vests, and were met with speeches and flowers from the official South Vietnamese welcoming committee. Two hours later BLT 1/3 began landing at Da Nang Air Base in Marine KC-130 transports.

Marine operational involvement in the Viet Nam war had begun three years earlier when on Palm Sunday, 15 April 1962, Medium Helicopter Squadron 362 had arrived at Soc Trang in the Delta south of Saigon with its Sikorsky UH-34s. The task unit was called "Shu-fly" and its first operational employment, lifting Vietnamese Army "little people" into battle, had come a week later on Easter. In September 1962 Shu-fly had moved up to Da Nang, South Viet Nam's second largest city, and set itself north on the west side of the airfield in a run-down French compound. By early 1965 half the medium helicopter squadrons in the Marine Corps had rotated through Da Nang for a tour of duty. Then in 1964 the Marines began to supply advisors for service with the Vietnamese Army in addition to those already with the Vietnamese Marine Corps.

Once ashore, 9th MEB was given the mission of reinforcing the defenses of the air base and such other installations as might be agreed upon with Major General Nguyen Chanh Thi, the tigerish commanding general of I Corps and I Corps Tactical Zone. The 3d Battalion, 9th Marines, moved out to a ridgeline west of the field dominated by Hill 327. Behind them was the Bay of Da Nang, formed by the embracing arms of Hai Van peninsula on the northwest and Tiensha peninsula on the southeast. The Trans-Vietnam Railway was still intact north to Hue, going behind Red Beach, across Nam O Bridge and then up through the blue-green Hai Van mountains by way of a half-dozen tunnels to Thua Thien province. Highway One, the old Mandarin Road, roughly paralleled the railroad, zigzagging through the Hai Van Pass which the French, for good reason, called *Col des Nuages* ("Pass of the Clouds"). Tiensha peninsula was flat and sandy but at its end was Monkey Mountain, 621 meters high and once an island. Below Monkey Mountain, beautiful China Beach curved southward for some twelve kilometers to Marble Mountain, monoliths of marble jutting up out of the sand, and highly regarded as a Buddhist shrine.

Looking south from Hill 327 the Marines could see virtually all the rest of the populated area of Quang Nam province, the hamlets like dark-green islands in a checkerboard sea of green and brown rice paddies. The rivers twisted and turned through the lowlands, following a hundred different courses and changing their names a dozen times, but the main ones were the Thu Bon and the Vu Gia. Thirty kilometers due south were the Que Son mountains, another spur coming out of the

Annamites and, as the Marines would learn, honeycombed with a thousand caves which would serve the Viet Cong well.

The 1st Battalion, 3d Marines, stayed on the airfield to provide close-in security. At that time Da Nang had one of only three jet airfields in South Viet Nam, a crazy-quilt of activities, some military, some civilian, some Vietnamese, some American. Northernmost of the four Vietnamese corps areas, I Corps Tactical Zone included five provinces: Quang Tri, Thua Thien, Quang Nam, Quang Tin, and Quang Ngai, stretching some two hundred and twenty-five miles from north to south and as narrow as thirty miles. General Thi's corps headquarters was in a handsome French compound on the east side of the field.

On 11 April the first fixed-wing Marine squadron arrived, VMFA-531, flying the superb McDonnell F4B Phantom. That same day, BLT 2/3, which had been on an exercise in Thailand, landed across Red Beach, and three days later BLT 3/4 arrived from Hawaii and was put in at Phu Bai, seven miles southeast of Hue, Viet Nam's third largest city and the old imperial capital.

Major General William R. ("Rip") Collins, commander of the 3d Marine Division, moved his flag to Da Nang on 3 May and three days later 9th MEB was dissolved to be replaced by the III Marine Amphibious Force. Ground elements were grouped under the 3d Marines and air elements under Marine Aircraft Group 16. On 11 May, Major General Paul J. Fontana, one of the Guadalcanal air aces, arrived with the advance headquarters of 1st Marine Aircraft Wing. All three headquarters—Force, Division, and Wing—were crowded into the same ramshackle compound that had been occupied by Shu-fly. On 4 June, Major General Lewis Walt (in the intervening years "Silent Lew" of World War II had become "Uncle Lew" to the troops) took over command of III MAF and 3d Marine Division from General Collins in a ceremony held rather furtively in the Officers Mess because the display of U. S.

North Viet Nam

D.M.Z.
Con Thien
Khe Sanh Dong Ha
QUANG
TRI Quang
Tri

D.M.Z.
Con Thien
Gio Linh
Rock Pile
cua Viet river
Cam Lo Dong Ha
Camp Carroll
Khe Sanh
Combat Camp Ca Lu Quang Tri
9 Khe Sanh Quang Tri River 1

Hue
PhuBai
THUA THIEN

VIET NAM
I CORPS TACTICAL
ZONE

A Shau

Hai Van
Tiensha
DaNang

Marble Mt

QUANG NAM
ThuongDuc Thanh Quit
An Hoa

Hoi An
Thang Binh

KhamDuc QueSon
Hiep Duc

Tam Ky
Chu Lai

QUANG TIN

SOUTH CHINA SEA

Van Tuong
Batangan
Quang Ngai

QUANG NGAI

II CTZ

Duc Pho

25
0 miles 50

LAOS

national colors was not yet permitted. Next day, Brigadier General Keith McCutcheon (the brilliant theoreti-
cian of close air support and helicopter tactics) relieved
General Fontana.

Chu Lai

A second jet-capable airfield was urgently needed in I
Corps Tactical Zone and on 7 May, the 3d Marine
Expeditionary Brigade, commanded by Brigadier General Marion Carl (the same Carl who had scored
eighteen Japanese aircraft in World War II) had landed
the 4th Marines at "Chu Lai," a sandy pine barren
fifty-five miles south of Da Nang. By Memorial Day
four thousand feet of aluminum matting had been laid
and on 1 June eight Douglas A-4 Skyhawks arrived
from the Philippines and flew their first combat mission.

The steady parade of Marine battalions and squadrons into Viet Nam continued. On 1 July the Seventh
Fleet's Special Landing Force, then BLT 3/7, landed at
Qui Nhon, one hundred and seventy-five miles south of
Da Nang to cover the impending arrival of the 1st Air
Cavalry Division. A week later BLT 3/7 was re-embarked, having been relieved in place by 1st Battalion,
7th Marines. On 6 July the headquarters of the 9th
Marines arrived at Da Nang and was given the area
immediately south of the airfield. On 14 August the
headquarters of the 7th Marines landed at Chu Lai.
Thus by late summer 1965, four Marine infantry regiments—the 3d, 4th, 7th, and 9th Marines—were in Viet
Nam. In this new war Marine regimental headquarters
would tend to function as brigade headquarters with
battalions moving in and out of regimental operational
control, as available and as required, much the same
way squadrons moved in and out of Marine aircraft
groups.

There were also four Marine aircraft groups: MAG-
12 with its A-4s was at Chu Lai; MAG-11, a fixed-wing

group, came into Da Nang from Japan on 7 July; MAG-16 detached its fixed-wing squadrons to MAG-11, and in September moved with its helicopters to the new Marble Mountain Air Facility on China Beach; at about the same time MAG-36, also a helicopter group, arrived from California and set itself up on Ky Ha peninsula northeast of the Chu Lai strip.

Operation Starlite

By 15 August good intelligence indicated that the 1st Viet Cong Regiment, some two thousand strong, was concentrated on Van Tuong peninsula, fifteen miles south of Chu Lai, with intentions of attacking the airfield. To thwart those ambitions, Operation Starlite was launched 18 August, the first regimental-size battle fought by U. S. forces since Korea. The 7th Marines converged on the 1st Viet Cong Regiment, one battalion making a river crossing from the north in LVTs, another landing to the west in helicopters, and a third battalion coming in from the sea in an amphibious landing. By 24 August nearly a thousand Viet Cong had been killed.

Pacification

South of Da Nang, the 9th Marines had cleared one-third of the way to Hoi An by October. The theory of pacification was deceptively simple. A hamlet or village would be liberated from VC domination, would be provided security, the seeds of Government of Viet Nam control would be sown, and then nurtured with a carefully worked out civic-action program. The test zone would be the nine villages of the Hoa Vang district that lay south of the Song Cau Do. By October 1965 this area had been cleared by the 9th Marines and the province chief had developed his Nine Village program. Until sufficient Popular Forces were ready to take over, the specially formed 59th Regional Force

Battalion would provide close-in security while Marines provided an outer ring of tactical protection.

The same kind of thing was happening at Chu Lai and Phu Bai as the Marines moved out from their base areas in clearing operations. Drawing on tribal memories of Nicaragua, Haiti, and Santo Domingo, the Marines recognized that the key to pacification was an effective grass-roots gendarmerie. They therefore set about to improve the quality of the Popular and Regional Forces. The Vietnamese rule-of-thumb called for providing a PF squad to each hamlet and a PF platoon to each village or township. Weapons were scarce, mostly carbines and festoons of grenades. Many units were no more than the personal bodyguards of the hamlet or village chiefs. During the summer the 3d Battalion, 4th Marines, at Phu Bai had organized something called a "Joint Action Company" (later the name would be changed to the more accurate "Combined Action Company"). A squad of Marines, all volunteers, was assigned to work with each of five Popular Force platoons in the hamlets north and east of Phu Bai. The combination seemed to work. From the PF the Marines got a feel for the local situation and the Marines gave the PF the stiffening provided by good communications, adequate fire support, and a little basic military training. When 3d Battalion, 4th Marines, came down to Da Nang in January 1966 to serve as air-base-defense battalion it brought along the Combined Action concept and Marine squads were paired off with the seven Popular Force platoons located around the airfield. From these beginnings the Combined Action Program would grow eventually into a regimental-size force.

The night of 27 October 1965 was an unhappy one for Marine aviation. Viet Cong sappers under cover of a mortar barrage got onto the air facility at Marble Mountain. Forty-one were killed but six reached the flight line with bangalore torpedoes and satchel charges, destroying twenty-four helicopters and damaging twenty-three more, almost all of MAG-16's aircraft. That same night at Chu Lai there was a similar attack and two A-4s were destroyed and six damaged before the raiders could be cut down. It was an embarrassment, but later, as the war wore on, it would come to be accepted that no number of American defenders could guarantee an absolute defense against rockets or mortars or even determined sappers.

BLT 2/7 at Qui Nhon was finally released by the Army and loaded out in amphibious shipping on 7 November, it having been decided to combine the move to Chu Lai with a tactical landing. A Vietnamese Marine battalion was also embarked in the Amphibious Task Group and on 10 November, the Marine Corps birthday, the two battalions landed northeast of Tam Ky, midway between Da Nang and Chu Lai. There was no opposition and the chief result was historical: the first combined landing by U. S. and Vietnamese Marines. The Vietnamese Marine Corps, shaped in the U. S. Marine Corps mold, had been formed after the departure of the French in 1954 and had grown to five infantry battalions, an artillery battalion, and an amphibious support battalion. The brigade was highly valued by Saigon as a strategic reserve, and before the war's end it would grow to a light division.

Meanwhile, the northeast monsoon had begun to blow and by November the rain was averaging an inch a day. Outlines of the Viet Cong monsoon strategy were soon clear. After Starlite he avoided stand-up battles against the Marines in anything larger than a company-size formation, but small units—fire teams and squads, even platoons and companies if they were unwary—would be surprised and struck and there would be attacks by fire and sappers against the major bases. As for the ARVN, the Viet Cong were still willing to take them on in battalion or even regimental strength. But the main targets for the monsoon season were the isolated district capitals and market towns garrisoned by the RFs and PFs.

Hiep Duc, a district headquarters twenty-five miles west of Tam Ky, was overrun the night of 16 November. Two ARVN battalions were flown by Marine helos through a solid wall of cotton-wool clouds and rain and then through a gantlet of ridgeline machine guns into the valley. After a bitter fight the ARVN retook the town. Then General Thi, because he had too few regular troops to leave them there, ordered the town abandoned.

After Hiep Duc, the Viet Cong moved next against Que Son district headquarters. Beleaguered Que Son lay in a valley completely dominated by the Viet Cong. To remove the pressure against Que Son it was planned that an ARVN column would move southwest along the axis of one of two roads entering the valley. After the ARVN had developed a contact, two Marine battalions would heli-lift behind the enemy with a third battalion held ready in reserve. The operation was called Harvest Moon.

The ARVN 5th Regiment with two battalions started down the road from Thang Binh the morning of 8 December. About 1330 the right-flank battalion was knocked out of the fight by a heavy close-in attack. Marine helicopters brought in another ARVN battalion before dark. Next morning the commanding officer of the 5th ARVN Regiment (a brave man who had done well at Hiep Duc three weeks earlier) was killed and his faltering regiment driven south and east. To salvage the fast-disintegrating situation, General Walt landed the 2d Battalion, 7th Marines, west of the line of contact and put the 3d Battalion, 3d Marines, in southeast of the battle area. Next morning the Special Landing Force—in this case, the 2d Battalion, 1st Marines—landed mid-way between them and the Marine battalions were put under Task Force Delta with headquarters at Que Son. Meanwhile the shaken ARVN had caught their breath. They came back into the valley under the personal command of Major General Hoang Xuan ("Ho Ho") Lam, commander of the 2d ARVN Division, and moved against the northern rim while the Marines moved south. The Marine climb into the hills was prefaced by four B-52 strikes, the first to be delivered in direct support of Marine operations. By 16 December Viet Cong resistance had faded and three days later the Marines were out of the valley.

An ambitious operation, Double Eagle, was begun on 28 January 1966 targeted against the 325A NVA Division which was believed to be straddling I Corps' southern boundary. Task Force Delta which had been formed for the Que Son operation was given four battalions for the new job. It was a hop-scotch kind of battle; played in concert with the 1st Air Cavalry Division which was operating across the Corps boundary in Binh Dinh province. Task Force Delta returned to Que Son valley in Quang Tin province in mid-February and for the next several months, with a changing array of subordinate battalions, did some hard fighting against the 36th NVA Regiment and the reconstituted 1st Viet Cong Regiment.

1st Marine Division Arrives

The 1st Marine Division had moved its flag forward from Camp Pendleton to Okinawa in August. Its 7th Marine regiment and the 1st and 2d Battalions, 1st Marines, were already in country as 1966 began. The rest of the Division, including the 5th Marines, was now scheduled to come into country. In March, with two-thirds of his Division in place, Major General Lewis J. ("Jeff") Fields opened his command post at Chu Lai. He was given the southern two provinces of the Corps area, Quang Tin and Quang Ngai, as an area of operations to be shared with General Lam's 2d ARVN Division.

Buddhist Revolt

General Thi had been running I Corps Tactical Zone almost semi-independently of Saigon. He and Premier

Ky were old rivals and on 10 March, Thi was relieved of his command and ordered out of the country. Pro-Thi, antigovernment protests under Buddhist leadership bubbled up in Saigon, Da Nang, and Hue. The dissidents coalesced into something called the "Struggle Force." By 3 April the 1st ARVN Division was in the streets of Hue demanding the overthrow of the Saigon government. Ky responded by bringing three battalions of Vietnamese Marines to Da Nang the night of 4 April. On 9 April a Struggle Force column started up Route 1 from Hoi An toward Da Nang. It was met at Thanh Quit bridge, twelve kilometers south of the air base, by Company F, 9th Marines. For several tense hours, U. S. Marines stood gunpoint to gunpoint with the Struggle Force but the Hoi An column did not seek to force the bridge. Elsewhere, General Walt was using his good offices to help negotiate a solution.

A kind of accommodation was reached which lasted until 15 May when Ky landed four battalions at the airfield and overran the semiabandoned corps headquarters (the deposed Thi was in Hue). A week of confused, nasty fighting in and around Da Nang followed. On 22 May active resistance in Da Nang collapsed. Government troops then marched north to Hue and on to Quang Tri, and by 22 June the Buddhist revolt was over and Thi was on his way to exile.

All of this played havoc with the pacification program south of Da Nang, which in late February and early March, before the internecine troubles, had begun to pick up momentum. The 9th Marines had developed several new techniques. One was the "County Fair," a kind of elaborate cordon-and-search operation. Another was "Golden Fleece," in which they protected the rice harvest.

The chronic enemy south of Da Nang was the R-20, or Doc Lap Battalion, a Viet Cong Main Force formation which in the first year showed great willingness to accept appalling losses in night attacks against Marine

company and battery positions. The enemy then settled
down to sapper and terrorist activities and in his use of
mines, both antipersonnel and antivehicular, he had a
cheap and effective means of exacting Marine casualties. Throughout the six years that Marines would
work south of Da Nang, the percentage of casualties
caused by these insidious devices would hang at 50 per
cent.

In March, just before the Buddhist Revolt began,
General Walt had returned from Washington where he
had gone for a month's leave and promotion to lieuten-
ant general. He continued as Commanding General, III
Marine Amphibious Force, but command of the 3d
Marine Division now went to Major General Wood B.
Kyle (they had been in the same Basic School, had also
served together in Shanghai and on Guadalcanal).
General Kyle started a deliberate, systematic advance
to Hoi An, a kind of scrubbing action, using first the 9th
Marines and then moving the 3d Marines in on the
right flank and the 1st Marines on the left.

North to the DMZ

General Kyle's careful campaign was interrupted in
July 1966 by solid intelligence that the 324B NVA
Division had crossed over the DMZ into Quang Tin
province. Task Force Delta was dispatched north with
three battalions and on 15 July Operations Hastings
began. By the end of the week three more U. S.
battalions and five Vietnamese battalions had been fed
into the action and the Marines became acquainted
with the "Rockpile," a seven-hundred-foot hill which
formed a cork to the valleys leading down from the
north and west. The Marines met a new kind of enemy:
fresh, well-equipped North Vietnamese regulars
fighting with secure supply lines to their rear. There
was a pause the first week in August, then the 324B
tried again, this time accompanied by the 341st NVA

Division. The new action was called Operation Prairie,
it would be fought in four phases, and it would last
until 31 May 1967.

The battleground was the strip between Route 9 and
the DMZ. In general the Marines were west of Route 1
and the ARVN east of the road. Fortunately the 1st
ARVN Division had recovered from the Buddhist Re-
volt and was once again a first-class fighting division.
In October 1966, General Kyle moved his 3d Marine
Division command post northward to Phu Bai with an
advance CP at Dong Ha where Route 9 intersects with
Route 1. Essentially, General Kyle had his 3d and 9th
Marines in Quang Tri province, fighting the main battle
of the DMZ from a series of combat bases along Route
9. Kyle's other regiment, the 4th Marines, was in Thua
Thien province covering the western approaches to
Hue.

Major General Herman Nickerson, Jr., a flinty native
of Maine who had had the 7th Marines in Korea, now
commanded the 1st Marine Division. With the shift of
the 3d Marine Division northward he moved his headquarters up from Chu Lai into the bunkered command
post vacated by General Kyle on the reverse slope of
Division Ridge. The 1st Marines were now in Quang
Nam province, the 5th Marines in Quang Tin, and the
7th Marines in Quang Ngai. Also in Quang Ngai was
the 2d Korean "Blue Dragon" Marine Brigade with
three battalions and very much like the U. S. Marines
in organization, training, and equipment.

On Okinawa the 9th Marine Amphibious Brigade
was organized to be CINCPACFLT's strategic amphibious reserve. In addition to overseeing the refitting of
the battalions and squadrons briefly rotated out of Viet
Nam, the Brigade also provided the BLTs and helo
squadrons which served afloat as the 7th Fleet's Special Landing Force. On 1 April 1967, 7th Fleet activated
a second Amphibious Ready Group, doubling its Special Landing Force capability. The two SLFs, each a
battalion landing team and a medium helicopter squad-

ron, were designated Alpha and Bravo. In California, the 5th Marine Division had been reactivated as a temporary division and by late 1966 its first infantry regiment, the 26th Marines, was echeloning its battalions forward to the Western Pacific.

In the south of I Corps Tactical Zone, the U. S. Army's 196th Light Infantry Brigade landed at Chu Lai on 9 April. It was joined later by the 3d Brigade, 25th Infantry Division. Both were placed under Task Force Oregon, commanded by Major General William B. Rosson, USA, and TF Oregon in turn was put under III MAF and for the first time since the unpleasantness at Saipan, a Marine corps-size headquarters had the equivalent of an Army division subordinate to it. The two battalions of the 5th Marines in Quang Tin province, joined later by their 1st Battalion which was then Special Landing Force Alpha, had heavy fighting in Que Son valley during late April and through the month of May, called Operation Union.

Meanwhile, there was even bloodier fighting going on in the northwest corner of Quang Tri province. On 20 March, tall, athletic Major General Bruno A. Hochmuth replaced General Kyle as Commanding General, 3d Marine Division. In late March the enemy pounded Gio Linh and Con Thien with rockets, artillery, and mortars. In early April, most of the fighting centered around Cam Lo. Then on 24 April a patrol from 1st Battalion, 9th Marines, bumped into an NVA force five miles northwest of Khe Sanh. Next day 3d Battalion, 3d Marines, arrived from Dong Ha by helicopter and by nightfall was in contact with at least a battalion on Hill 861. On 26 April, the 3d Marines command group came in along with the regiment's 2d Battalion. Hill 861 was secured by evening of 27 April and next day the 2d and 3d Battalions went forward in a two-pronged attack against Hill 881 North and Hill 881 South. Hill 881 South was taken in a one-day assault but 2d Battalion fought until 3 May before winning Hill 881 North.

On 12 May, with the First Battle of Khe Sanh over,

the 26th Marines arrived and relieved the 3d Marines. East of Khe Sanh the Marines now went on the offensive with the mission of ridding the DMZ south of the Ben Hai of the enemy. A complicated maneuver began on 18 May 1967. Five battalions of the 1st ARVN Division worked along the axis of Highway 1 between Gio Linh and the Ben Hai while three Marine battalions plus the Special Landing Force worked along the river itself. The Prairie series came to a close on 31 May with a hard action on Hill 174 southwest of Con Thien.

Changes

On 1 June 1967, Lieutenant General Walt, after two years of commanding III MAF, was relieved by Lieutenant General Robert Cushman, a big, bluff fifty-two-year-old, former military assistant to Vice President Nixon and holder of the Navy Cross from Guam. Two years of fighting in Vietnam had brought visible changes in the appearance of the Marine rifleman. He had begun the war with the M-14 rifle, essentially an improved M-1, rechambered for the 7.62-mm NATO cartridge and with a twenty-round box magazine. In the spring of 1967, in time for the fighting at Khe Sanh, he had been rearmed with the M-16. A 5.56-mm weapon of terrific velocity (3250 feet per second), the M-16 was at its best in delivering high-volume fire at short ranges. The Marine rifleman had worn the standard green utility uniform into Viet Nam and with General Greene's permission had cut off the sleeves at the elbow. There had been some experimentation with light-weight, quick-drying materials and now there was a loose-fitting camouflaged cotton uniform reminiscent of that worn by the French paratroopers. There was also a "South-East Asia" boot with molded rubber soles and canvas uppers instead of the leather combat boot.

A "fire break" was being cut from Con Thien through Gio Linh to the sea. It was to be filled with barbed wire heavily seeded with sensors and mines and was to link a series of hardened strong points along Route 9. There was no great enthusiasm amongst the Marines for the barrier and the press quickly pounced upon it as McNamara's Wall, comparing it with the Great Wall of China and the Maginot Line. Violent fighting broke out around Con Thien on 2 July, marked by massive supporting fires. With the NVA pushed back from Con Thien, three battalions of Marines and three battalions of ARVN on 14 July went into the southern half of the DMZ for a two-day sweep while the 1st Amphibian Tractor Battalion worked the sandy area between Route 1 and the sea.

At this time, the 3d Marine Division had three infantry regiments in Quang Tri province. The 9th Marines were in "Leatherneck Square," formed by Gio Linh and Con Thien up along the border and Dong Ha and Cam Lo along Route 9. West of Leatherneck Square, the 3d Marines were operating in the vicinity of Camp Carroll, the Rockpile, and Ca Lu. Farther west, the defense of Khe Sanh continued under the 26th Marines. There was hard fighting that September going on around Con Thien. The press was calling it "little Dien Bien Phu." The hill itself, 158 meters high and scraped down to the bare laterite, was never occupied by much more than a battalion and while it was a continuing target for enemy artillery and mortars most of the fighting was some distance away as the enemy tried to get within attack range.

The 4th Marines in Thua Thien province were having a relatively quiet time of it, but it was becoming increasingly apparent that A Shau valley, empty of allied effort since March 1966, was being developed as a major NVA logistical base. The introduction of 122-mm and 140-mm rockets into the enemy's arsenal had increased the problems of defending the base areas from stand-off attacks. Dong Ha, Da Nang, and Chu Lai continued to be regular targets. Nevertheless, security of the populated coastal area was steadily improving. It was now possible to drive along Route 1 from Dong Ha south to the Binh Dinh province border. In all, it was a strange blurry kind of war where every scrap of statistical evidence—enemy killed, weapons captured, rice caches found—had to be collected and fed into a computer so that Washington could measure progress. Sometime in mid-summer 1967 total Marine casualties in Viet Nam went past the total for the Korean War and Viet Nam had become the second largest war in Marine Corps history.

On 14 November Major General Hochmuth was killed when his UH-1E helicopter exploded and crashed and Major General Rathvon Tompkins, holder of the Navy Cross from Saipan, came out from Parris Island to be the new 3d Marine Division commander. Donn J. Robertson, who had his Navy Cross from Iwo Jima, was now in command of the 1st Marine Division and in September there had been heavy fighting in Que Son valley.

Tet Offensive (1968)

Farther south, additional brigades joined TF Oregon which in late September was redesignated the Americal or 23d U. S. Infantry Division. This new Army strength set in motion a whole sequence of moves which the Marines called "Operation Checkers." The Korean Marine Brigade moved up from Chu Lai in late December 1967 to an area of operations radiating out from Hoi An. This made it possible to start sending some additional 1st Marine Division battalions north. The idea was to allow the 3d Marine Division to concentrate on the defense of the DMZ and Quang Tri province and have the 1st Marine Division take over responsibility for Thua Thien and the approaches to Hue. The 1st Marine Regiment's headquarters had already moved to Quang Tri and it was supposed to flip-flop with the 4th Marines headquarters in Thua Thien, thus getting the regiments realigned with their parent divisions. On the enemy side, six NVA divisions threatened Quang Tri and Thua Thien.

The second battle of Khe Sanh began on 20 January 1968 with a sharp fight between the 3d Battalion, 26th Marines, and an NVA battalion entrenched in the saddle between Hills 881 North and South two miles northwest of the base. Next day the enemy overran the village of Khe Sanh and pushed against the base itself. An ammunition dump went up under the barrage. General Tompkins sent the 26th Marines a fourth battalion, the 1st Battalion, 9th Marines, and on 26 January the lightweight 37th ARVN Ranger Battalion joined the defenders. Cushman's battle plan was to put no more troops than necessary into Khe Sanh, realizing that they must be resupplied by air through the tag end of the monsoon, and to put his dependence upon massive air and ground firepower to destroy the attackers.

The Tet holiday was about to begin and the Viet Cong announced a nationwide truce to run from 27 January until 3 February 1968. This illusory truce was interrupted on 29 and 30 January by rocket attacks against Da Nang, Marble Mountain, and Chu Lai. On the thirtieth and thirty-first there were ground attacks against all five province capitals. In Da Nang, before dawn on 30 January, infiltrators reached the I Corps headquarters compound; their mission was to disrupt command and control while the 2d NVA Division launched its attack from south and west of the city. The 2d NVA columns which were to make the main effort were caught by Marine air and artillery as they came down from the hills west of An Hoa. Some North Vietnamese made it almost to the river south of the Da Nang airfield where they were engaged by Marine infantry.

The enemy had more success, at least temporarily, at Hue. Several regiments had been infiltrated into the city in civilian clothing. At midnight, 30 January, they changed into their uniforms, let go a rocket and mortar barrage, and revealed themselves as essentially in control of the city. There were pockets of Allied resistance. 1st ARVN Division headquarters was still intact as was the MACV advisers' compound south of the Perfume River.

Early next morning, 31 January, 1st Battalion, 1st Marines, at two-company strength, started up the road to Hue from Phu Bai, fought their way through scattered resistance, and arrived at the MACV compound in the early afternoon. They were then ordered to open a route to the 1st ARVN Division headquarters. There was a hard fight getting over the bridge, they reached the Citadel wall, could not breach it, and withdrew south again to the MACV compound. On 1 February the battalion was given the task of clearing the part of the city that lay south of the river. By 4 February, 2d Battalion, 5th Marines, had also arrived. The counterattack was put under command of the 1st Marines. It was house-to-house street fighting of a kind that Marines had not done since Seoul in 1950. By 9 February the city south of the river had been cleared.

Across the river, the ARVN had been attacking from the northeastern corner of the city toward the Citadel. On 12 February the 1st Battalion, 5th Marines, went in on the ARVN left flank. The 3d ARVN Regiment was in the center and the Vietnamese Marines were on the right flank. After ten grinding days the U. S. Marines reached the southeast wall of the Citadel. Mopping up continued for another week and on 2 March the Battle for Hue was declared over. Three understrength U. S. Marine battalions and thirteen Vietnamese battalions had virtually destroyed at least eight, and possibly eleven North Vietnamese battalions. In retaliation, thousands of civilians had been executed by the enemy or marched off into oblivion. Much of the beautiful old city lay in ruins.

In Washington, on 1 January, General Leonard Fielding Chapman, Jr., had succeeded General Greene as Commandant. An artillery battalion commander in World War II and Greene's chief of staff, Chapman would give the Marine Corps four years of leadership characterized by cool managerial efficiency.

Second Battle of Khe Sanh

At Khe Sanh, during the early morning of 5 February, sensors told the 26th Marines that the enemy was coming. The NVA attempted to assault Hills 881 South and 861A, were hit heavily with air and artillery, and thrown back. Next day the enemy continued the attack, coming in from the west along the axis of Route 9 and successfully overran the Special Forces camp at Lang Vei, six miles from Khe Sanh, using Russian-built PT-76 amphibian tanks.

On 9 February, Westmoreland had sent his Deputy, fifty-three-year-old, cigar-chewing General Creighton W. Abrams, to Phu Bai to establish a MACV forward command post (which later became XXIV Corps). Many interpreted this as a questioning of Marine generalship at Hue and Khe Sanh. Not so, said General Westmoreland—and General Abrams was scrupulously correct in his dealings with General Cushman.

Regimental Landing Team 27, the second RLT to be drawn off from the new 5th Marine Division, began arriving on 17 February and went into the still-troublesome area south of Marble Mountain, permitting the rest of the 5th Marines to go north to Phu Bai. Brigades from the 101st and 82d Divisions also arrived in Thua Thien province, and by the end of February there were twenty-four U. S. Marine and twenty-eight U. S. Army infantry battalions in I Corps Tactical Zone and General Cushman was commanding the equivalent of a field army.

On 10 March, Westmoreland made General William W. Momyer, CG, Seventh Air Force, the "single manager" for tactical air and gave him "mission direction" of the 1st Marine Aircraft Wing's fixed-wing strike aircraft. The Marines had fought this assignment on doctrinal grounds, but found in practice it could be accommodated and Marine ground operations continued to get first priority for Marine tactical air support. Tactical air had gotten its greatest testing of the war in its support of the Khe Sanh defenders. Unprecedented tonnages of bombs churned the green hillsides into a red-orange moonscape. Aerial resupply by C-123s and C-130s and by helicopter transports continued in what Westmoreland called the "premier air logistical feat of the war." On 18 March the NVA tried to crack the portion of the perimeter held by the Vietnamese 37th Rangers and failed. On the thirtieth, the 1st Battalion, 26th Marines, counterattacked and dislodged an NVA battalion from the hills a mile south of the airstrip.

Spring Counteroffensive (1968)

Cushman's plan for a Spring counteroffensive had three phases: relief of Khe Sanh, a raid into A Shau valley, and an attack into the DMZ.

The relief of Khe Sanh, called Operation Pegasus, got under way 1 April 1968. The 1st Marines and three Vietnamese battalions moved westward along Route 9 while the 1st Air Cavalry Division and an ARVN airborne battalion leapfrogged toward the beleaguered base. On 4 April the 26th Marines attacked southeast from Khe Sanh and two days later made contact with the Air Cav. By 12 April, Route 9 was open to truck traffic. Next came a spoiling attack by the 1st Air Cavalry and 101st Airborne Divisions into the A Shau valley, from 19 April until 16 May, costing the enemy the largest materiel losses he had yet suffered in I Corps Tactical Zone.

The thrust into the DMZ was delayed by an attack by the 320th NVA Division beginning 29 April against 3d Marine Division elements at Dong Ha. There was a bitter six-day seesaw action at Dai Ho hamlet northeast of Dong Ha and heavy fighting continued through most of May. The enemy's attack on Dong Ha was part of his second major offensive for the year. The Marines called this new offensive "mini-Tet." In Quang Nam province four NVA regiments were south and west of Da Nang. The 1st Marine Division's defense of the Da Nang vital zone had resolved itself largely into a thickly-manned, heavily-patrolled "rocket belt" arcing around the city. In early May, to keep the NVA regular formations at arm's length, the 7th Marines were sent on a sweep through "Go Noi Island," a delta west of Hoi An formed by the many-channeled, many-named Ky Lam or Thu Bon river, and then on westward into the Thuong Duc corridor.

During May, Major General Raymond Davis, Medal of Honor holder from Korea, took command of the 3d Marine Division and Tompkins moved up to Deputy Commander, III MAF. Tactical headquarters at Khe Sanh was now Task Force Hotel under Brigadier General Carl W. Hoffman. Earlier in May there had been a series of sharp actions with the rejuvenated 304th NVA Division in the hills and along Route 9. At the end of the month, the 304th was replaced by the 308th, which had two regiments—the 88th and 102d— fresh from Hanoi. Davis gave Hoffman the 1st and 4th Marines for a fast-moving, high-mobility operation. The objective area was a salient south of Khe Sanh formed by a loop in the Laotian border. Two fire-support bases, Robin and Loon, were blasted through the canopy. The first battalions were inserted on 2 and 3 June and when it was over on 19 June, the 308th NVA Division, after only two weeks in combat, was on its way back north for refitting.

Next mission assigned Task Force Hotel was the evacuation of Khe Sanh. Cushman had argued for such a move immediately after Operation Pegasus. Westmoreland agreed militarily but was concerned over the timing politically and asked that the decision to execute be deferred until Abrams had taken over as COMUSMACV. This occurred on 11 June. The planned evacuation got into the press prematurely and caused much speculation and debate. Why, if Khe Sanh had been worth defending at all costs just a few months before, was it being abandoned now? The White House quickly announced that it was a military decision, not President Johnson's. Hanoi equally quickly claimed that the "fall" of Khe Sanh was a "grave defeat" for the Americans. The official MACV explanation stressed the switchover to more mobile tactics, making "the operation of the base at Khe Sanh unnecessary." Meanwhile, the 1st Marines and the 11th Engineer Battalion had razed Khe Sanh and withdrawn east along Route 9, almost without incident.

In July, General Cushman got on with the third phase of his spring counteroffensive, a general cleansing of the area between Route 9 and the DMZ. There was a series of convoluted attacks by the 3d and 9th Marines coordinated with actions by the 2d ARVN Regiment. Contact was frequent but small scale. At the end of July the 1st Brigade, 5th U. S. Mechanized Division, arrived in Quang Tin as the numerical relief for the temporarily deployed RLT-27, which would return to Camp Pendleton in September.

West and south of Da Nang, the 1st Marine Division, now commanded by artilleryman Major General Carl A. Youngdale, fought sharp actions near Hill 55 and in and around Go Noi Island, and it became increasingly obvious that the enemy was preparing the battlefield for another major attack. The enemy's "Third Offensive" of 1968 began on 18 August with rocket and mortar attacks and some sapper action against provincial and district headquarters. The main target, though, was Da Nang. Before dawn on 23 August a VC sapper battalion got across the Cau Do River and into the Hoa Vang district headquarters and also seized the southern end of the Cam Le bridge, one of two bridges which carry Route 1 into Da Nang. The ARVN Rangers threw the VC out of Hoa Vang district headquarters and those on the bridge were caught between two companies of Marines. Four miles south of the bridge, the

38th NVA Regiment was badly mauled in a three-day battle with three Vietnamese battalions and elements of the 27th Marines. It was the enemy's last serious effort to enter Da Nang by force. As part of the August offensive, the 320th NVA Division came across the DMZ but was ejected in a counteraction by the 9th and 3d Marines west and north of the Rockpile, followed by a sweep through the DMZ which gutted the 320th NVA Division's carefully positioned ammunition stockpiles.

Monsoon (1968)

September and October were quiet months, the coming of the monsoon causing seasonal problems for both sides. The 1st Cavalry Division (AirMobile) was redeployed to III Corps Tactical Zone and the 3d Marine Division and 101st Airborne Division adjusted their boundaries accordingly. The 3d Marine Division and the 1st Brigade, 5th Mechanized, would continue to work in Quang Tin province and the 101st in Thua Thien province.

Thuong Duc Special Forces Camp lay in the valley of the Song Vu Gia about halfway between Da Nang and the Laotian border. On 28 September 1968 the NVA attacked the camp, briefly held two outposts, were driven out by air and artillery, and then settled down to a more deliberate siege. On 6 October, the 7th Marines launched a relief column down the axis of Route 4, feinted an attack, developing the enemy positions, while other battalions went in deeper by helo. The fight coalesced into a struggle for Hill 163 two miles from the camp. This was taken and held and by 19 October the road to Thuong Duc was once again open. The 5th Marines, meanwhile, were operating close by in the "Arizona" territory south of the Vu Gia and Thu Bon. Almost half of the 1st Marine Division kills that summer and fall were attributed to the 1st Reconnaissance Battalion using what were called "Sting Ray" techniques, quiet insertions of six-man patrols who watched for enemy movement and then called in Marine air and artillery.

November saw the beginning of the Accelerated Pacification Plan designed to win back all that had been lost in territorial confidence and security as a result of the Tet offensive. Operation Meade River, an enlarged County Fair, was begun by the 1st Marine Division on 20 November. The target area was "Dodge City," ten miles south of Da Nang and lying between the La Tho and Ky Lam rivers, where there had been much hard fighting since the 9th Marines first went there in 1966. Six Marine battalions were used for the cordon which worked out to one Marine for every five meters along the perimeter. Inside the box there were thought to be 1300 NVA and about 100 VCI. When the operation ended on 9 December, the total enemy body count was put at 1210.

New Year (1969)

As 1969 began, it was estimated that there were about 90,000 enemy either in I Corps Tactical Zone or poised on its borders. South and southwest of Da Nang, the 1st Marine Division, now commanded by Major General Ormond R. Simpson, followed up the success of Meade River with a deep thrust into the enemy's mountainous base areas. Farther south, on 13 January, the 2d and 3d Battalions, 26th Marines, landed on the northern face of Batangan peninsula, the old Starlite battlefield, in what was the largest Special Landing Force operation of the war. In an amphibious application of the County Fair concept, the two SLF battalions closed a cordon formed on the land side by two battalions of the Americal Division, and together the joint operation killed 239 enemy and screened 12,000 Vietnamese, of whom 256 were identified as Viet Cong cadre.

To the north, in Quang Tri province's southwest corner, the 3d Marine Division had begun Dewey

Canyon, perhaps the most successful high-mobility regimental-size action of the war. On 22 January the 9th Marines went into the enemy's Base Area 611 in Da Krong valley. Depending entirely upon helicopters for logistic support, the battalions leapfrogged from fire-support base to fire-support base, these quickly hacked out of the jungle to provide a helo landing zone and room for a mixed battery of artillery. By 18 March the enemy's base area had been cleaned out, 1617 enemy dead had been counted, and 1461 weapons and hundreds of tons of ammunition and supplies taken.

Tet 1969 in mid-February was only a pale shadow of the violence of Tet 1968. The enemy sought once again to mount a full-scale attack against Da Nang. The attack was launched on 23 February and in three days it had petered out.

Pacification seemed to be going well. Goal for the year was to bring all the populated area under government control and to raise the security level of the population to 90 per cent. III MAF's largest contribution to the security of the rural areas continued to be the Combined Action Program. The Program had grown to four battalion-size Combined Action Groups, with headquarters at Da Nang, Chu Lai, Phu Bai, and Quang Tri. These Groups totaled 19 Combined Action Companies. Under the companies, in turn, were 102 Combined Action Platoons—the specially selected and trained Marine rifle squads which were paired off with Popular Force or Regional Force platoons to provide hamlet and village security.

On 26 March 1969, Lieutenant General Herman Nickerson, Jr., who on his previous Viet Nam tour had commanded the 1st Marine Division, relieved General Cushman as the CG, III MAF. Cushman on his return to the States became the Deputy Director of the Central Intelligence Agency.

Troop Withdrawals Begin

In April the arrival of a fresh NVA regiment in the vicinity of Cam Lo caused some sharp exchanges with the 9th Marines. In May, the 9th Marines passed this sector to the 3d Marines and went back into Da Krong valley in a replay of Dewey Canyon. Finding it virtually empty, in June they moved up into the salient formed by the Laotian border south of Khe Sanh. This is where the war ended for the 9th Marines. The first major U. S. troop withdrawal had been announced and the 9th Marines were to return in July to Okinawa. Proportional slices of combat support and service support as well as elements of the 1st Marine Aircraft Wing also left. At this time the Wing was operating from 5 major airfields with 6 aircraft groups and 26 tactical squadrons with a total of 186 helicopters and 242 fixed-wing aircraft.

The 1st Marine Division continued its less spectacular but arduous operations west and south of Da Nang. Battles would be fought and refought against the almost invisible enemy on the same ground: "Barrier Island," the sandy waste south of Hoi An dotted with poverty-stricken fishing villages; the "Arizona Territory," the piedmont agricultural area northwest of An Hoa made desolate by the war; "Dodge City," south of Da Nang; and "Go Noi Island," one-time center of silkworm and mulberry culture. At the end of August the boundary between the 1st Marine Division and the Americal Division was realigned and the Marines were again given responsibility for Que Son valley, first entered by them in December 1965. The 7th Marines began moving back into the valley on 15 August, displacing the 196th Light Infantry Brigade.

In September, the second increment of the U. S. troop withdrawal was announced. By mid-October the rest of the 3d Marine Division was gone; Headquarters and the 4th Marines to Okinawa, the 3d Marines to Camp Pendleton. All helicopter squadrons remaining in country were consolidated under MAG-16 at Marble Mountain.

The last Special Landing Force operation was conducted in September 1969, one more sweep of Barrier Island. Since 1965, Seventh Fleet had carried out seventy-two of these SLF landings, of which fifty-three had been in ICTZ. There were no World War II style beach assaults; the enemy never did more than lightly harass the landing force. The SLFs were most profitably used as highly mobile reserves with which to exploit opportunities presented by ongoing operations. This was particularly true of the big battles fought along the DMZ by the 3d Marine Division in 1967 and 1968. Coastal operations, such as the repeated visits to Barrier Island and Batangan Peninsula, helped keep those areas free of the enemy and aided the U. S. Navy's Market Time blockade of infiltration from the sea.

By this time the enemy in Quang Nam and Quang Tin provinces had reverted almost completely to guerrilla and terrorist operations and it was once again monsoon season. In December, Major General Edwin B. Wheeler, who as a colonel had commanded the 3d Marines, the first regiment to come in-country in 1965, succeeded General Simpson as commanding general, 1st Marine Division. The Division had just ended a six-month effort to clean out, once again, the Dodge City–Go Noi Island areas. By the end of the year, in the northern five provinces, the percentage of the population judged to be living in secure areas had climbed to an optimistic 94 per cent and a goal of 100 per cent was set for 1970.

XXIV Corps Takes Over

It was now time for another troop withdrawal. Between January and April 1970, the Marines reduced their in-country strength another 12,600 "spaces." The 26th Marines went back to Camp Pendleton and eventual deactivation. A helicopter squadron and three fixed-wing squadrons also departed. With these reductions, the U. S. Marines were no longer the dominant U. S. service in I Corps. On 9 March 1970, upon the detachment of Lieutenant General Nickerson, the roles of III MAF and XXIV Corps were reversed. Lieutenant General Melvin Zais, USA, moved his headquarters from Phu Bai down to Da Nang and into the old III MAF compound on the Tourane River. The new III MAF commander was Keith McCutcheon, now a lieutenant general. McCutcheon moved his headquarters to Red Beach, close to where the Marines had originally landed in 1965.

The "tactical area of responsibility" of III MAF had shrunk to that held by the 1st Marine Division, essentially Quang Nam province. The Division was now down to its three organic infantry regiments, the 1st, 5th, and 7th Marines and its artillery regiment, the 11th Marines. It had lost some of its amphibious elements but was heavy with engineer and motor transport reinforcements. The Division's overriding mission was still to keep the enemy at arm's length from Da Nang. "Ed" Wheeler broke his leg in a helo crash on 18 April and was succeeded by Charles F. ("Chuck") Widdecke, who had won a Navy Cross at Guam and who had commanded the 5th Marines in Vietnam in 1966.

On 2 July 1970, I Corps Tactical Zone was redesignated Military Region 1. There were sweeping organizational changes with more responsibility for territorial security going to the province chiefs. General Lam, commanding in Military Region 1 and knowing that further U. S. troop withdrawals were imminent, planned a last large-scale broad-front combined offensive westward into enemy base areas. In Quang Nam province a Vietnamese Marine brigade was added to the 51st ARVN Regiment and the Ranger Group so that a division-equivalent was available. The 7th Marines followed behind Lam's attack in a supporting operation, Pickens Forest, 16 July to 24 August. The results were not great, but the pattern was significant:

the ARVN were out in front and the Marines were in a supporting role. Marine strength was scheduled to go down 18,600 more "spaces" by 15 October. The 7th Marines would begin one more operation before leaving for home. On 31 August, behind a thunderous air and artillery preparation, they went back into the Que Son mountains, beginning Imperial Lake, the Marines' last effort to clean out that enemy stronghold.

The 7th Marines went home to Camp Pendleton in September and the 5th Marines took their place in the Que Sons. The 1st Marines, alone now in the Da Nang area, fanned out to take over the 5th Marines' zone north of the Thu Bon. The great combat base at An Hoa, most of it razed, was turned over to the ARVN just as the monsoon rains began.

On the air side, Major General Alan J. Armstrong now commanded the 1st Marine Aircraft Wing. As part of the withdrawals, VMCJ-1, the hard-working reconnaissance and electronic countermeasures squadron, left for Iwakuni. MAG-13 turned Chu Lai over to the U. S. Army and left for El Toro. Remaining in country were two aircraft groups, MAG-11 at Da Nang with about 80 fixed-wing aircraft, and MAG-16 at Marble Mountain with about 150 helicopters.

In October, Typhoon Kate caused the worst floods in Quang Nam since 1964. Strenuous rescue efforts by the Marines—particularly by the Marine helicopters—evacuated perhaps 30,000 civilians. The province chief estimated that, otherwise, as many as 10,000 might have died.

There was a big celebration of the Marine Corps Birthday on 10 November, capped by a pageant in one of the hangars on the west side of Da Nang Air Base. General McCutcheon officiated, but he wasn't feeling well, and on 13 December he left for the U. S Naval Hospital at Bethesda. It was a terminal illness for the Marine aviator who had done so much to develop close air support and to bring helicopters and vertical-lift aircraft into the Marine Corps. He was placed on the

retired list on 1 July 1971 in the grade of four-star
general and died of cancer two weeks later.

Phase Out

Donn Robertson, who had commanded the 1st Marine
Division in 1967 and 1968, came out to Viet Nam just
before Christmas as a lieutenant general to take command of III MAF. The next troop reduction was being
negotiated and the days of the III MAF in-country were
literally numbered. The intensity of combat experi-
enced by the 1st Marine Division continued to decline.
In 1969, the Division had had 1051 killed and 9286
wounded. In 1970, casualties were down to 403 killed
and 3626 wounded. They continued to tail off in the
first months of 1971. General Chapman paid his last
visit as Commandant to the combat zone in January.
He charged the remaining Marines to come out of
Viet Nam in good order, leaving behind nothing worth
more than "five dollars."

In February, General Lam launched the major incur-
sion into Laos called Lam Son 719. It was supposed to
be a spoiling action to prevent a large-scale enemy
offensive into the northern province. Unlike the Cambodian offensive of the year before, U. S. ground forces
did not go into Laos. For many reasons, including bad
weather and the lack of American advisors with the
ARVN units, the operation went badly. U. S. Marine
participation was limited to tactical air support, a few
heavy-lift helicopters, and some engineer and transportation help on the Vietnamese side of the border.

The 5th Marines started its stand-down on 15 February, coming out of the Que Son valley and mountains.
Two fixed-wing and one helicopter squadron also departed. Just the 1st Marine regiment remained in the
field. In January, the 1st Marines had put a battalion
for the last time up onto Charlie Ridge west of Da Nang
to look for the NVA's elusive rocketeers who were still
sporadically shelling the city and air base. Another

bobtailed battalion was put up into the Que Sons. Any Marine finding a rocket was rewarded with a short leave, if he wished to go, to Hong Kong or Bangkok.

On 14 April 1971, General Robertson took the flag and headquarters of III MAF to Okinawa. That same day the headquarters of the Wing left for Iwakuni in Japan and the flag of the 1st Marine Division departed for Camp Pendleton. The remaining combatant elements were briefly combined into the 3d Marine Amphibious Brigade under Major General Armstrong. Ground and air operations stopped on 7 May and by 26 June 1971 all elements of the Brigade had been redeployed. The Marines' place in Quang Nam province was taken by the U. S. 196th Light Infantry Brigade.

Easter Offensive 1972

This left about five hundred Marines in Viet Nam—embassy guards, air and naval gunfire spotters, and advisors to the Vietnamese Marines—and this was about the number that was present when the North Vietnamese began their Easter offensive at the end of March 1972. The four-division NVA thrust across the DMZ and sliced through the new and green 3d ARVN Division. The brigades of the Vietnamese Marine Division were hurriedly moved into blocking positions. At sea, by the end of the first week in April, the 9th Marine Amphibious Brigade had taken station in amphibious shipping with four battalion landing teams and two composite helicopter squadrons. At Da Nang air base, MAG-15 had begun arriving with four squadrons of F-4 Phantoms. Most of this air support was used in Military Regions I and II; some strikes were flown north into Laos and North Viet Nam. Farther south, at Bien Hoa, a field not previously used by the Marines, MAG-12 moved in during mid-May with two squadrons of A-4 Skyhawks to support Military Regions III and IV, with some sorties into Cambodia.

From on board the USS *Coral Sea*, VMA(AW)-224,

with the A-6 Intruder, flew most of its missions in Laos and North Viet Nam. HMA-369, with the new AH-1J Sea Cobra, arrived off the coast on 20 June and began flying armed helicopter strikes from the decks of the USS *Denver*.

No Marine ground-combat troops went ashore, but with this kind of air and naval gunfire support—every available cruiser and destroyer in the Seventh Fleet took its turn on line—the crack Vietnamese Airborne and Marine Divisions, widely held to be the two best divisions in South Vietnam's armed forces, fought a series of delaying actions, finally stopped the North Vietnamese drive at My Chanh, north of Hue, and then counterattacked. The Marine advisors to the Vietnamese Marine Division—some forty-one officers and thirteen enlisted men—never left the side of their counterparts. Helicopters from the 9th MAB were used to lift the Vietnamese Marines and in one operation, U. S. Marine amphibian tractors landed a battalion across the beach.

Task Force Delta, reactivated for the occasion, went to Nam Phong in Thailand in late May to set up an expeditionary airfield and, in June, MAG-15 moved from Da Nang to Nam Phong, promptly named it "the Rose Garden," in derisive reference to the then-current recruiting slogan, "The Marine Corps didn't promise you a rose garden."

Restructuring for Peace

The Viet Nam war was the longest and, in some dimensions, the biggest war in the history of the Marine Corps. At its peak strength in 1968, III Marine Amphibious Force had a total of 85,755 Marines, more Marines than had been ashore at Iwo Jima or Okinawa. By mid-1972, 12,926 Marines had been killed, another 88,542 Marines wounded (about half of whom required hospitalization), casualties that compare to the 19,733 Marines killed and 67,207 wounded in World War II.

Overall strength of the Corps during the Viet Nam war peaked at 317,400, far under the 485,053 peak reached in World War II. But because Viet Nam was fought using peacetime personnel policies, more Marines actually served in the Corps during the seven years of major involvement in Viet Nam than served during the four years of World War II, some 800,000 as opposed to 600,000.

18

1972-1975
"...getting back into the amphibious business..."

Restructuring for Peace

On 1 January 1972, General Robert Everton Cushman, Jr., took over as Commandant from General Chapman. General Ray Davis retired as Assistant Commandant on 1 April. The new Assistant Commandant was General Earl E. Anderson, the first Marine aviator to reach four stars on active service. The Corps, by then, was down to about 200,000 men. The post-Viet Nam redeployments had put the 3d Marine Division back on Okinawa, and the 1st Marine Brigade had been reconstituted in Hawaii. The 1st Marine Division was back in Camp Pendleton and the 3d Marine Aircraft Wing remained at El Toro. On the East Coast, the 2d Marine Division continued at Camp Lejeune and the 2d Wing at Cherry Point.

At Quantico, as after previous wars, the lessons of Viet Nam were being analyzed and digested. In April 1971, at about the same time that President Nixon was welcoming the 1st Marine Division home from Viet Nam, VMA-513 at Beaufort, South Carolina, received its complement of AV-8As, the British-built Hawker-Siddeley Harrier. With its vertical take-off and landing capability, the Harrier promised to be as revolutionary in the area of close air support as the helicopter had proved for tactical troop lifts. "Sea-basing" was the name given to the new concept aimed at greatly increasing seaborne logistic support, so that future operations would not need the great sprawling logistics complexes such as had grown up in Viet Nam. General Cushman said in April 1972, "I don't want to give the impression that we are rewriting the book on amphibious warfare. Sea-basing represents an evolutionary refinement, not a revolutionary new concept. We have deployed forces which were essentially sea-based since the end of World War II, including our Caribbean and Mediterranean ready forces and our Special Landing Forces in Viet Nam."

Then in words that Nicholas, Henderson, and Lejeune would have appreciated, Cushman said tautly: ". . . we are pulling our heads out of the jungle and getting back into the amphibious business . . . we are redirecting our attention seaward and re-emphasizing our partnership with the Navy and our shared concern in the maritime aspects of our national strategy. . . ."

The numbers of amphibious ships had shrunk with the overall contraction of the U. S. Navy but the quality was good, and the objective of a twenty-knot speed of advance for the amphibious forces had been attained. The new capital ship for the amphibs was to be the LHA, a multipurpose amphibious assault ship that could handle helicopters from its flight deck and amphibian vehicles from its hold. The first of these, USS *Tarawa* (LHA-1) began its operational tests in 1975. It was to be followed shortly by USS *Saipan* (LHA-2). The three remaining ships of the class were to have delivery dates stretching out through the late 1970s.

Paris Peace Accords

In Paris, on 27 January 1973, after four frustrating years of negotiation, the "Peace Accords" were signed

by four parties: South and North Viet Nam, the Viet
Cong, and the United States. Fighting was to stop while
the Vietnamese themselves worked out South Viet
Nam's political future. Until free general elections
could be held, the Saigon government was to remain in
power. The U. S. and other foreign troops were to be
out of country in sixty days (most had already departed) and their bases dismantled. No requirement
was imposed, however, for the pull-back of the 150,000
North Vietnamese soldiers then encysted in South Viet
Nam. The cease-fire was to go into effect at midnight,
Greenwich Mean Time, 27 January.

For the United States, the Peace Accords offered a
face-saving formula: they permitted the release of U. S.
prisoners of war and the end of participation in an
unbearably unpopular war—without the appearance of
utter abandonment of an ally. The Nobel Peace Prize
for 1973 went jointly to U. S. Secretary of State Henry
A. Kissinger and North Vietnamese negotiator Le Duc
Tho. Kissinger accepted his prize, but Tho said he
would be able to consider it only after "real peace is
established in South Viet Nam."

In February and March 1973, 649 American prisoners of war came home from Hanoi. Twenty-six of them
were Marines. Twelve other Marines had either escaped or were exchanged earlier. Three were known to
have died in captivity. As of mid-1975, forty-seven
were still listed as missing-in-action.

The cease-fire was to be monitored by a four-nation
International Commission of Control and Supervision
(ICCS)—1160 members to be drawn equally from
Canada, Indonesia, Hungary, and Poland. Almost immediately, violations began to be reported on both
sides. The work of the commission was effectively
blocked by Hungarian and Polish intransigence and
North Vietnamese obstructionism. In July 1973 Canada
withdrew in frustration from the ICCS and was replaced by Iran. North Vietnamese forces continued to
march into South Viet Nam. Much of northernmost

Quang Tri Province was now in Communist hands and
heartsick U. S. Marines read in the newspapers that
Khe Sanh and Dong Ha, scene of their hard-won
victories, were now North Vietnamese airfields.

Israel and Cyprus (1973–1974)

On the other side of the world, on 6 October 1973, Syria
and Egypt launched their twin offensives against Israel—in what quickly came to be called the October or
Yom Kippur War (it was not only the Jewish holy day
but was also the tenth day of Islam's sacred month of
Ramadan). Afloat in the eastern Mediterranean was the
Landing Force, Sixth Fleet—the 34th Marine Amphibious Unit (34th MAU) and the headquarters of the 4th
Marine Amphibious Brigade (4th MAB) under the
command of Brigadier General Andrew W. O'Donnell.
The skeleton brigade was quickly reinforced by the
arrival of the 32d MAU, so that O'Donnell had under
his command 4400 Marines, organized provisionally
into a regimental landing team, a helicopter group, and
a logistics support group. But this was not 1956, when
the mere presence of the U. S. Sixth Fleet could halt a
Suez war. Ashore, out of sight of the Marines, the greatest tank battles of history were being fought, and from
these battles the Marines would derive certain lessons
as to their own antitank and antiaircraft defenses.

The following summer, in July 1974, the 34th MAU,
then consisting of Battalion Landing Team 1/8 and
Medium Helicopter Squadron 162, was engaged in a
landing exercise in Lakinikos Gulf, some one hundred
miles southwest of Athens, when word reached them
that Archbishop Makarios of Cyprus had been over-
thrown on the fifteenth by Greek Cypriot factions
seeking *enosis*, or union, with Greece. On 20 July, in a
countermove, the Turks landed on the north coast of
Cyprus. The next day, the 34th MAU in its amphibious
shipping took station off the south coast of the embat-
tled island and on 22 July began the evacuation of U. S.

citizens and other foreign nationals. Some were evacuated from Dhekalia airfield by Marine helicopters; others were delivered to the ships by the British. In all, 752 persons, 498 of them Americans, were taken out and given safe passage to Beirut. The warm glow of this successful evacuation was chilled a month later, on 19 August, when a Cypriot mob attacked the U. S. Embassy in Nicosia and, despite the best efforts of a handful of Marine security guards, ransacked the building while a sniper's bullet killed U. S. Ambassador Rodger P. Davies.

Viet Nam (1975)

In January 1975 the North Vietnamese boldly took possession of Phuoc Long province, only forty miles north of Saigon. The United States did nothing and President Nguyen Van Thieu accepted the loss. Having tested South Vietnamese resolve and U. S. reaction, North Viet Nam followed up this initial probe with a full-scale offensive, pressing forward on a broad front that swung in a great arc from the DMZ in the north, through the Central Highlands, down Route 14 to Tay Ninh in the south. To meet the attack, the South Vietnamese had, on paper, an imposing numerical superiority: 850,000 combatants to 305,000. But the South Vietnamese had only 13 divisions in the field and these were widely dispersed as compared to the 18 to 20 lean and concentrated North Vietnamese divisions.

In March, Ban Me Thuot, Montagnard city and capital of Dar Lac province in the Highlands, fell after a week's fighting. This apparently triggered a decision on Thieu's part to withdraw from both the Highlands and the north so as to concentrate his regular forces in the vital coastal regions and around Saigon. (The word "enclave," much discussed in the strategic debates of 1965 and 1966, was rediscovered.) On 14 March, Thieu met secretly at Nha Trang with Lieutenant General Pham Van Thu, commander of Military Region II. Thu was to evacuate the Highlands and shift his corps headquarters from Pleiku to Nha Trang on the coast. Thieu then flew north to Da Nang to meet with Lieutenant General Ngo Quang Truong. Truong, admired by the U. S. Marines, had the reputation of being the best fighting general in the South Vietnamese army. He had already lost most of the Airborne Division, which had been ordered back to Saigon. His best remaining troops were the ARVN 1st Division and the Vietnamese Marine Division. Thieu ordered him to pull back from Quang Tri, the northernmost province.

All along the front, from north to south, the withdrawal became a rout. Provinces were lost at the rate of one a day. Kontum, Pleiku, and Dar Lac were the first to go, then Quang Tri, and in the south, Binh Long and Quang Duc. In Military Region I, the old battleground of the III Marine Amphibious Force, General Truong was outflanked and overextended. He thought he could hold Hue. Then he changed his mind and withdrew. U. S. Marines, listening to the news and watching their maps, waited for their old comrades, the Vietnamese Marines, heroes of the 1972 counteroffensive, to make their stand. A defense line, swung in an arc around Da Nang from the Hai Van peninsula (what the Marines had called "the Rocket Belt") to Hoi An seemed feasible. The Vietnamese Marines were marched and countermarched as orders changed, but there was no stand. This time there were no U. S. advisors, no U. S. close air support, no B-52 raids in the north, no mining of Haiphong harbor, no seemingly endless onrush of U. S. logistical support. Da Nang fell without a fight.

Cambodia (1975)

The end was also fast approaching in neighboring Cambodia. The Khmer Rouge had begun their dry-season offensive, and by March had completed the encirclement of the capital, Phnom Penh, cutting off the vital Mekong River supply line. Only a fifteen-hundred-ton-a-day airlift of ammunition, food, and medical supplies—flown into Pochentong airport by U. S. civilian pilots in chartered U. S. Air Force C-130s—kept the city alive. The Khmer Rouge noose tightened around Phnom Penh and Pochentong came within easy range of Soviet-supplied rockets and artillery.

On 1 April ailing President Lon Nol left his capital for an "official visit" to Indonesia (and thence to exile in Hawaii). His departure signaled the irreversible collapse of his government. Out in the Gulf of Siam, amphibious ships of the Seventh Fleet, with the 31st Marine Amphibious Unit embarked, waited for President Ford's decision to execute Operation Eagle Pull, the evacuation of the few remaining Americans and such foreign nationals who chose to leave. The order came on 12 April 1975.

It was a Saturday and in the early morning hours a Ground Combat Force (GCF) of about 300 Marines came in by helicopter and threw a perimeter around the soccer field (near the U. S. Embassy), which had been designated as the evacuation site. Two Marine helicopter squadrons, flying CH-53 Sea Stallions from the decks of amphibious assault ship *Okinawa* (LPH-3) and attack carrier *Hancock* (CVA-19), swiftly shuttled 276 Americans, third-country nationals, and high-ranking Cambodians to safety. The operation went smoothly and was over in a little more than two hours. The Marines from the embassy guard then brought down the U. S. flag and left in the last helicopter. As it lifted from the landing zone, three Khmer Rouge recoilless rifle rounds impacted on the soccer field, killing or wounding, it was reported, several Cambodian children who had been watching the evacuation.

The End in Saigon

In South Viet Nam, the collapse of the Thieu government was accelerating. The Communists had taken the coastal cities of Qui Nhon, Tuy Hoa, Nha Trang, and Cam Ranh. Only at Xuan Loc, forty miles east of Saigon on Route 1, and covering Bien Hoa, South Viet Nam's next-to-last jet air base, was there determined resistance to the invaders. The Vietnamese Marines, those who weren't captured or surrendered, had left Da Nang in great disorder, many on board the SS *Pioneer Commander* which took them to the great base at Cam Ranh Bay, where the breakdown in order and discipline seemed complete. Only a single brigade of combat-effective Vietnamese Marines could be fed in at Xuan Loc to reinforce the battered ARVN 18th Division.

On 21 April 1975 President Thieu resigned, leaving office with bitter words of denunciation for the United States. He was replaced by feeble seventy-one-year-old Vice President Tran Van Huong. After a week, Huong transferred the presidency to General Duong Van ("Big") Minh, the neutralist Buddhist who had helped engineer the overthrow of Ngo Dinh Diem in 1963 and who was now eager to turn over the Saigon government to the North Vietnamese. Xuan Loc fell; the Communists were in the outskirts of Saigon and were playing cat-and-mouse, perfectly able to enter the city whenever they wished.

As so many times before in those waters, the 9th Marine Amphibious Brigade (which had made the original landing at Da Nang ten years before) was standing by in its amphibious ships, waiting for the order to go ashore and take out the Americans. The brigade was commanded by Brigadier General Richard E. Carey, a Marine aviator who had cut his combat teeth as a rifle and machine-gun platoon leader in Korea. He had under him Regimental Landing Team 4, Provisional Marine Aircraft Group 39, a Brigade Logistical Support Group, and an Amphibious Evacuation Security Force. The last was made up of hastily organized security platoons, which were to preserve some semblance of order and discipline on board the Navy and merchant ships which were carrying off distraught Vietnamese refugees by the tens of thousands.

A five-man advance party from the Brigade went ashore at Saigon on 20 April to assist in the evacuation planning and was dismayed by the "business-as-usual" attitude of the American community. It was thought that some six thousand Americans were still in the city. No one was sure. The number of potential Vietnamese evacuees was astronomic. Most of the Americans and some of the Vietnamese were gotten out in fixed-wing transports, some chartered, some U. S. Air Force, from Tan Son Nhut airport before Communist rockets and artillery closed down flight operations. On 26 April a platoon from Company C, 9th Marines, was landed at Tan Son Nhut to augment the thinly spread Marine Security Guard from the embassy. Before dawn on Tuesday, 29 April, Communist rockets killed two Marines standing guard at the Defense Attaché Office compound at Tan Son Nhut. By Washington time, it was the evening of the twenty-eighth. President Ford convened the National Security Council and at 2245 ordered Operation Frequent Wind, the final evacuation of Saigon, to begin.

Shortly after noon, Saigon time, 29 April, 9th MAB received the order to execute Frequent Wind. An hour and a half later, Dick Carey arrived at the DAO compound at Tan Son Nhut from the amphibious command ship *Blue Ridge* (LCC-19) and opened his command post ashore. Two heavy helicopter squadrons, HMH-462 and HMH-463, began shuttling in the Ground Security Force (GSF). (After Phnom Penh, someone had decided that Ground *Combat* Force was too warlike.) Some 865 Marines from BLT 2/4 came into the tennis-court landing zone in the DAO compound. In the early evening, three platoons were heli-lifted from there into the city to help out the Marine Security Guard. This brought a total of 171 Marines at the embassy.

Meanwhile, the outbound flights of the CH-53s were

carrying the evacuees back to the ships. Things went smoothly at the DAO compound. In all, 395 Americans and 4475 Vietnamese were safely gone by midnight. The last Marines to leave set the buildings, once known as "Pentagon East," on fire.

Things went less well at the U. S. Embassy. Besieged by a combination of frantic would-be refugees and anticipatory looters, the gates had to be locked and late-arriving Americans lifted over the walls. There were two spots where helicopters could be landed. The embassy roof could take the medium CH-46s and the heavy CH-53s could go in, one at a time, at the embassy parking lot. Plans had called for only 100 Americans to be taken out of the embassy, but the evacuation went on all night and, before it was over, 978 Americans (including some rather strange ones who had come out of the "woodwork") and 1120 foreign nationals and Vietnamese were evacuated. The Vietnamese mob used a fire truck to bash its way into the embassy. The Marine guards withdrew to the roof, floor by floor. The last CH-46 lifted off at 0753 in the morning with the last 11 Marines on board. The North Vietnamese were already into the heart of the city, primed for a May Day takeover of South Viet Nam.

Overhead, the Marine helicopters had been covered by U. S. Air Force jets flying from Thailand bases and U. S. Navy jets from offshore carriers. There had been much harassing ground fire, apparently from both the Communists and disgruntled South Vietnamese. Because of the dense civilian population, and with iron discipline, the Americans did not return the fire. There were also a number of reported surface-to-air missiles; but there were no U. S. combat casualties, either in men or aircraft. Two Marine helicopters were lost to operational causes: one, a CH-46 with its pilot and co-pilot, the other, a UH-1E.

An aftermath to the collapse of the Thieu government was the influx of some 150,000 refugees into the United States. A mixture of the high and the low, the threatened, the desperate, the opportunistic, and the simply frightened, they were staged through three principal areas: Guam, Wake Island, and Clark Air Base in the Philippines. Retired General Leonard Chapman was the Director of the Immigration and Naturalization Service. A large share of the processing of the refugees fell to him and he handled it with the same cool efficiency that had marked his years of active Marine Corps service. Temporary camps for the arriving refugees were opened at three military bases— Camp Pendleton, California; Fort Chaffee, Arkansas; and Eglin Air Force Base, Florida—and later a fourth one, at Indiantown Gap, Pennsylvania. The tent camp at Pendleton (immediately and predictably nicknamed "Little Saigon") was closest to the points of arrival and was soon filled to its 18,000-person capacity. Among the temporary guests was the flamboyant and controversial former premier, Air Marshal Nguyen Cao Ky, still wearing his lavender scarf, familiar to thousands of Marines who had seen him in his frequent visits to I Corps.

The *Mayaguez* Incident

At 1420 on Monday, 12 May 1975, a Cambodian gunboat fired across the bow of the thirty-one-year-old, 10,766-ton container ship SS *Mayaguez*, tramping its way from Hong Kong to Sattahip, Thailand. The *Mayaguez* prudently hove to, a boarding party came over the side brandishing weapons, and the American ship was ordered to follow the Cambodian gunboat at half-speed. The ship was led to an anchorage off Koh Tang, a two-by-three mile heavily jungled island thirty-four miles from the Cambodian mainland port of Kampong Som. The thirty-nine-man crew was taken ashore and then, on the fourteenth, moved to Kampong Som. En route, their gunboat was strafed and tear-gassed by American jets. The attacking aircraft were U. S. Air Force F-4s, A-7s, and F-111s sent up from

Thai bases to interdict any Cambodian boats moving between Koh Tang and the mainland. The jets sank five gunboats and hit at least two others. The sight of Caucasian faces had saved the gunboat carrying the *Mayaguez* crew from sinking or more serious damage.

The National Security Council had met on Tuesday, 13 May, and President Ford had decided upon a rescue mission. The decision had gone from the President through the Secretary of Defense and the Joint Chiefs of Staff to Commander-in-Chief, Pacific, in Hawaii, and thence for execution to Lieutenant General John J. Burns, Commander, Seventh Air Force, at his headquarters in Nakhon Phanom air base in Thailand. There were to be two Marine assaults: one to board the *Mayaguez*, the other to land on Koh Tang, where the crew was thought still to be. Over the protests of the Thai government, 2d Battalion, 9th Marines, reinforced, was airlifted in Air Force C-141s from Okinawa to Utapao air base in Thailand. Meanwhile, the attack carrier *Coral Sea* (CVA-43), the guided-missile destroyer *Henry B. Wilson* (DDG-7), and four destroyer escorts were steaming into the Gulf of Siam. There were no amphibious assault ships or Marine helicopter squadrons in the vicinity, so helilift for the assault was to be provided by two Thai-based U. S. Air Force squadrons—eight CH-53s from the 21st Special Operations Squadron and eight HH-53 ("Jolly Green Giants") from the 40th Aerospace Rescue and Recovery Squadron. (During the marshaling, one of the CH-53s crashed thirty-seven miles west of Nakhon Phanom and all twenty-one airmen on board were killed.)

The first echelons of Marines began arriving at Utapao at 0430 on 14 May. Their leaders made an air reconnaissance of Koh Tang that afternoon and saw nothing to cause them to think there would be any resistance. At midnight, General Burns decided that the raid on the island and the retaking of the *Mayaguez* would be undertaken simultaneously the following morning.

Lift-off from Utapao was made at 0415, Wednesday, 15 May, in six HH-53s and five CH-53s. The first part of the operation went well. Three HH-53s delivered sixty-nine Marines from Company D, 1st Battalion, 4th Marines, to the destroyer escort *Harold E. Holt* (DE-1074) at 0550. The *Holt* came alongside the *Mayaguez* at 0830, the Marines went over the rail, found the ship deserted, and ran the U. S. flag up over the fantail, Iwo Jima style. At this time, the *Mayaguez* crew was in fact being returned in a captured Thai fishing boat. This fishing boat was intercepted by the *Wilson* at 0945, the *Mayaguez* crew taken safely on board; and the Thai fishermen, also rescued, were separated from their Cambodian guards and allowed to head for home. Meanwhile, Navy A-6s and A-7s from the *Coral Sea* were pounding Ream airfield outside of Kampong Som.

The raid on Koh Tang was also under way. At 0600, under cover of U. S. Air Force fighter-bombers, the 210-man raiding force—Company G, 2d Battalion, 9th Marines—under Lieutenant Colonel Randall W. Austin began to land and immediately ran into devastating ground fire. Heavy counterfires were brought to bear on the island and included the dropping of a 15,000-pound bomb—the kind that had been used to blow away jungle canopy in the Viet Nam war. The Marines were divided between two landing zones and their position was precarious until their eventual evacuation the night of 16 May. By then the crew of the *Mayaguez* had her under way again and were headed for Singapore.

Of the fifteen U. S. Air Force helicopters employed, three had been shot down, ten others had received battle damage, and only two had escaped unscathed. Personnel casualties were also proportionately high: eleven Marines, two Navy men, and two airmen killed; three Marines missing in action; forty-one Marines, two Navy men, and seven airmen wounded.

The Marines: 200th Birthday

On 30 April, the same day that the North Vietnamese marched into Saigon, President Ford announced the nomination of Lieutenant General Louis Hugh Wilson of Brandon, Mississippi, to be the next Commandant of the Marine Corps. Wilson, who as a captain had been in Cushman's battalion at Fonte Hill on Guam and had a Medal of Honor for it, was Commanding General, Fleet Marine Force, Pacific, at the time of his nomination. In the years since World War II, he had, among other assignments, served in Korea, was commanding officer of The Basic School, attended the National War College, and had been with the 1st Marine Division in Viet Nam. General Cushman chose to retire six months early and, on 1 July, General Wilson became the twenty-sixth Commandant of the Marine Corps.

The tenth of November 1975 was approaching. The Corps' celebration of its 200th Birthday was intertwined with the Nation's Bicentennial, but the Marine Corps Birthday (always "birthday," never "anniversary") had been for many years something special, celebrated for as long as anyone could remember each tenth of November around the globe wherever two or more Marines or former Marines (there are no "ex-Marines") might get together.

John Lejeune, the thirteenth Commandant, who understood these things so well, in 1921 had published the following order which is still read to all Marines on the Marine Corps Birthday:

> *(1) On November 10, 1775, a Corps of Marines was created by a resolution of Continental Congress. Since that date many thousand men have borne the name "Marine." In memory of them it is fitting that we who are Marines should commemorate the birthday of our corps by calling to mind the glories of its long and illustrious history.*

(2) The record of our corps is one which will bear comparison with that of the most famous military organizations in the world's history. During 90 of the 146 years of its existence the Marine Corps has been in action against the Nation's foes. From the Battle of Trenton to the Argonne, Marines have won foremost honors in war, and in the long eras of tranquillity at home, generation after generation of Marines have grown gray in war in both hemispheres and in every corner of the seven seas, that our country and its citizens might enjoy peace and security.

(3) In every battle and skirmish since the birth of our corps, Marines have acquitted themselves with the greatest distinction, winning new honors on each occasion until the term "Marine" has come to signify all that is highest in military efficiency and soldierly virtue.

(4) This high name of distinction and soldierly repute we who are Marines today have received from those who preceded us in the corps. With it we have also received from them the eternal spirit which has animated our corps from generation to generation and has been the distinguishing mark of the Marines in every age. So long as that spirit continues to flourish, Marines will be found equal to every emergency in the future as they have been in the past, and the men of our Nation will regard us as worthy successors to the long line of illustrious men who have served as "Soldiers of the Sea" since the founding of the corps.

Acknowledgments and Short Bibliography

This book had its beginning in 1969 when Mr. Leo Cooper of London asked Mr. Henry I. Shaw, Jr., the civilian Chief Historian of the U. S. Marine Corps to suggest someone who might write a short history of the U. S. Marines for Mr. Cooper's Famous Regiments series. The U. S. Marines were the first American fighting formation to be asked to join this distinguished series and the book was meant to be a companion work to Major-General J. L. Moulton's *The Royal Marines*, which came out in 1972.

My own book was delayed by a second tour, on my part, in Vietnam. Also, I don't think that either Mr. Cooper or I realized the problems we would encounter in trying to fit two hundred years of history of a United States Marine Corps that had grown larger than the British Army into a format originally designed for individual British regiments. *The United States Marines*, as eventually published by Leo Cooper, Ltd., in 1974, was about twice the length of the other books in the Famous Regiments series. Still, it was shorter than I would have liked to have had it, as was the similar edition which was serialized in the *Marine Corps Gazette*, under the title *The United States Marine*

Corps, in monthly installments from November 1973 until December 1974.

This Viking edition, although still short (I would say *compact* or *concise*, but both of these have been used in the titles of other Marine Corps histories) is half again as long as the earlier versions. I have been able to finish out the first two hundred years of Marine Corps history and the book is indexed—which I think makes a book of this sort much more useful. It also has maps made by Major Charles Waterhouse, USMCR, from my sketches.

Many persons have contributed in many ways to the putting together of this short history and to cite only a few is to slight the many; however, I would be completely ungrateful if I failed to thank the late Colonel John H. Magruder III, USMCR, for his trenchant and useful criticism of early drafts; Captain Benis M. Frank, USMCR (Ret.) for his thoughtful comments and the indexing of this edition; Sergeant Major Ethyl M. Wilcox, USMC (Ret.), Master Sergeant Philip R. Mackinnon, USMC, and Mrs. Cathy Bakkela for their clerical assistance; and Miss Gabrielle Neufeld for verifying the Battle Honors.

The expansion of the Corps in successive wars, particularly during and since World War II, necessarily forced me into a shift of perspective to correspondingly higher echelons. Thus the narration as it moves to division and corps level gets further and further away from the individual Marine who makes up the heart and soul of the Corps. Realizing that some readers will want to make up for this deficiency, in the Bibliography which follows I have been less concerned with documentation of sources than with pointing the interested reader in the direction of additional material.

Any historian of the U. S. Marines owes a great debt to the early work of Major R. S. Collum, USMC, including his *The History of the United States Marine Corps* (1903), and Major E. N. McClellan, USMC, whose mimeographed history, compiled during the 1920s and

1930s, regrettably exists in only a very few copies. The standard history until World War II was Colonel C. H. Metcalf's *A History of the United States Marine Corps* (1939), somewhat dry and patchwork, but nevertheless full of substance. Its place has now been largely taken by Colonel R. D. Heinl's magnificent *Soldiers of the Sea* (1962). Shorter, less comprehensive general histories include the *Compact History of the Marine Corps* (1960) by Lieutenant Colonels P. N. Pierce and F. O. Hough and the official *A Concise History of the United States Marine Corps, 1775–1969* (1970) compiled by Captain William D. Parker, USMCR.

The evolution of U. S. amphibious doctrine and practice is brilliantly developed in *The U. S. Marines and Amphibious War* (1951) by J. A. Isely and P. A. Crowl. The two best aviation histories are Robert Sherrod's *History of Marine Corps Aviation in World War II* (1952) and Colonel J. A. DeChant's *Devilbirds* (1947). For more information on uniforms I recommend Colonel R. H. Rankin's *Uniforms of the Sea Services* (1962).

There is now a definitive history of the Continental Marines, the official *Marines in the Revolution* (1975) by C. R. Smith. There is also some Marine content in the standard naval histories of the Revolution, most notably G. W. Allen's *A Naval History of the American Revolution* (1913) and C. O. Paullin's *The Navy of the American Revolution* (1906). Similarly, Allen should be consulted for *Our Navy and the Barbary Corsairs* (1905) and *Our Naval War with France* (1909). The role of Marines in the War of 1812 can also chiefly be found in more general naval histories and biographies such as Theodore Roosevelt's *The Naval War of 1812* (1882). For these early years, James Fenimore Cooper's *Naval History of the United States* (1839) has some interesting material. A more recent book, *Surf Boats and Horse Marines* (1969), by K. J. Bauer deals with the Marines in the Mexican War. There is no comparable book for the Civil War.

For the first half of the twentieth century some of the most colorful reading can be found in the biographies of various Marine leaders including Lowell Thomas's *Old Gimlet Eye: The Adventures of Smedley D. Butler* (1933), Colonel F. W. Wise's *A Marine Tells It to You* (1929), General J. A. Lejeune's *The Reminiscences of a Marine* (1930), and Burke Davis's *Marine! The Life of Lt. Gen. Lewis B. (Chesty) Puller* (1962). No one of course captures the color and flavor of the Marine Corps in this period as well as does Colonel J. W. Thomason, Jr., in *Fix Bayonets!* (1926) and . . . *and a Few Marines* (1945).

The bibliography for World War II is very full and varied and only a few of many excellent titles can be listed here. At the top of the list must go the five-volume official *History of Marine Corps Operations in World War II.* Good one-volume histories include F. O. Hough's *The Island War* (1947), Fletcher Pratt's *The Marines' War* (1948), and Robert Leckie's *Strong Men Armed* (1962). The Korean War also has its five-volume official history, *U. S. Marine Operations in Korea.* Two other works of particular importance are Lynn Montross's *Cavalry of the Sky* (1954) and R. D. Heinl's *Victory at High Tide* (1968). Not much has yet gotten into print in the way of operational histories of the Vietnam conflict and I have drawn chiefly on my own *Marine Corps Operations in Vietnam, 1965 . . . 1972* which has been published sequentially by the *Naval Review.*

The Marine Corps History and Museums Division has been particularly prolific in producing historical reference pamphlets, monographs, unit histories, bibliographies, and chronologies. Among the titles I found most useful were *The United States Marines in Nicaragua* (1968), *United States Marines at Harpers Ferry* (1966), *The United States Marines in the War with Spain* (1967), and *The United States Marines on Iwo Jima* (1967), all by B. C. Nalty; *The United States*

Marines in North China 1945–1949 (1968) and *The United States Marines in the Occupation of Japan* (1969), both by H. I. Shaw, Jr.; *Marine Corps Women's Reserve in World War II* (1968) by Lieutenant Colonel Pat Meid, USMCR; *The United States Marine Corps in the World War* (1968 reprint of 1920 edition) by Major E. N. McClellan, USMC; and *The Eagle, Globe and Anchor, 1868–1968* (1971) by Colonel J. A. Driscoll, USMCR. (A complete listing of all these pamphlets can be obtained by writing the Director of Marine Corps History and Museums; Headquarters, U. S. Marine Corps; Washington, D.C. 20380.)

I also found the oral history transcripts held by the History and Museums Division very illuminating and I have made large use of the file of official biographies and clippings I have collected over the years. Such a file is not readily available, but there are Karl Schuon's *U. S. Marine Corps Biographical Dictionary* (1963), Jane Blakeney's *Heroes, U. S. Marine Corps, 1861–1955* (1957), and C. L. Lewis's *Famous American Marines* (1950). There are also good biographical sketches of the Commandants in Karl Schuon's *Home of the Commandants* (1966 and 1974). The two periodicals I found most useful, not surprisingly, were the *U. S. Naval Institute Proceedings* and the *Marine Corps Gazette*. The *Gazette* has been published since 1916 and is the professional magazine of the Marine Corps Association which, incidentally, was formed in 1911 at Gauntanamo by officers of the 1st Provisional Marine Brigade while they were waiting for a decision to be made as to whether or not they would be landed in Mexico.

And finally, unless otherwise specifically attributed, all opinions expressed are my own and are certainly not to be construed as official.

Alexandria, Virginia   E. H. Simmons
1 July 1975

The Marine Hymn

From the halls of Montezuma
  To the shores of Tripoli,
We fight our country's battles
  In the air, on land, and sea.
First to fight for right and freedom,
  And to keep our honor clean,
We are proud to claim the title
  Of United States Marines.

Our flag's unfurl'd to every breeze
  From dawn to setting sun;
We have fought in every clime and place
  Where we could take a gun.
In the snow of far-off northern lands
  And in sunny tropic scenes,
You will find us always on the job—
  The United States Marines.

Here's health to you and to our Corps
  Which we are proud to serve;
In many a strife we've fought for life
  And never lost our nerve.
If the Army and the Navy
  Ever gaze on Heaven's scenes,
They will find the streets are guarded
  By United States Marines.

Battle Honors

The official Battle Color of the Marine Corps is held by the Marine Barracks, Washington, D.C.; a duplicate is maintained in the office of the Commandant of the Marine Corps; and a third Battle Color is displayed at the Marine Corps Museum, Quantico, Virginia. These colors bear streamers representing U. S. and foreign unit awards as well as those periods of service, expeditions, and campaigns in which the U. S. Marine Corps has participated since the American Revolution. The list that follows shows the honors, as of early 1975, commemorated by attachments to the Battle Color either by an unadorned streamer, as in the case of early wars, or by added stars or other devices for more recent actions. In general, a bronze star or oak leaf cluster indicates an additional award and a silver star five such awards.

1. Presidential Unit Citation (Navy) (1941–1968)
   Streamer with six silver and two bronze stars (33 awards).
2. Presidential Unit Citation (Army) (1942–1969)
   Streamer with one silver oak leaf cluster (6 awards).

3. Navy Unit Commendation (1942–1973)
   Streamer with sixteen silver stars (81 awards).
4. Valorous Unit Award (Army) (1968).
5. Meritorious Unit Commendation (Navy–Marine Corps) (1965–1973)
   Streamer with twenty-five silver stars (126 awards).
6. Meritorious Unit Commendation (Army) (1967–1968).
7. Revolutionary War (1775–1783).
8. Quasi-War with France (1798–1801).
9. Barbary Wars (1801–1815).
10. War of 1812 (1812–1815).
11. African Slave Trade Patrol (1820–1861).
12. Indian Wars (1811–1812; 1836–1842).
13. Operations Against West Indian Pirates (1822–1830s).
14. Mexican War (1846–1848).
15. Civil War (1861–1865).
16. Marine Corps Expeditionary (1874–1962)
    Streamer with ten silver stars, four bronze stars, and one silver "W" (56 expeditions). (The silver "W" is for the defense of Wake Island, 7–22 December 1941.)
17. Spanish Campaign (1898).
18. Philippine Campaign (1899–1904).
19. China Relief Expedition (1900–1901).
20. Cuban Pacification (1906–1909).
21. Nicaraguan Campaign (1912).
22. Mexican Service (1914).
23. Haitian Campaign (1915; 1919–1920).
    Streamer with one bronze star.
24. Dominican Campaign (1916)
    (Marine occupation 1916–1924 is commemorated on the Marine Corps Expeditionary Streamer.)
25. World War I Victory (1917–1918; 1918–1920)
    Streamer with one silver and one bronze star for combat operations in France, 1918; one Maltese

cross for service in France, 1918–1919; West Indies clasp, 1917–1918; and Siberia clasp, 1918–1920.

26. Army of Occupation of Germany (1918–1923).
27. Second Nicaraguan Campaign (1926–1933).
28. Yangtze Service (1926–1927; 1930–1932).
29. China Service (1937–1939; 1945–1957)
    Streamer with one bronze star.
30. American Defense Service (1939–1941)
    With bronze star indicating service outside continental limits of the United States.
31. American Campaign (1941–1946).
32. European-African-Middle Eastern Campaign (1941–1945)
    Streamer with one silver star and four bronze stars representing nine actions.
33. Asiatic–Pacific Campaign (1941–1946)
    Streamer with eight silver stars and two bronze stars representing forty-two operations and actions.
34. World War II Victory (1941–1946).
35. Navy Occupation Service (1945–1955)
    With Europe and Asia clasps.
36. National Defense Service (1950–1954; 1961–1974).
37. Korean Service (1950–1954)
    Streamer with two silver stars representing ten campaigns.
38. Armed Forces Expeditionary (1958–1975)
    Streamer with one silver and three bronze stars (nine expeditions).
39. Vietnam Service (1962–1973)
    Streamer with three silver and two bronze stars representing seventeen campaigns.
40. French Croix de Guerre (1918)
    Streamer with two palms and one gilt star (three awards).
41. Philippine Defense (1941–1942)
    With bronze star indicating participation in engagements against the enemy.

42. Philippine Liberation (1944–1945)
    Streamer with two bronze stars representing three campaigns.
43. Philippine Independence (1941–1945).
44. Philippine Presidential Unit Citation (1941–1942; 1944–1945; 1970; 1972)
    Four citations.
45. Korean Presidential Unit Citation (1950–1954)
    Six citations.
46. Republic of Vietnam Meritorious Unit Citation of the Gallantry Cross with Palm (1965–1969).
47. Republic of Vietnam Meritorious Unit Citation, Civil Actions (1969–1970).

INDEX

"If the Army and the Navy ever gaze on Heaven's scenes, they will find the streets are guarded by United States Marines."

Defense Dept. Photo (Marine Corps)

Brigadier General
Edwin H. Simmons, USMC (Ret.)

Born at Billingsport, New Jersey, in 1921, almost on an American Revolution battle site, Brigadier General Edwin H. Simmons claims to have done his first bit of historical research and writing at the age of fourteen. Since then he has been published widely, mostly on military subjects. He came into the United States Marine Corps in 1942 and is now, as a retired officer on active service, Director of Marine Corps History and Museums. He has a B.A. in journalism from Lehigh University (1942), and an M.A. in journalism from Ohio State (1955), and is a graduate of the National War College (1967). His numerous personal decorations from World War II, Korea, and Vietnam include the Distinguished Service Medal, the Silver Star, two Legions of Merit, two Bronze Stars, a Meritorious Service Medal, and an unavoidable Purple Heart.